SCHOOL
FINANCE
AND
EDUCATION
EQUITY

SCHOOL FINANCE
AND
EDUCATION EQUITY

Lessons from Kansas

BRUCE D. BAKER

HARVARD EDUCATION PRESS

Cambridge, Massachusetts

Paperback ISBN 978-1-68253-680-3

Library of Congress Cataloging-in-Publication data is on file.

Published by Harvard Education Press,
an imprint of the Harvard Education Publishing Group

Harvard Education Press
8 Story Street
Cambridge, MA 02138

Cover Design: Ciano Design
Cover Photo: TriggerPhoto/E+ via Getty Images

The typefaces used in this book are Anko, Open Sans, and ITC Century.

CONTENTS

INTRODUCTION

This book explores the story of Kansas school finance, a saga that spans decades, three waves of court cases, plenty of political bluster, and a handful of intriguing characters. The forces, structures, events, and characters addressed in these pages have protected Kansas public schools from suffering a much worse fate than might otherwise have occurred in their absence. The goal of this book is to provide the more casual reader of education- and public policy–oriented books an entertaining tale of school finance reform in Kansas, with implications for reforms in other states. The casual reader of education policy may have heard that in the most recent decade, Kansas schools suffered thanks to the largest funding cuts in the nation, a result of Governor Brownback's "real live experiment" in cutting taxes. While states in many parts of the country and in particular those neighboring Kansas significantly disinvested in their public schooling systems over the past ten years, Kansas, despite the Brownback era setbacks, has remained ahead of the pack. This book unpacks how and why.

School finance isn't a particularly riveting topic. Kansas is probably not considered by many to be a particularly entertaining state. So writing about the intersection of the two would seem to be a monumentally bad idea. After all, Kansas's main tourist attractions include a barbed wire museum and the world's largest ball of twine. Kansas is nearly a perfect rectangle, but for the broken northeastern corner, and for the most part, Kansas is flat—damn flat. Kansas is flyover country at its finest and flattest.

Kansas has captured the intrigue of political media and authors in search of Middle America for the past few decades. Kansas is the geographic center of the US, but not so much the political center. Perhaps the best-known political commentary on Kansas is Thomas Frank's 2002 book, *What's the Matter with Kansas?* In the book, Frank paints a facile portrait of largely ignorant, low-income white voters unable to break the self-destructive habit of voting against their own economic interests. Recently, Frank's caricature of Kansans has been countered by more nuanced perspectives from a pair of books published in 2018: Sarah Smarsh's *Heartland: A Memoir of Working Hard and Being Broke in the Richest Country on Earth* and *What's Right with Kansas?* by Ed O'Malley, former Kansas state representative and head of the Kansas Leadership Center. Ed O'Malley shows up as a character in this book at a few points in time. Sarah Smarsh would have been an undergraduate at the University of Kansas soon after I arrived there as a faculty member, though our paths never crossed to my knowledge.

The Kansas school finance saga is one of the more interesting stories in both recent Kansas history and in school finance—admittedly, a low bar. More importantly the Kansas school finance story provides useful insights for strengthening public education in other states and protecting public schooling from outright dismantling and complete disinvestment in politically conservative states. In fact, many of the lessons of Kansas school finance may also inform productive change in bluer states, from California and Colorado to Connecticut and Vermont. Kansas offers a unique constitutional structure for both protecting educational rights and maintaining judicial independence, which in combination are essential to providing equitable and adequate schooling in politically and economically volatile times. The history behind how all of this comes into being and the involvement of Kansas courts in interpreting those constitutional protections includes a cast of characters and events, captured in court documents themselves, as well as often clever reporting and political cartoons that keep it all entertaining.

Through multiple rounds of state and federal constitutional challenges and shifting political tides in the state legislature, Kansas has maintained a degree of balance, stability, equity, and adequacy in the financing of its public schools that not only exceeds what we more liberal coastal elites might expect, but also exceeds that of most surrounding states and many other states across the country. This book explores the how and why.

ORGANIZATION OF THIS BOOK

This book combines historical background, legal analysis, and political and economic contextual data. Some chapters are primarily historical. Others focus on data and context. Other chapters focus on legal analysis, and still others on the characters involved, including the key role of strong female leadership in the governor's office, legislature, and the high court. Throughout the middle portion of the Kansas school finance saga, I was an active, in-person participant, and much of that portion of this book is presented from a first-person perspective. My involvement as an expert and consultant continued for the decade since my departure. But this book also includes a deep historical dive into the constitutional history of the state and the reshaping of Kansas's government and institutions over time, including the 1966 amendments to the education clause of the constitution—all of this long prior to my own arrival.

Anyone who knows me or my work knows that I can't possibly write a book, or even a simple blog post, without some data, tables, graphs, and charts. The thesis of this book, that Kansas is better off than it might have been, requires some validation in data, including evaluating long-term trends in taxes and public expenditures and in education spending equity and adequacy, and comparisons with neighboring states. This book takes advantage of a publicly available longitudinal data set my team and I have compiled over the years: the School Finance Indicators Database (SFID), which includes a multitude of measures of the level and fairness of school funding.[1] Extensive comparisons are made between Kansas and each of its four neighboring states: Colorado, Oklahoma, Missouri, and Nebraska.

I also draw on data on the political context of Kansas to address how Kansas compares with its neighbors and the nation as a whole on measures of political leanings and on the gender balance within state legislatures over time, in order to illustrate that Kansas is not always what outsiders might expect. I use Michigan State University's Correlates of

State Policy data set, which includes indices of the political disposition of state legislatures and policy context itself, as well as numerous useful background attributes of state legislators and governors.[2]

Much of the school finance saga itself is told through the words, arguments, and decisions of the various lawyers and judges who have participated in multiple rounds of litigation. This book includes deep dives into the texts of trial court and state supreme court rulings, which both illustrate the evolution of the interpretation and application of the state's 1966 constitutional requirements for financing and governing public schooling and provide a window into the personalities of the judicial characters involved. I also explore in detail herein the three separate attempts the legislature has made to conduct empirical analyses of the costs of meeting the constitutional requirements to *make suitable provision for finance of the educational interests of the state.* The legislature engaged in these efforts, using outside consultants, to inform their response to court orders and to appease the court itself. I explore the backstory and individuals involved in each study, in addition to the technical aspects of the studies themselves. These studies are not only central to the saga in terms of how they inform the court and legislature but also contribute to what sets Kansas apart from most other states. Few other states have engaged as extensively or rigorously and independently in such endeavors.

Then there are the various characters who bring the Kansas school finance saga to life, many of whom I had the pleasure to interact with personally. One of those characters was Shawnee County District Court Judge Terry Bullock, loved by some but hated by just as many, who recently passed away on August 2, 2019. Judge Bullock receives much attention in the pages that follow. In the second round of legal challenges to the state's school funding system over which Judge Bullock presided, he was faced with evaluating evidence offered by the state in its defense that more money really wouldn't help improve schools. Thus, from the state's standpoint, it would be inappropriate for the court to rule current funding levels inadequate. Bullock responded in his decision with the proclamation: "Money doesn't matter? That dog won't hunt in Dodge City."

Finally, this book relies heavily on state and local news coverage of the events as they happened, from both serious and satirical outlets.

Yes, there was indeed satirical media coverage of school finance (go fig-ure!), including but not limited to numerous political cartoons from the *Wichita Eagle*'s cartoonist, Richard Crowson. Satirical portrayals of the school finance saga also occasionally made their way into the *Kansas City Pitch*'s KC Strip column—a column written from the perspective of an observant, sarcastic slab of meat (a Kansas City strip steak, to be precise).

At the core of this book are descriptions, analysis, and discussion related to eight key elements. I argue these elements are the reasons that Kansas, despite the general political disposition of the state (Kan-sas has supported Republican presidential candidates in every election since 1968),[3] has managed to continue providing a reasonably equitable and adequate system of public schools—more so than three out of four of its neighbors. Those eight elements include the following:

1. The 1966 ratification of the Education Article of the Kansas Con-stitution,[4] which established an independently elected Kansas State Board of Education, with self-executing constitutional powers to oversee elementary and secondary education (general supervision of schools) and required that the legislature "shall make suitable provision for finance of the educational interests of the state."
2. A judicial selection and retention process, which reduces the role of political ideology among state high court justices and limits turnover, providing the opportunity for state high court judges to develop a deep understanding and institutional history of complex ongoing litigation.[5]
3. A panel of high court judges with in-depth understanding of the complexities of school finance policy and the intersection with state constitutional requirements.
4. A legislature that has been generally responsive to the state high court in terms of orders to increase and/or redistribute state aid and in terms of meeting its obligation to provide empirical evidence to guide school finance reforms.
5. An independent and trusted (bipartisan) legislative research divi-sion (Division of Post Audit), which has played a role in perform-ing and digesting empirical evidence pertaining to school finance reform, including collaborating with outside scholars.

6. The availability (as a result of elements 4 and 5) of high-quality evidence for (a) informing judicial evaluation of the state of school finance in Kansas and (b) guiding legislative reforms.[6]
7. Tireless legal counsel with deep knowledge and institutional history, representing plaintiffs in several rounds and decades of litigation, from 1990 to the present day.
8. The role of informed media, covering the story from a variety of angles, providing historical context and background, and occasionally offering insightful, satirical perspectives on a topic that's really just not that funny.

Importantly, all of these elements provide policy guidance for other states—red and blue—to strengthen their public education systems and solidify the role of public schooling in their states' future. Illuminating that policy guidance and providing a detailed roadmap for other states is the primary goal of this book.

THE SAGA

This book would not exist if there was not a saga around which to spin the tale and develop the characters in the chapters that follow. But what is the Kansas school finance saga? And why is it, or should it be, of interest to anyone outside of Kansas, or even outside of those immediately involved in or affected by the saga within Kansas? Well, on that last point, nearly everyone in Kansas has been affected in one way or another by either taxes or the quality of public schools available in the state, or both, over the past several decades. The Kansas school finance saga is often described by other authors in exceedingly manly, Old West terms, as if it was a gunfight in Dodge City between awesomely mustached foes. While this book does include a few awesomely mustached characters, the Kansas school finance saga, so dramatized by others, has really been an ongoing process of mediation, frequently negotiated by the women of the high plains.

The saga mainly involves two distinct teams: plaintiff school districts and their legal counsel, challenging the constitutionality of the state school finance system to achieve more equitable and adequate funding, with *the state* meaning primarily the legislature, but also the state board of education (it's complicated); and a team of *referees*, meaning the state judicial system, from district courts to the Kansas Supreme Court. The saga occurs in three major phases, including five event periods, as shown in figure I.1, but it requires some important backdrop info. None of the legal battles that followed would have been possible without the 1966 amendments to the state constitution, which both altered the distribution of responsibilities for the governance of the public education system and clarified the legislature's obligation to fund it.

The first wave of modern era litigation and mediation came about in the *Mock v. State of Kansas*, 1991 (*Mock*) case, wherein school districts across the state brought multiple legal challenges to growing

FIGURE I.1   Kansas School finance saga

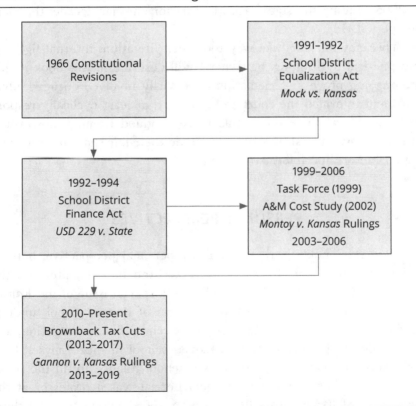

disparities in school funding, exacerbated by recent tax cuts. *Mock* in particular is most often shared in Kansas school finance lore as a great mediation orchestrated by a uniquely Kansan and boisterous judge, Terry Bullock. That period came to a close when the state's high court decided that the solutions adopted by the legislature to the problems identified by Bullock were good enough!

Good enough didn't last for long: the school finance system was back in court for a protracted period and parallel challenges in state and federal court from 1999 to 2006 (*Montoy* in state court and *Robinson* in federal court), when again, at the end of it all, the high court decided that the legislature had sufficiently fulfilled the court's demands. Soon thereafter, the great recession hit, and fiscal austerity and tax cuts became the policy preferences du jour under a conservative Kansas governor, Brownback, and an increasingly conservative Kansas legislature. Their efforts and the recession undermined the solutions adopted in 2006, landing the state back in court for another decade: the *Gannon* period.

This may all seem like way too much litigation, internal fighting, and political positioning, but what I will describe in this book is that the ongoing process of mediation necessarily involved engaged advocates and informed the court and a largely, at least cyclically responsive legislature. Even under this more subdued framing, however, I assure you that the stories herein include their fair share of entertaining characters and informative events.

PERSONAL PERSPECTIVES

Much of this book is written from my personal perspective, both as insider and onlooker. To date, I have written book chapters on the history of Kansas school finance reforms, a special issue of the *Kansas Policy Review* that covered various aspects of Kansas school funding, numerous law review articles on Kansas school finance litigation, and peer-reviewed journal articles on Kansas school finance. I myself have written more than enough on Kansas school finance to fill the pages of this book, but that is not the goal here. I was a professor at the University of Kansas from 1997 through 2008, having traveled there for my first academic position after completing my doctorate at Teachers College, Columbia University. I went to Kansas with typical East Coast views of what Kansas would be, and even by the time I left eleven years later, I had not entirely dispensed with those views. It's a process. I continued working with plaintiff attorneys in the *Gannon* litigation, traveling back for trial in 2011 and most recently drafting reports in 2018 (a review of the most recent cost studies). I returned to Kansas City in the spring of 2019 for an academic conference in which we convened various parties discussed in this book to talk about the most recent episodes in the saga.

By my third year in Kansas, I found myself sitting on the governor's task force on financing K–12 education, which recommended the first of three studies that would address the "costs" of meeting the state's constitutional obligation toward its schools. (I was very much involved in drafting that recommendation.) We traveled the state for hearings, giving me newfound respect for the vastness, and flatness, of the high plains of western Kansas. New to Kansas, I had little understanding of the prominence and influence of many of my peers on that task force, which included a former US senator from Kansas. Soon thereafter, I found myself consulting for attorneys representing plaintiffs bringing two new lawsuits against the state over funding inequities and inadequacies—one in federal court (*Robinson v. Kansas*) and another in state court (*Montoy v. Kansas*). These lawyers have carried on these fights from the late 1980s to present. My involvement in these cases would eventually lead to days on end of the most tedious depositions through which I've ever sat, walking page by page, word by word, number by number through every opinion and analysis I had provided in that case. Annoyed as hell, while trying to stay composed, I had little idea that the state board attorney deposing me at the time would himself end up sitting on the Kansas Supreme Court.

I also had the pleasure (albeit a terrifying one) of testifying as an expert before the famed (or infamous, depending on your perspective) Judge Terry Bullock and in front of the three-judge panel (for hours on end) that heard the *Gannon* case nearly a decade later. I spent time on the side crafting simulations and trying to come up with solutions over lunch with young representative Ed O'Malley, and then sharing the same with his legislative colleagues in an attempt to get traction—to try to come up with solutions outside of litigation. My twenty-plus-year involvement in this story, while short of the thirty-plus-year involvement of many other characters involved (fifty-three years for one!), gives me unique insight into what actually went down, which I will do my best to share herein.

THE CHAPTERS THAT FOLLOW

The first section of the book provides a largely sequential tale of the Kansas school finance saga, from the historical backdrop through the three major waves of litigation. But I begin in chapter 1 with a prologue, providing some background on my personal perspectives and how they shaped my perceptions of Kansas on my arrival there in 1997, versus my perceptions of Kansas now, having left the state over a decade ago (2008). In my years prior to moving to Kansas, I was attending graduate school in New York City while teaching science at a progressive, liberal, elite private school. Clearly a contrast with Kansas, but also a contrast with my own upbringing in small-town northern New England.

Chapter 2 provides some historical context, from the era before the US Supreme Court decision in *Brown v. Board of Education* through the adoption of the 1966 Kansas constitutional amendments that shape how the state's high court evaluates school funding concerns to this day. The year 1966 and the term of then governor Avery also marked the introduction of the state's first statewide aid program for public schooling. Much of what I know about the *real* history of the Kansas constitutional amendments I learned in a lengthy conversation with Governor Avery outside a bathroom at a daylong economic conference at the University of Kansas in 2002.[7] Of course, that conversation is supplemented herein with other research and documentation.

Chapter 3 ushers in the modern era of Kansas education policy, still prior to my own arrival. Chapter 3 digs into the first high drama on the high plains, in which Judge Terry Bullock arrived on the scene to mediate legal complaints brought against the state, from all corners of the state (forty-two separate school districts), decrying growing inequities in school funding, lack of sufficient state aid, and vastly uneven local taxes required to provide adequate schooling from town to town and one corner of the state to the other. Bullock, sidestepping writing any formal trial court ruling—or even holding a trial—instead fired a warning shot, convening legislators, the governor, those bringing the complaints, and other key officials, suggesting that they fix the problem—and quickly—to avoid trial and an inevitable ruling against the state. Governor Joan Finney responded quickly by convening a citizen task force, which provided recommendations to the legislature. Not without significant drama, by the close of the 1992 legislative session, a new school funding formula was adopted: the School District Finance Act. That formula was eventually evaluated, and upheld in part but overturned in part, by then district court (now high court chief justice) judge Marla Luckert, and eventually it was upheld by the state's high court under Chief Justice Kay McFarland.

Chapter 4 introduces the modern era of school finance litigation in Kansas, the increased role of the courts, and the soap opera–like reshuffling of characters that would occur over the next two major rounds of judicial battles: *Montoy*[8] and *Gannon*.[9] It turned out that the solution negotiated by Bullock and upheld by the high court (a) wasn't quite as game-changing as many had first assumed and (b) was also vulnerable to erosion over time—and not much time. Within only a few years (after 1994), several districts were again feeling the financial squeeze and concerned about spending and taxing inequities, leading to the filing of the *Montoy* challenge in 1999. The story repeated itself a decade later, with the filing of *Gannon*. Chapter 4 focuses mainly on the mid-2000s and the *Montoy* case, in which empirical evidence of education costs begin to play a role in informing court rulings and legislative responses, and in which the unique structure of the Kansas government and the balanced constitutional roles and obligations of the legislature and state board of education are clarified and affirmed. Chapter 4 is also where I begin to cut my teeth, both as an academic researcher and an advisor and expert witness in school finance litigation. Finally, chapter 4 also explores the rhetoric and reality of highly publicized showdowns between the Kansas high court and legislature.

Chapter 5 takes us into the economic recession, when the Kansas political pendulum swung back to the right and Governor Brownback promised that sweeping tax cuts would provide a shot of adrenaline to the Kansas economy. Instead, it was more like a shot of sedative. In chapter 5, I take a look at outside analyses of the Kansas tax cuts and their failure, and I walk through data on the effects of those cuts in the wake of the recession, on state revenue and on public school funding in particular. But still, Kansans persisted. Chapter 5 also addresses the follow up litigation to *Montoy*: *Gannon v. Kansas*, which was filed as the recession hit and funding increases promised in the wake of *Montoy* came to a halt. The *Gannon* case was tried and deliberated by the state's lower and high courts throughout the period of budget decimation that resulted from the Brownback tax cuts. Judicial involvement clearly played at least some role in the Kansas comeback. But chapter 5 explains that this comeback would not have been realized without the political rebalancing of the state legislature and the eventual departure of Brownback.

The second section of the book focuses on analyzing specific topics and issues that I believe played critical roles in keeping Kansas in balance and in funding Kansas schools better than might have been the case otherwise in the absence of these conditions. These conditions include the presence of strong women leaders as governors, in the legislature and the court; the use of high-quality evidence to inform judicial analysis and policy remedies; and a collection of persistent structures, organizations, and individuals, often assuming more than one role in different chapters in the saga.

Chapter 6 profiles the women of Kansas. Literature in political science on state and local governments suggests that women as elected officials are more likely to support spending on social programs, in particular on programs that provide services to children and families. Of course, literature in political science also suggests that more liberal state governments are more likely to spend more and more equitably on these same services. Kansas presents an odd contrast. For a politically conservative state, Kansas has had more women as governors (three to date) than most other states; a large share of women on the high court, including two chief justices; and a larger share of women in the legislature than many other states, including much bluer states. Especially notable figures discussed in chapter 6 include the governor at the time of the first major overhaul of school funding in Kansas, Joan Finney, who ushered in the modern era, and Justice Carol Beier, who penned an impressive dissent for the court on the question of whether the state constitution provides for a fundamental right to an education and who has often asked the most challenging questions, leading to sharp exchanges in oral arguments before the court.[10]

Chapter 7 explores the role of evidence in influencing the state's high court and legislature. In the more visible national context of the evolution versus creationism and intelligent design debates, Kansas might be viewed by many coastal elites as being decidedly antiscience.[11] One might argue that the state took a similarly dogmatic and antiempirical approach to its reliance on the suspect economic advisement of Arthur Laffer[12] to guide Governor Brownback's tax cut policies. But when it comes to school finance, Kansas has arguably led the nation in both conducting rigorous analyses to guide school funding policy and then, perhaps more importantly, paying some attention to those analyses when revising and adopting policy. This is despite the apparent direct conflict with the cult of Lafferism idea that increased taxes can only ever cause economic harm. Chapter 7 summarizes those analyses, but also explores the characters behind them and how they came to be. In that chapter, I admit and disclose my personal role at each of three critical junctures in the recent history of Kansas school finance.

Chapter 8 explores the persistent individuals, organizations, and interest groups that have shaped Kansas school finance policies over the past several decades. My speculations about the importance of persistence and persistent individuals is drawn less from academic literature and more from my personal perspective as a participant in this story. Testifying in front of a judge who is familiar with how schools are funded, what children need, what outcomes matter, and how to evaluate the intersections of these is far easier than testifying in front of judges who are not. It's also helpful that judges have deep knowledge of how to link broad, at times ambiguous constitutional requirements to this evidence. This process is communicated through lawyers, and thus their deep knowledge of the same in setting up and communicating their case to the judge is critical. And it's equally important that legislators tasked with redesigning a school finance system to meet judicial demands understand what they are doing. Developing that understanding takes time—usually more than one or a few terms. By virtue of dealing for decades with both the technical and legal issues involved in constitutional litigation over school funding, the individuals chronicled herein know their stuff and its context.

Attorneys Alan Rupe and John Robb have been representing plaintiff families and school districts in state and federal legal challenges over school funding for three decades. Their worthy opponent in early rounds of litigation, Dan Biles, represented the Kansas State Board of Education as defendant, then migrated toward a middle ground position in the mid-2000s, when the attorney general's office began more actively representing the interests of the governor and legislature, and now sits on the high court. Marla Luckert sat as district court judge upholding (in part; also overturning in part) the legislature and the governor's remedy response to Judge Terry Bullock's heavy-handed, orchestrated resolution in 1991. Bullock himself returned a decade later to hear trial testimony in *Montoy v. Kansas*, penning a highly entertaining 2003 ruling and several equally entertaining and insightful orders to follow. Chapter 8 chapter explores the various lawyers, judges, legislators, other public officials, and interest groups involved, as well as state, local, and national media. One man persisted through it all, from immediately after ratification of the state's 1966 constitutional amendments to the latest rounds of *Gannon v. State*, as chief purveyor of any and all data pertaining to the state school finance system: Dale Dennis. My own personal involvement, beginning with my membership on a governor's task force in 1999, is now running into two decades.

Chapter 9 of this book provides contextual data illustrating that Kansas school funding is, in fact, less bad than it might otherwise have been, by comparison with national trends and with neighboring states. I'm often pressed in academic conferences and other contexts about what I hope to gain from participating in these lengthy legal challenges over school funding or from preparing reports and analyses for courts or legislatures on costs of meeting specific outcome standards. Critics argue that legislators don't ever really fully comply with court orders or design formulas that take fully into account any cost analyses anyone might provide. My response has been that even small shifts matter. That if judicial pressure—even if never-ending—combined with sound empirical evidence can *bend* school finance in the *right* direction, toward more equitable and adequate education for all, then that's a good thing and it was all worth it. That is, the modest goal is to make school funding less bad than it might otherwise have been if left entirely to political self-interest and preservation! Chapter 9 brings us to the lessons that can be learned from decades of litigation, political activity, empirical research, and the often explosive, sometimes mundane, frequently entertaining saga of Kansas school finance. Some lessons can be learned from governance structures, which, while difficult to change, might provide the greatest long-term leverage, in part *because* they are difficult to change. Should other states consider constitutional revision, separating standard setting and oversight from financing of schools? Does the less political judicial selection and retention process in Kansas lead to a more stable and thus more knowledgeable court? Is it better able to understand and thus manage the complexities of school finance over time? What can be learned from advocacy groups and political actors in the state over time? How have those individuals ensured that (a) the legislature and governor will respond, at least in part, to judicial rulings, and (b) the legislature would request and rely on credible expertise and empirical analyses?

Before we move to these reflective questions about what we can learn from the Kansas saga, we first need to step back in time to my arrival on the scene in the late 1990s, and then even further back in time, to the state's founding and its original and revised constitutions. And now, our story begins.

SECTION

I

The Kansas School
Finance Saga

1

GOING WEST

How I Got Schooled in Kansas

"Not all those who wander are lost."

—J. R. R. Tolkien, *The Fellowship of the Ring*

I literally wandered into the middle of the Kansas school finance saga in 1997 with no idea how the events that followed would shape my own life, career, values, and beliefs from that point on. I left Kansas in 2008, but never really left in spirit. In retrospect, even by the time I'd left, I really didn't understand all that had gone on before my arrival or what would continue to go on after I left. Even from a distance after leaving Kansas, I've remained an active participant.

MY ENTRY TO THE SAGA

In the summer of 1997, I drove away from my apartment overlooking the Hudson River in Yonkers, New York, to go west: 1,228 miles and nineteen hours west, to Overland Park, Kansas. As a newly minted doctoral graduate from Teachers College of Columbia University, in New

FIGURE 1.1 My entry to the saga

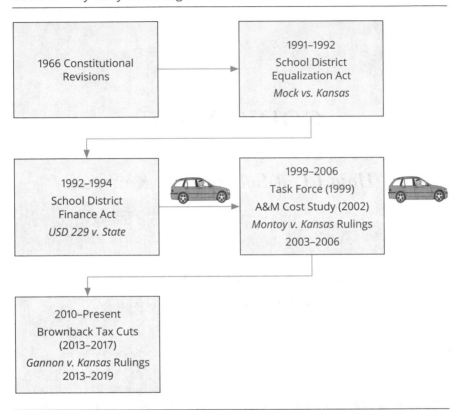

York City, I had taken a tenure-track faculty position at the University of Kansas in Lawrence. I got the job late in the academic job search season, when their first-choice candidate backed out and accepted another, presumably better or more desirably located position. I had no other offers and a rather large stack of rejection letters from across the country. I was just happy to have an academic job, even though this meant I'd be leaving the East Coast, where I'd spent my whole life, and leaving the best teaching job I ever had (perhaps still!) as a middle school science teacher at the Fieldston School, an elite, progressive private school in Riverdale (Bronx), New York City. Fieldston is the kind of place where media executives, authors, and Broadway producers send their kids, a place that, to this day, lingers in the back of my head as an example of what schools for all children should be—and could be, if they just had the resources. It's a school that was later highlighted in a *This American Life* two-part series on NPR, "3 Miles," as representing the home of the extreme "haves" in a "haves versus have nots" story of schooling in the Bronx.

I grew up in Vermont in a republican family. After completing my undergraduate degree in biology in Pennsylvania, I tried my hand at high school teaching at a military boarding school in Virginia. Among other things, the school wasn't particularly thrilled when I started the chapter on evolution or happy about my frequent absences from morning chapel service, for which I was admonished by the dean, who informed me the services were nondenominational and catered to both Methodists and Baptists. While I liked teaching, that school wasn't really a good fit for me. I pursued a master's degree in the Teaching the Talented (gifted education) program at the University of Connecticut and landed a job in New Hampshire. While working as a teacher in the Live Free or Die state of New Hampshire, I gravitated toward libertarian views. I attribute some of my libertarian leanings at the time to hours of listening to then local talk radio host David Brudnoy (WBZ, Boston). The two ideologies—libertarianism and old New England republicanism—at the time were not too far apart, but both were unlike what one might consider today's Republican or Tea Party views, ones favoring a gun-wielding, conservative Christian theocracy—views that an east coaster like myself tend to project onto Kansas, not entirely without justification. I simply believed in individual responsibility, small government, and local control and had adopted a naive skepticism of the economic efficiency of any and all government-operated programs—especially at the state or federal level, and including public schools. Equity concerns were not on my radar. To a large extent, my values were a product of my upbringing as an upper-middle-class white kid, from an almost entirely white New England town, where income and racial inequality were not a part of my daily lived experience.

In the early 1990s, as a teacher in a nonessential program (gifted and talented) in a New Hampshire middle school, I learned quickly about the local politics of school funding in a state where all politics, taxes, and school funding are local. This was around the time of the

1992 presidential primaries, which were later parodied in the film *Primary Colors*, caricaturing the rise of a Bill Clinton–like figure to his first presidential term. (New Hampshire being New Hampshire, it voted instead for nearby moderate Massachusetts native Paul Tsongas in that Democratic primary, and Pat Buchannan in the Republican primary.)

While the presidential candidates were making their rounds at local donut shops, I too realized that the local donut shop was where politics in New Hampshire was done. I'd sit at the Donut Depot before school each morning, have my coffee and my blueberry muffin, warm, with butter, and chat with the other regulars at the counter. When town meeting time came around— when school and municipal budgets and tax rates are set by popular vote—I would hope that at least one person from the local donut shop might step up and advocate to keep my program (and thus my job) in the district for another year. That's how school budgeting was (and largely is) done in old New England. Having never studied the topic formally, I had no comparison basis, nor any understanding of the vast inequities that resulted from one town to the next as a result.

A few years later, I found myself teaching science at the Fieldston School in New York. As a teacher at Fieldston, I was provided the opportunity (and financial support) to take courses at Teachers College, Columbia University. I had a bachelor's degree in biology, but no formal, general education courses up to that point. I had a master's degree (educational psychology) with a very specific focus on education of the gifted and talented, which I had pursued after having spent several summers working at a private residential program for academically talented youth. But I really wasn't sure where to begin this next endeavor and was skeptical of the value of more typical "ed school" classes. Recalling my days of donut shop politicking and thinking I might someday want to be a school district administrator, I chose a class on school finance. I figured a class on school finance might have some real teeth to it. It did, for sure. And the professor even managed to bring a few other graduate students in that class to tears when handing back our first assignments.

Within the semester, I found myself dragged into research projects ranging from studies of a specific state's school finance systems (Connecticut) to a study of the first significant attempt at private management of urban public schools, which occurred in Baltimore.[1] My new passion—strange as it seems—was designing spreadsheet simulations and dynamic, interactive simulation models of state aid formulas to figure out how to equitably and efficiently distribute state aid to local school districts—and, perhaps most importantly, how to distribute aid to enough districts, without spending too much, to get enough votes to pass the formula.[2] That was always the trick. In those days, the winner/loser counts on any state aid run still overshadowed partisan alliances in state legislative deliberations. Breaking partisan gridlock has become more difficult over the past two decades. These early research projects helped to both shape and shake up my perspectives on the politics of public education.

Like many critics of public schools in the mid to late 1990s, I felt that private managers might just have a shot at more efficiently running public schools. I thought, How could they do worse than government bureaucrats? I also believed that vouchers, charter schools, and competition were logical—if not simply the best—policy solutions for any and every ailment of government-operated schools (and my first academic article was a voucher proposal[3]), and that deregulating the teaching profession would necessarily lead to a higher quality workforce (a later article in the same journal[4]). I had an especially bleak view of schools of education and teacher preparation programs (reflected in a 2006 article[5]) and the role of teachers' unions, perhaps because I had never attended a teacher-preparation program myself and had refused to participate in the local unions, leading to a rather contentious relationship with local union leaders in one of my previous jobs. I believed vehemently that maintaining local control over taxing, financing, and budgeting was important, but had acquiesced by this point to the idea that state aid would be necessary to counterbalance disparities in local capacity.[6] My academic training had begun to influence my thinking.

I had developed my own preconceived notions about what might and might not work for improving public schools and my own naïve perspectives on how these issues aligned with traditional partisan values of conservatism, liberalism, Republican, and Democrat. My understanding in this regard was not academic and was regionally skewed for sure. Being raised a Vermont Republican put me out of step with most of the political spectrum, much like my own local hometown

US senator and high school graduation speaker, Jim Jeffords. In 2001, after having an "R" by his name for decades, Jeffords decided he had little in common with "Rs" from other regions and states, like Kansas, perhaps, and defected from the party. In my own lifetime, Vermont had shifted from being politically similar to New Hampshire to being an emerging socialist outpost, due largely to decades of migrants to the Burlington area from New York City and other mid-Atlantic states: Bernie (Sanders, that is), Howard Dean, Ben and Jerry, and members of the band Phish. My hometown, though, remained largely untouched by this political revolution.

As I was wrapping up my time in New York and transitioning into my new life in Kansas, state supreme courts in both Vermont and New Hampshire struck down their state school finance systems because of the inequities in funding and tax rates that resulted from heavy reliance on local property taxes. By this point, I had studied these issues enough academically to know that similar rulings had occurred across the country, as early as the 1970s in California[7] and New Jersey,[8] and later in more conservative states, including Kentucky[9] and Texas.[10]

Early in 1997, Vermont's high court explained, "The evidence demonstrates, in sum, that the system falls well short of achieving reasonable educational equality of opportunity."[11] Vermont's legislature and governor complied with the court ruling by adopting statewide property taxation and aggressive revenue sharing.[12] In December of that year, New Hampshire's high court declared: "In this appeal we hold that the present system of financing elementary and secondary public education in New Hampshire is unconstitutional. To hold otherwise would be to effectively conclude that it is reasonable, in discharging a State obligation, to tax property owners in one town or city as much as four times the amount taxed to others similarly situated in other towns or cities. This is precisely the kind of taxation and fiscal mischief from which the framers of our State Constitution took strong steps to protect our citizens."[13] "Fiscal mischief" indeed, but New Hampshire resisted change nonetheless and continues to resist to this day, over twenty years later. Neither state has made as much progress in improving educational equity or in relying on high-quality evidence to guide school finance reforms as Kansas has.

By this point, I had it pretty clear in my head that conservative, Republican education policy involved deference to local control for both financing and accountability, a preference for school choice involving vouchers and charter schools (which were just emerging at the time). Little did I understand at the time the conflicting values between choice and competition and local democratic control. It turns out, the two are highly incompatible. Who knew? (Scholars who had studied and written about it, that's who![14]) Conservative education policy in my view generally meant less regulation, including deregulation of the teaching profession and decentralization of governance more generally.

Step 1 after my arrival in Kansas was to begin to get a handle on how school funding, and public education governance more generally, worked in my new home state. After all, I was going to have to start teaching classes on school finance in the Kansas context, at the University of Kansas, to Kansans, within a matter of weeks. Even though the university was out in Lawrence, about forty minutes west of Kansas City, I had relocated to the suburban sprawl of Overland Park, outside of Kansas City, not too different from where I had lived in Nashua, New Hampshire. Most faculty lived out in Lawrence, which was, as I learned, a politically liberal bubble. This decision significantly shaped my Kansas experience, providing more connectedness with the politics of Johnson County and suburban Kansas City than I would have experienced if I had remained in the Lawrence safe space.

During that first year, I had to find some time to figure out Kansas school finance in between college basketball, figuring out where to go when the tornado sirens blared, and learning where to find the best BBQ (the answer to that most vexing question, by the way, is Oklahoma Joe's on Forty-Seventh Street in Kansas City, KS). Kansas was politically a red state, and I was surrounded by the politically red suburbs. This was an entirely new context for me, personally and professionally. I hadn't lived it, nor had I even really studied it or read about it academically. It had a Republican (albeit moderate) governor at the time, Bill Graves. However, his predecessor had been a Democrat, and woman who I came to learn presided over a sea change in public school financing in Kansas, ushering in the modern era. From early on, Kansas shook my understanding of the intersections between education policy and political ideology.

One of the first great tales I heard from my new university colleagues was of the sea change presided over by Governor Joan Finney, which had been instigated in 1991 by Shawnee County District Court Judge Terry Bullock. Judge Bullock is perhaps deserving of an entire chapter in this book. Judge Bullock's order in *Mock v. Kansas* and the reforms that followed occurred years before courts in Vermont and New Hampshire addressed similar concerns, though state courts elsewhere had intervened for decades (since the 1970s). Kansas had responded with a highly state-controlled system for financing schools and a prescriptive system for monitoring schools and districts: the School District Finance and Quality Performance Accreditation (SDFQPA) Act. This politically red state had, in effect, adopted a statewide property tax like the one adopted in far more liberal Vermont. Moreover, Kansas adopted strict limits on taxation above prescribed spending levels in order to maintain equity, something neither Vermont nor New Hampshire had achieved, though Vermont had adopted an aggressive revenue-sharing scheme for supplemental tax revenue.

I also came to learn that the state had forcibly consolidated non-K–12 school districts years earlier from over a thousand to just over three hundred, something Vermont still hasn't achieved to any significant extent, for all of its trying.[15] Kansas had also adopted curricular and program standards and a statewide system of assessments run through the University of Kansas. There were few to no rumblings of vouchers or charter school expansion—what I perceived as more typical conservative education policies.

There were downsides. I also observed some of what I perceived to be more typical red-state uses of these seemingly blue-state policies.[16] Legislators had used the tightly controlled state school finance system to reinforce disparities funding that existed prior to such tight state control, shortchanging schools and districts serving low-income and minority populations.[17] That is, they actually designed the school funding system to give more money to those who had more to begin with and less to those who had less. They had also used consolidation and reorganization of district boundaries to reinforce racial segregation, which also reinforced the financial disparities.[18] And over time, legislators in the know would introduce clever formula adjustments to exacerbate racial and economic disparities.[19] Centralization of curriculum and standards provided an opportunity for special interests to advance agendas such as pushing for adoption of "intelligent design" as part of the state science curriculum. But the net effect of the highly centralized, seemingly liberal policy structures in Kansas and the conservative pushback has been a system that is more good than bad, more balanced than not—and more successful on many measures than systems in surrounding states.

As I mentioned in the introduction, when working with state legislatures to mitigate school funding inequities or when testifying in court about those inequities, I often explain that the modest goal is to achieve a system that is *less bad than it otherwise might have been*. Kansas has achieved this modest goal, at least more than the typical coastal elite like me might expect. It will forever be a work in progress. No school finance system will ever be empirically, scientifically perfect. After all, school finance formulas are complex calculations that redistribute millions to billions of taxpayer dollars, and they must be adopted through political deliberation among elected officials. That can't always end well. In fact, we may be lucky when it ever does. Despite the conservative political leanings of the state, despite the draconian tax cuts pushed through under recent governor Sam Brownback, Kansas schools are doing relatively well—and Kansas school funding is more equitable and more adequate than that of most of its neighbors and the nation as a whole. It's less bad than it might otherwise have been, and that's a good thing.

Kansans owe this miracle to a set of conditions outlined in the introduction and to a cadre of unique characters I will discuss throughout this book. In a 2019 academic presentation in Kansas City, Missouri, I proposed seven conditions (I've now added an eighth), as listed in the introduction, that I believe are responsible for Kansas's success in improving school funding equity and adequacy:

1. The 1966 ratification of the education article of the Kansas Constitution, which established an independently elected Kansas State Board of Education, with self-executing constitutional powers to oversee elementary and secondary education (general supervision

of schools). It also required that the legislature "shall make suitable provision for finance of the educational interests of the state."

2. A judicial selection and retention process that reduces the role of political ideology among state high court justices and limits turnover, providing the opportunity for state high court judges to develop a deep understanding and institutional history of complex ongoing litigation.

3. A panel of high court judges with in-depth understanding of the complexities of school finance policy and the intersection with state constitutional requirements.

4. A legislature that has been generally responsive to the state high court in terms of orders to increase and/or redistribute state aid and in terms of meeting its obligation to provide empirical evidence to guide school finance reforms.

5. An independent and trusted (bipartisan) legislative research division (the Division of Post Audit), which has played a role in performing and digesting empirical evidence pertaining to school finance reform, including collaborating with outside scholars.

6. The availability (as a result of points 4 and 5) of high-quality evidence for (a) informing judicial evaluation of the state of school finance in Kansas and (b) guiding legislative reforms.

7. Tireless legal counsel with deep knowledge and institutional history, representing plaintiffs in several rounds and decades of litigation from 1990 to the present.

8. Engaged, knowledgeable, and experienced state and local media.

But it's more than just these eight conditions in play. There are stories and individuals behind the scenes, stories of persistence, vigilance, individual knowledge, and institutional history. One modest goal of this book is to be less boring than it might otherwise be if I wrote it like any other academic book on school funding and public policy. The topic just isn't innately riveting. Nor is the setting, Kansas—though some of the characters, from Shawnee County District Court Judge Terry Bullock to the *awesomely mustached* John Robb and the local writers and reporters who've chronicled the events of Kansas school finance, have provided much entertainment value along the way.

In February 2004, in the wake of Bullock's lower court ruling in *Montoy v. Kansas*, *The Pitch* reporter Joe Miller interviewed the judge. Among other things, Miller asked Bullock why he specifically was called upon to mediate the dispute, after having mediated a similar dispute a decade earlier: "'There are people who have perfect pitch, and they're meant to become singers,' he says, explaining what motivated him to seek the bench in the first place. 'There are people who are quick and coordinated, and they make great athletes. I've always believed that my knack, my little niche, if you will, is to listen to a lot of stuff and very quickly find the peanut and figure out what to do. 'In short, it's what I'm good at,' he says. 'And I'm sure you can get a different opinion on that.'"

Joe Miller and I had met at a tea shop a few months prior to the release of his story on Judge Bullock, in the Westport district of Kansas City, to discuss the Kansas school finance litigation more broadly. Miller was looking for the story to tell—knowing there probably was a story to tell, but not knowing at the time exactly what that story was. I can't recall how we first got in touch. But on more than one occasion, my own plotting on Kansas school finance occurred on the Missouri side of State Line Road. By that time, I lived just a few blocks west of State Line in Fairway, Kansas, in Johnson County. In our tea shop conversation, Joe gravitated immediately to the apparent main character in the drama—Judge Bullock—eventually crafting a 4,500-word feature article on the judge and the case, boldly titled, "You Got Schooled," with a full-page mug shot of Bullock.[20] That's right: a long-form, deep bio on a judge in a school finance case, including extensive discussion of the substance, context, and history of the case itself. I had provided quotes previously to reporters on issues related to school funding. But this was new, different, and refreshing to see.

Over time, I would get to know several local education reporters, from more and less serious media outlets. I met and spoke with writers from the *Pitch* on several occasions, who had a special knack for making the Kansas school finance saga accessible and entertaining. One such reporter was Tony Ortega, then editor of the *Pitch*, who would stop by the afternoon drive show at the local alt-rock radio station (96.5, "the Buzz") on Wednesdays to discuss what was going on that week. Tony regularly offered edgy political commentary on state and local issues. Kansas politics and politicians were often convenient political targets of Kansas City (Missouri) political commentary. If I recall, I reached out to Tony after hearing him discuss a related issue on one of those Wednesday segments, though I can't recall details. It was the local alt-rock station that at times offered the edgiest political commentary, including regarding school funding in Kansas on at least a few occasions. Notably, this same station, and its morning host a few years later, helped bring forward the story of Megan Phelps-Roper of the Westboro Baptist Church.[21]

Writers at the *Pitch* dedicated a hearty helping of their *KC Strip* columns to Kansas's legislative follies in school finance. As mentioned in the introduction, this particular column was written from the perspective of a sarcastic slab of meat—a KC strip steak, to be precise. In the midst of the *Montoy* litigation, when Kansas legislators were pressed to develop and fund a formula that would pass muster with the courts, legislators slipped through a modification to the formula that would allow (if not encourage) the state's wealthiest (and whitest) communities to raise additional revenues for their schools. At the time, I had just presented an academic paper with colleague Preston Green explaining how the steps the legislature had taken were merely codifying its long history of racially discriminatory behavior into new policies.[22] Tony Ortega had stopped by my house one day (in Leawood, Kansas) in search of story lines on Kansas politics, so I walked him through this particular series of examples. Intrigued, Tony eventually voiced the tale in the words of the *KC Strip*:

> Our great white leaders don't get much thanks for it, but over the past several decades, they've found **the most clever ways** to see to it that those darker school districts get treated like bull calves on castration day.
>
> Take the ingenious move they made in the early 1990s, for example. Back then, it looked like the jig was finally up. The damned activist courts were pushing the Legislature to make things "equitable," and it was obvious that our lawmakers were going to have to come up with more cash for the crappy schools that black kids were attending.

But then—a stroke of genius! The Legislature decided that school districts with a lot of **new construction needs** could increase their budgets and spend more money per pupil than other districts. The "new construction" adjustment they dreamed up wasn't money to pay for the building boom itself—oh, no, that's handled through capital-improvement bonds and the like—it was merely a bonus given to districts because they had new buildings to populate.

. . .

But then this clown **Terry Bullock**, a district court judge who had forced those early 1990s changes, tried to ruin the whole arrangement. In a 2004 court order, Bullock demanded that the Legislature quit playing games and finally start paying enough so that all students, no matter where they were from in Kansas, could get a good education.

. . .

Then, once again, inspiration struck.

If leaders couldn't reward rich white folks for building new schools, why not reward them for the expensive things they already owned? Namely, their **overpriced palatial homes!**

Sweet Jesus! What an insight![23]

In fact, the court never did take away that new facilities adjustment, but it did suggest that other adjustments, ones that actually addressed student needs, required attention. And the court chose to leave that adjustment alone for the sixteen (now seventeen) districts with the highest priced houses, but only because they were part of a new law that had not been fully vetted at trial through the lower court. They got by on a technicality.

I may be wrong, but it certainly seems plausible that these more entertaining portrayals of the dirty details of Kansas school finance helped to engage an audience in the Kansas City metro area. These were serious points of contention, in the context of state constitutional litigation. When presented so clearly, so bluntly, these legislative actions were plainly and obviously wrong. In the summer of 2005, Ortega again used the *KC Strip* column to address Kansas school finance, ridiculing Kansas legislators' battle with the court in a piece titled "The Wussies of Oz." Here's an excerpt, in which Munchkins are the legislators and Glinda the court—presumably, Chief Justice McFarland specifically:

> **Munchkin No. 3:** We promised the other Munchkins we wouldn't raise taxes! You can't make us go back on our word!
>
> **Glinda:** Oh, rubbish. Your promises are silly. The only real responsibility you have is to follow your constitutional duty to pay for a decent school system in Munchkinland. And it was you *yourselves* who paid for a study to figure out how much a suitable education costs in our land. For years, you've been increasing per-pupil spending by tiny amounts and ignoring how much a decent school system really costs. It's your own fault that the report found that you need to spend $853 million more a year just to meet constitutional requirements.[24]

After Tony Ortega departed from the *Pitch*, Justin Kendall took on the task of ridiculing Kansas policymakers, eventually coining the moniker "awesomely mustached" for the school finance plaintiffs' attorney, John Robb, as the next rounds of school finance litigation commenced.[25]

Another source of frequent, biting, and always on point commentary regarding Kansas school finance was *Wichita Eagle* cartoonist Richard Crowson. On one occasion in May of 2005, which I will discuss at greater length later in this book, the counsel representing the state in front of the Supreme Court was ill-prepared and, to be blunt, took a verbal lashing at the hands of the high court judges. As described in the *Lawrence Journal World*: "At times during the questioning from judges, the state's attorney, Kenneth Weltz, of Overland Park, conceded he didn't know the rationale behind certain aspects of the new school finance law approved by Republicans in the Legislature. Even so, he argued, the court should uphold it as constitutional."[26] Weltz is portrayed in Figure 1.2 by Crowson, reporting back to the attorney general on just how well those arguments went.

Crowson also captured roughly that same moment in history for which Tony Ortega ridiculed Kansas legislators as the "Wussies of Oz," portraying legislators as whining infants complaining of mean old judges while actual school children pled maturely for adequate school

FIGURE 1.2   School finance defendants get a report from their lawyer

funding, in a cartoon titled "Arrested Development."[27] And there are so many more! Enough to tell this entire tale via cartoons.

Local print and radio media also provided more serious coverage of the Kansas school finance saga, including major news outlets in Kansas (*Wichita Eagle, Lawrence Journal World, Topeka Capital Journal*). Throughout my time in Kansas and beyond, major regional, state and hyperlocal print media carried front page headlines like these:

School Ruling Could Cost State $1 Billion
Lawrence Journal World, 145 (337), December 4, 2003

$1 Billion School Fix Ordered
Northeast Johnson County Sun, December 4, 2003

Fix or Close Schools, Judge Orders State
Lawrence Journal World, 146 (133), May 12, 2004

Reporters like Tim Carpenter; Peter Hancock, statehouse reporter for the *Topeka Capitol Journal*; and Scott Rothschild were eventually followed by a new generation of outstanding reporters like Celia Llopis-Jepsen (at the *Capitol Journal* and later KCUR, Kansas City's NPR station). They—the media—kept the subject entertaining. They also kept the public informed, and over time there emerged a network of reporters, radio personalities, and news writers, both serious and less so, all exceptionally well versed in the complex, often tedious topic of school funding.

Mundane and tedious as it can be, school finance made the list of the top ten news stories of 2005 on Kansas.com, placing second overall—after evolution, but ahead of gay marriage, abortion, and pornography, in one of the few occasions in which school finance and pornography are mentioned in the same context:

Editorial: Top 10 Political/Public Policy Issues of 2005

Certain events and issues drove the debate on *The Eagle*'s Opinion pages this year. Some were epic and integral to the daily lives of Wichitans and Kansans. Some weren't. In crafting this list, we focused on political/public policy issues, not just big news stories—so the capture and conviction of BTK didn't qualify. We also focused on local and state issues, and gave strong preference to the ones that generated the most buzz and public passion.

1. **Evolution**. The Kansas State Board of Education again attacked evolution theory and drew ridicule for the state, hosting kangaroo-court hearings and finally redefining science to encourage the teaching of criticisms of evolution. Then a University of Kansas religion professor took flak for his intolerant criticisms of the board. The classroom impact? Practically nil. But it sure produced a lot of letters to the editor.

2. **School finance**. The Kansas Supreme Court ordered the Legislature to find more millions for public education or invite a K-12 shutdown. The constitutional crisis forced a rare special session and produced, amid attempts to curb the court's power, a remarkable $290 million, no-new-taxes funding increase. 2006 could offer another round, fueled by a key cost study and more court orders.

3. Iraq . . .

4. Gay marriage . . .
5. Economy . . .
6. Downtown redevelopment . . .
7. Expanded gambling . . .
8. GOP infighting . . .
9. Abortion . . .
10. Pornography . . . [28]

In many markets, truly local media has died, and Kansas and the Kansas City region have not been spared. One of the state's most seasoned political reporters, Peter Hancock, who covered decades of Kansas school finance, has departed for Illinois. The *Pitch* is no longer what it was, though various local interests have kept it in publication with local coverage. Even the alt-rock radio station that introduced me to Tony Ortega has recently moved to a national syndicated format, having abandoned edgy political commentary about a year earlier, replacing its morning show personalities. These may seem like unconnected or trivial events with respect to school finance reform. But I remain convinced that local media involvement in so many forms, at so many levels, and with such persistence helped keep Kansans informed about school funding in ways I've not witnessed elsewhere.

One final condition that might be added to the aforementioned list of what makes Kansas different is Kansas's and Kansans' stubbornness to *be Kansas*! The wheat state, the state with a barbed wire museum and the world's largest ball of twine as its major tourist attractions. Kansas has largely avoided, or at least approached cautiously and slowly, the multitude of education reform fads rippling across other states—including Colorado, Kansas's "progressive" neighbor to the west. These fads in recent years include tying teacher evaluation, compensation, and dismissal to student test scores and expanding school choice through charter schooling, vouchers, and tuition tax credits. These fads are argued to make education more efficient and thus improve quality without new money—and perhaps spending even less! In short, they are most often pitched as money-free or "revenue-neutral" solutions to education woes. States that have most aggressively pursued these reforms have often done so instead of funding schools adequately or even as an excuse for cutting funding dramatically. But Kansas has mostly avoided these fads, though the legislature did adopt a small tuition tax credit program and eliminated public school teacher tenure in 2014.[29] States like Colorado and Arizona in particular have taken an *anything but funding* approach to K–12 schooling, while Kansas has largely adopted a *funding-first* approach.

REFLECTIONS ON KANSAS

To put my time in Kansas into the historical context, college basketball references are obligatory. I was there from the end of Paul Pierce's career at the University of Kansas (1997), which sadly ended in an early-round upset loss in the 1998 NCAA tournament to Rhode Island, until the year of Mario Chalmer's buzzer-beating three-pointer that sent the NCAA finals into overtime against Memphis, leading to KU's first national championship since 1988. This was also the time period in which Kansas gained national exposure for its conservative politics around the teaching of biological evolution in the schools. The same state board of education that has wielded its independent constitutional authority to establish standards for schools, increasing pressure on the legislature to provide suitable funding, has at times strayed into controversial territory, at one point in 2005 holding its own revisionist version of the Scopes trial.[30] And this was the time period when the not yet nationally famous Fred Phelps and members of his Westboro Baptist Church would picket daily outside the University of Kansas Natural History Museum in protest of exhibits on human evolution.

National media latched on to Westboro Baptist's anti-LGBTQ protests, which eventually extended beyond the state's own borders to funerals of fallen soldiers and to the Kansas State Board of Education debating the introduction of intelligent design into the state science curriculum, because those stories comported with the portrayal of the state in *What's the Matter with Kansas* (released in 2004).[31] Eventually, the national media would focus on the dreadful failure of the Brownback tax cuts both as evidence of the self-destructive political preferences of stereotypical middle-American voters and to reinforce the caricatures of Kansans favoring ideology over evidence to their own detriment.

Meanwhile, Kansas and Kansans continued to quietly self-correct, counterbalance, and chart their path forward, one that is *less bad than it might otherwise be.* They have continued to maintain a minimally politicized judicial branch, which provides a critical counterbalance on politically divisive issues.[32] Despite consistently voting conservative in national elections, the pendulum has swung in state and local elections—if only between more and less conservative Republicans, with the latter often having been strong supporters of traditional public schools. Kansas and Kansans have continued to both seek and rely on high-quality, impartial evidence, to guide their decision-making both via outside experts and via their own highly competent, independent, nonpartisan research arm. And they have largely continued to resist off-the-shelf education reform fads and trends. [33]

POSTSCRIPT

As a postscript to this chapter, recall that as I left for Kansas, both my home state of Vermont and New Hampshire, where I once taught, had been ordered by their state supreme courts to address inequities and inadequacies in school funding. Of the two, Vermont did over time seek outside advisement to help reform its school funding system and did adopt significant reforms in 1998, mostly around tax equity issues.[34] But most recently, I, along with colleagues, finally had the chance to consult for Vermont legislators, providing them with a new approach to evaluating and reforming their school funding system, built largely on lessons learned and empirical methods and models applied previously in Kansas.[35] Within a few months after completing this work, our team was contracted to provide similar empirical analyses and policy guidance for New Hampshire, which has, as of the time of writing, done little to address concerns raised by its high court in 1998. A significant amount of the advisement provided to New Hampshire was built on methods and models used previously in Kansas and the lessons learned there.[36]

2

AVERY'S LAW

The Amendments that Reshaped Kansas' Constitution

"Matters intended for permanence are placed in constitutions for a reason—to protect them from the vagaries of politics or majority. A change in the messenger does not change the message."

—*Gannon v. State*, 319 P.3d 1196, 298 Kan. 1107 (2014)

To understand the story I'm going to tell throughout this book, first you need some historical context, which long predates my arrival on the scene. This chapter takes us back to the era before the US Supreme Court decision in *Brown v. Board of Education*, moving through the adoption of the 1966 Kansas constitutional amendments that shape how the state's high court evaluates school funding concerns to this day. The year 1966 and the two-year term of then governor William Avery also mark the introduction of the state's first statewide aid program for public schooling. Much of what I know about the *real* history of the Kansas constitutional amendments I learned in a lengthy conversation with Governor Avery (in his nineties at the time), outside a bathroom at a daylong economic conference at the University of Kansas in 2002.[1]

The 1966 constitutional amendments come about in a now typically Kansas way: beginning with the formation of a citizen task force, or advisory panel, to consider the issue and provide a report to the governor and legislature. As Charles Berger explains: "In their suggestions to the state legislature, they sought to 'provide constitutional guarantees of local control of local schools,' while maintaining the authority of the legislature, acting through an elected board of education, to 'shape the general course of public education and provide for its financing.'"[2] These recommendations led to uniquely split and constitutionally balanced responsibilities: the independently elected state board of education to oversee (general supervision of) public schools and set standards, and the legislature to make suitable provision for financing the educational interests of the state. Presumably, those interests were articulated and overseen by the state board. As the high court later opined: "We conclude from this constitutional assignment of different roles to different entities that the people of Kansas wanted to ensure that the education of school children in their state is not entirely dependent upon political influence or the voters' constant vigilance. As the panel declared, '[m]atters intended for permanence are placed in constitutions for a reason—to protect them from the vagaries of politics or majority. A change in the messenger does not change the message.'"[3]

I'll explore the historical path to these amendments, and the various motives involved, which complicate any superficial political analysis and include issues of racial segregation, school district consolidation, and the state's desire to exert greater control over its schools while lacking constitutional authority to do so. This points to the need for a new constitution, or at least a significantly amended one. I'll also provide a primer on the structure of Kansas government, roles of branches and agencies, and changes over time and the first major tests of that constitutional structure and the education clause in particular.

KANSAS FROM 1854 TO 1965: SOME BACKGROUND

We often speak of constitutions, state or federal, as if they are ancient documents scribed by uncountable generations past, perhaps etched in stone tablets or penned on ancient scrolls. At the very least, we commonly think of constitutions as documents shaped primarily at the founding of our nation and each state. In doing so, we ponder what those founders or authors living in very different times may have thought when they penned a certain phrase. Constitutional "originalists" like to assert that the constitution can thus only mean what was in the minds of those who penned those phrases at that time. Much of the foundation of the Kansas constitution was first laid out in the Organic Act of 1854 and affirmed in the state's 1859 constitution.

This included establishing the state's role in providing common schools (lower grade schools). As my colleague Preston Green and I explained in a chapter we wrote some time ago:

> The Organic Act of 1854 set aside certain sections of land to be used for education and designed a Territorial Superintendent of Common Schools, who certified teachers and organized school districts (Montoy v. State, 2005). Article 6 of the 1859 constitution provided funding for public education through taxation and the sale of public lands (Montoy v. State, 2005). Article 6 also specified that the "legislature shall encourage the promotion of intellectual, moral, scientific and agricultural improvement, by establishing a uniform system of common schools, and schools of a higher grade, embracing normal, preparatory, collegiate and university departments" (p. 316, emphasis added).[4]

Of particular importance was that the adopted language specified that the legislature was compelled (as indicated by the use of *shall*) to encourage promotion of intellectual, moral, scientific, and agricultural improvement by establishing a uniform system of common schools and schools of a higher grade. It was not optional. Further, that system was to be uniform, suggesting not only a preference for the minimum adequacy of schooling—sufficient to "encourage the promotion of" improvement—but also a preference that all Kansas children would have access to equitable common schools and higher schools, regardless of their location in the state or arguably even the color of their skin. One cannot understate the importance of the word *shall* here, a word that, in this context, could have its own chapter in this book. Words matter. Word selection matters in the context of documents like state constitutions, where rights and responsibilities are spelled out. The choice to use the word *shall*—rather than, say, *may* or *sure . . . whatever*—in the original constitution, and later in amendments to that constitution, may be among the most important word selections in regard to the current state of education in Kansas and the rights of the state's children within that system.

Kansas had established itself as a "free state" in the run up to the civil war, aligning with northern interests in part due to the influence of New England settlers who had found their way to Lawrence, Kansas.[5] The period through which the state was seeking statehood and the constitution was being drafted was characterized by repeated skirmishes with slave state neighbors from Missouri. Most casual readers of education policy probably think of Kansas in terms of *Brown v. Board of Education*, where the namesake plaintiffs were from Topeka, Kansas. Racial segregation of schools doesn't seem to comport with Kansas being a free state, but that's Kansas—at least in my view. It's a constant series of seemingly unreconcilable contradictions, or at least political tensions. In part, at the outset, Kansas was able to duck the question of having Black and white children attend school together because so few Black families had migrated to Kansas at the time. In some cases, Black people who migrated to Kansas established their own all-Black, often remote towns, like Nicodemus.[6] In other cases, however, Black people migrated to the state's largest towns, including Topeka, in the post–Civil War era.[7] To address this issue, rather than imposing a statewide segregation mandate, Kansas lawmakers passed a statute in 1879 permitting cities of the first class (those of approximately fifteen thousand or more residents) to operate separate elementary (common) schools for Black children. Under the same legislation, cities of the first class were delineated as separate, autonomous school districts, while cities of the second class were governed partially by county superintendents (*Reynolds v. Board of Education of the City of Topeka*, 1903).

The education article of the state constitution at the time included a "uniform systems" clause, which applied to common schooling: lower grade schooling, as high school at the time was relatively uncommon. By establishing cities of the first class as separate, autonomous school districts, the legislature skirted the possibility that permitting them to operate differently with respect to segregation would violate this uniform systems clause (uniformity was assumed to apply within the system of common schooling, but not to these exempted autonomous districts). Very few Black Kansans attended high school. However, high school attendance increased for Black students, and in 1905, the legislature adopted a special statute allowing Kansas City, Kansas, to operate segregated high schools.

So yes, Kansas, the progressive "free state," did find numerous ways to craft laws to establish, reinforce, and protect racial segregation, though without making it any kind of statewide mandate. Even during this period, the Kansas judicial system, under a structure different from that which exists today, intervened to ensure equity—mainly between schools serving Black and white children within cities of the first class. Kansas had provided the option to operate separate schools, presumably "uniform" (within any one system), for Black and white children in 1879 and tweaked the law in 1905 to account for high school students. *Plessy v. Ferguson* was ruled on in 1896, declaring that separate was okay so long as the accommodations were equal. And the Kansas courts applied a relatively strict standard of uniformity to evaluate whether Black and white schools were substantively equal during the period from *Plessy* (1896) through *Brown* (1954).[8] Kansas courts also continually denied expansion of segregation beyond the class of schools established by the legislation.

In the final case in the run up to *Brown v. Board*, the Kansas Supreme Court denied the establishment of segregated schools in Johnson County, which had seen a significant housing boom in the post-war years, in the northeastern corner of the county, which bordered Kansas City, Kansas, and Kansas City, Missouri. Much of the housing growth had occurred under strict restrictions on deeds to properties and homes, excluding Black, Jewish, and other nonwhite ownership. Much of this development occurred under the direct watch of and while applying the creative real estate development strategies of native Kansas City developer J. C. Nichols, who is often cited as inventing the use of local homeowners' associations (HOAs) to adopt and enforce racially restrictive covenants as a way to preserve the value of homes.

Nichols perfected this art in Johnson County, and shared it with the real estate industry nationally. In 2001, Kevin Fox Gotham explained that between 1900 and 1947, 97 percent of the developed acreage in Johnson County, Kansas, was racially restricted and 96 percent of Johnson County subdivisions were racially restricted.[9] The fifteen black high school students who resided in the county at the time were shipped off to segregated schools in Kansas City, a few miles to the north.[10] No Black students attended the Shawnee Mission High School, which served primarily racially restricted neighborhoods and developments.

As Nichols's descendants described it—"He had to do what he had to do"[11]—he was merely acting in the best economic interests of (white, non-Jewish) homeowners and real estate investors, given the constraints of the day. In other words, he was quite literally capitalizing on racism. Of course, those economic issues led to vast wealth disparity between Black and white residents, quite specifically across boundaries of housing segregation established by Nichols, local government officials, and his peers in the industry.[12] Troost Avenue was a dividing line within Kansas City, Missouri, as a recent KCUR story explained: "Today, houses west of Troost can go for eight times as much as houses east of Troost, despite being priced similarly in the 1960s. Rising property values in Nichols's neighborhoods helped white Kansas Citians build wealth while black families lost equity as their homes depreciated."[13]

Not only are these effects persistent, but they have become exacerbated over time and the segregation of the region has largely held constant, with many zip codes in Johnson County, Kansas, still having very few Black homeowners. As Kansas Citians became more aware of this history in the mid-2000s, Kansas legislators were asked about adopting legislation to strike racial restrictions from HOA covenants. In 2005, when asked about whether the legislature should act, Kansas Senator John Vratil of Leawood asserted that this was an issue to be handled by local homeowners' associations: "It's a local issue, and a homes association issue. It's a question of, is it offensive enough that you're willing to pay $50 to $100 per homeowner to get it removed? And I think I know what the answer is. . . . It's one of those issues that politicians love to talk about because it resonates, but when you get below the surface, most people just aren't interested in going to the time and expense to deal with it."[14]

Figure 2.1 and Figure 2.2 are pulled from slide decks I used back when teaching at the University of Kansas in the mid-2000s, a time when I had become obsessed with mapping data and when I first became aware of the persistent problem of racial residential segregation. These maps focus specifically on the Kansas City metropolitan area, with the Missouri side of the line to the right and Kansas to the left—but the curvy line near the top left carves off the corner of Kansas. Kansas is roughly outlined by the dashed rectangle. Each dot represents, if I recall correctly, ten individuals. Figure 2.1 shows the overlay of white, Black, and Hispanic residents. Then, Figure 2.2 shows only Black residents. In Figure 2.1, you can see that Johnson County, Kansas, which was developed largely to be an all-white county, remained mostly white by 2003 (and remains that way today). In fact, many of the neighborhoods of homes built from the 1940s through the 1970s in the northeastern corner of the county remained less than 1 percent Black, while neighborhoods to the north in Kansas City, Kansas, and blocks to the east in Kansas City, Missouri, were majority Black.

Figure 2.2 is perhaps even more striking, showing where Black populations were relegated to home ownership, and the distribution of the Black population decades later, in the mid-2000s. To this day, Johnson County remains nearly 90 percent white, while Wyandotte County is only 67 percent white.[15] A striking feature of Figure 2.2 is the bounded box in Kansas City, Missouri, within which the majority of the Black population resides, with an especially clear boundary at its western edge (Troost Ave.).

These historical patterns remain highly relevant to this day, and they played a role during litigation over school funding in the mid-2000s and in steps taken by state legislators representing Johnson County to reestablish a position of advantage for the county's predominantly white schools. Johnson County's State Senator Vratil was at least partly responsible for a change to the state school finance

FIGURE 2.1   Zip code–level demographics: Kansas City metropolitan area

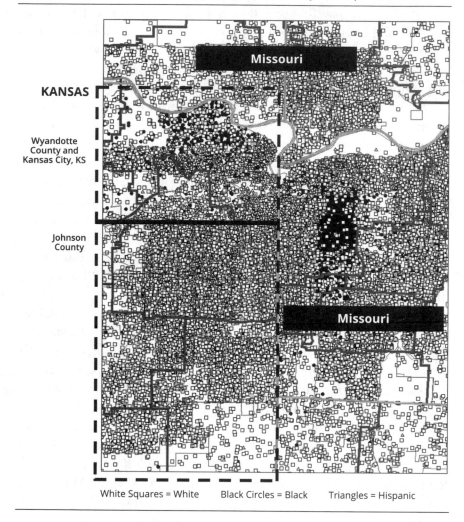

White Squares = White   Black Circles = Black   Triangles = Hispanic

formula, which provided the option for districts with higher valued homes to raise additional revenue to support higher teacher pay. As he explained to Tony Ortega of the *Pitch*: "Clearly, it costs more to live in certain counties of the state . . . therefore, it is a logical conclusion, an irrefutable conclusion, that it costs more to provide an education in those areas."[16]

FIGURE 2.2 Zip code–level demographics: Kansas City metropolitan area, Black residents only

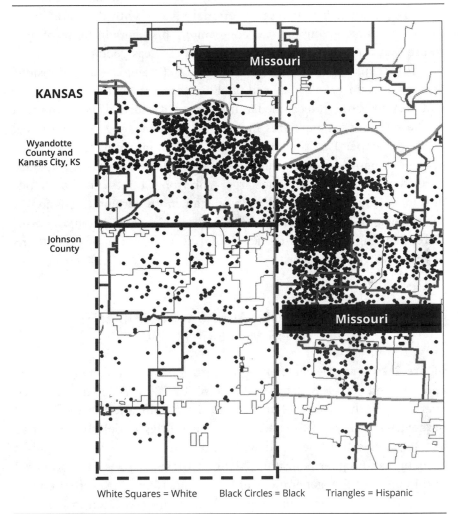

White Squares = White   Black Circles = Black   Triangles = Hispanic

Although these quotes paint Senator Vratil in a particular harsh light, at other points in this book he plays the role of a moderate republican—a supporter of quality education, increased funding for schools, and upholding constitutional obligations—and a coauthor of task force language leading to the first of many cost studies. The senator, like almost any elected official in state government, was primarily interested in what he could do for his constituents: residents of the largely white, segregated suburbs of Johnson County. He was also among the few with deep knowledge of and institutional history with the state school finance formula, giving him the edge among his peers in terms of how to use that formula—either for good or for . . . less good.

In the spring and early summer of 2020, amidst racial tensions across the country and renewed public interest in acknowledging past and present wrongs, local media in Kansas City turned their attention to the numerous monuments in the city honoring segregationist real estate developer J. C. Nichols. In June 2020, monuments to J. C. Nichols were removed from prominent locations in Kansas City, Missouri. In October 2020, one of the larger Johnson County neighborhoods developed under racial restrictions began more serious discussion of the removal of those restrictions.[17] But the racial segregation, the associated housing value, and the accumulated wealth gaps of generations of these restrictions persist.

EVOLUTION OF KANSAS GOVERNMENT TO ITS MODERN FORM

Figure 2.3 shows the number of constitutional amendments proposed and adopted for each decade from 1961 to 2000. A lot has changed over time, with substantial changes to the organization of the judicial branch, with changes to specific responsibilities under the executive and legislative branches, and with regard to the provision of public schooling and higher education. Many of these changes have occurred within the past few generations of state leadership. The current education article of the constitution was substantially rewritten in 1965 and ratified in 1966. I was lucky to have the opportunity to speak at length with the man who was governor during that time, William Avery. The man who implemented the first significant state school aid formula in the immediate aftermath of the adoption of the new Article 6, Dale Dennis, just retired this past year. What we are discussing are not, by any stretch, ancient texts. Many are texts of the 1960s and 1970s, a particularly progressive but politically volatile era. That Kansans could come to such agreement on such significant governance changes

FIGURE 2.3   Amending the Kansas Constitution

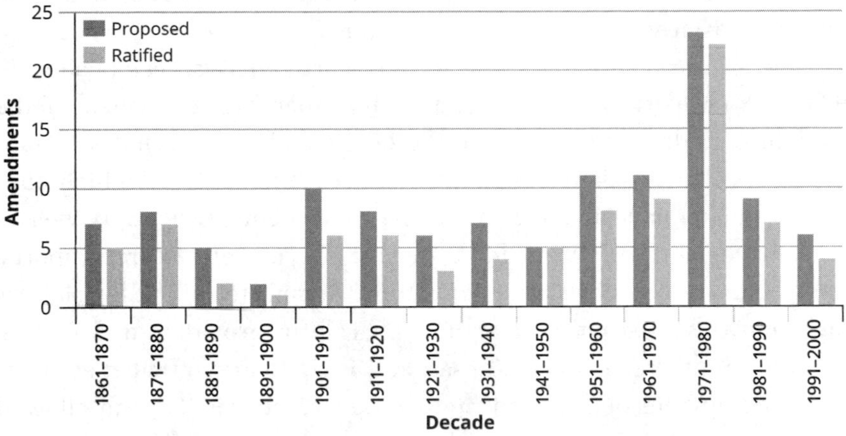

Source: J. W. Drury and M. G. Stottlemire, *The Government of Kansas* (Lawrence: University of Kansas, Division of Continuing Education, 2001).

during this period speaks volumes. Other changes occurred in the run up to this period, including establishment of a legislative coordinating council and legislative research entities, as well as judicial reform.

Legislative Coordinating Council

A unique feature of Kansas's government emerged in 1933, when Kansas became one of the first states to establish what it called a *legislative coordinating council* (LCC), in order to "prepare a legislative program in the form of bills or otherwise, as its opinion the welfare of the state may require, to be presented at the next session of the legislature."[18] The council consists of ten senators appointed by the lieutenant governor and fifteen by the speaker of the house, including most of the legislative leaders, ex officio. These are the officials who have been selected by their party caucuses and officially elected by their chambers. They are the speaker of the House, the president of the Senate, the majority leaders from both chambers, the minority leaders from both chambers, and the speaker pro tem.

It was this group that proposed and oversaw the first study of education costs in Kansas, released in 2002. The study has been argued to be the legislature's first, own study of costs. But questions persist as to whether a study overseen by the LCC necessarily represents the broader legislative interests and obligations.

The Kansas Legislative Research Department was established in 1934 as a nonpartisan fact-finding entity, operating on behalf of the legislature, under the oversight of the LCC (see Figure 2.4). Also established was the Legislative Division of Post Audit (LDPA), which conducts regular financial audits of state government services, as well as performance audits that include a variety of types of research reports, at the behest of the Legislative Post Audit Committee of the legislature. These entities have played a significant role in providing and vetting research to inform policy in Kansas, and I would argue that they have, over time, upheld quality and nonpartisan standards. Having allowed (for the purpose of timeliness) the LCC to contract and oversee the 2002 cost analysis that played a role in litigation from 2003 to 2006, the legislature itself assigned LDPA the responsibility for conducting and overseeing follow-up cost analyses, released in 2006. These analyses will be discussed in much greater detail in chapter 7.

FIGURE 2.4   The Kansas legislature

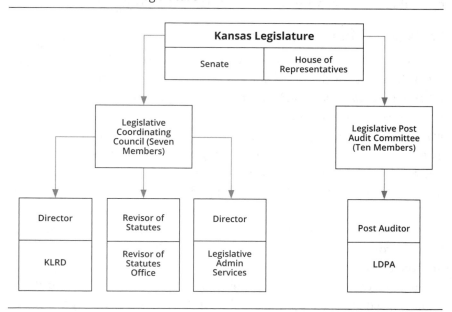

Judicial Reforms (1957–1958)

Kansas's judicial structure has also changed over time—most significantly in 1957, as Stephen Ware explains:

> Until 1958, Kansans elected their supreme court justices. The establishment of the Kansas Supreme Court Nominating Commission in 1958 was a reaction to events that had occurred after the most recently preceding general election.
>
> Kansas is the only state in the union that gives the members of its bar majority control over the selection of state supreme court justices. The bar consequently may have more control over the judiciary in Kansas than in any other state. This process for selecting justices to the Kansas Supreme Court is described by the organized bar as a "merit," rather than political, process.[19]

The purported virtue of this process is that it leads to a less politicized judiciary, or at least a less obviously partisan one. But Ware notes that "during this period, twenty-two people appointed by the governor served on the Commission. In all twenty-two cases, the governor appointed a member of the governor's party."[20]

It took multiple attempts to achieve the current structure, with resolutions proposed and defeated in 1953 and 1955 and eventually succeeding based on a resolution proposed in 1956.[21] The proposal was patterned after a system used in Missouri, in which the governor appoints from a list of three persons nominated by the nominating commission. In Kansas, that commission consists of a chairperson selected by the state bar association and two members from each congressional district, one of whom must be a lawyer selected by members of the bar association residing in that district; the other, a lay member, is appointed by the governor; and no members can be current office holders or hold official party positions.[22] Once appointed by the governor (from the short list), a justice serves for at least one year. At the first general election after that year, a retention vote is held. Thereafter, retention votes are held every six years.

Ware describes a complex series of events that led to election of democratic governor George Docking; the retirement of the supreme court chief justice, who had fallen ill just before Docking took office; and the last-minute replacement on the high court by Docking's would-be (but for a loss in the primary) republican opponent, then-current governor Hall, who had retired abruptly so that his lieutenant governor could appoint him to the court (referred to as the *triple play*). This appointment could not have happened under the new system—so with extensive lobbying from the state bar association, "the legislature submitted a proposal to amend the constitution to adopt the commission plan for the selection of supreme court justices only, and this amendment was passed by a wide margin in the 1958 general election." [23]

This new system, while criticized by some as veiled in secrecy, thus giving excessive control to the state's professional legal community, has in my view led to a court that in recent decades has been especially well equipped to deal with the constitutional complexities of state school finance litigation, especially in a state with an otherwise unique parsing of constitutional roles and responsibilities. Legal knowledge matters greatly in this context. Institutional knowledge and history also matter. And the process by which high court judges in Kansas are appointed and retained seems to have led to a system in which the high court as a whole possesses extensive institutional history and constitutional knowledge on school finance and other complex constitutional questions it faces.

1960S: PROGRESSIVE, AND NOT SO, REFORMS

As discussed earlier, key elements of the adopted 1859 Kansas constitution were that the "legislature *shall* encourage the promotion of intellectual, moral, scientific and agricultural improvement, by establishing a *uniform system of common schools*, and schools of a higher grade, embracing normal, preparatory, collegiate and university departments" (emphasis added). The original constitution also provided for the layered governance and control of Kansas schools, establishing autonomous, independent school districts of larger cities and towns and providing for election of state and county superintendents of public instruction, the raising and supporting of school funds, and establishment of a state university.[24] With the emergence of second-ary schooling over the ensuing decades, additional district types were added, and the number of self-governing school districts in the state exploded to over nine thousand by 1896. As early as the 1860s, the first state superintendent argued that many towns were operating school districts that were simply too small to be efficient and to provide a sufficient property tax base to run a school.

School district size, efficiency, costs, and local property taxes serve as a recurring theme decades later in school finance litigation and cost analyses. But these overlapping issues also set the stage for the constitutional amendments of 1966, which, like many bold changes in Kansas's history, may have been successful because they were both progressive and not at the same time. These amendments created tools that could be used by some to advance equity, but they had equal capacity to be used by others to exert control and pursue specific policy agendas.

The constitutional amendments to the Education Article (Article 6) came about from the recommendations of an eleven-member task force that was formed in 1965, under then governor William Avery (1965–1967). Key elements of the task force recommendations and the eventually adopted Article 6 include the following:

Section 1: The legislature shall provide for intellectual, educational, vocational and scientific improvement by establishing and maintaining public schools, educational institutions and related activities which may be organized and changed in such manner as may be provided by law.

Section 2: (a) The legislature shall provide for a state board of education which shall have general supervision of public schools, educational institutions and all the educational interests of the state, except educational functions delegated by law to the state board of regents. The state board of education shall perform such other duties as may be provided by law.

Section 5: Local public schools under the general supervision of the state board of education shall be maintained, developed and operated by locally elected boards. When authorized by

law, such boards may make and carry out agreements for coop-
erative operation and administration of educational programs
under the general supervision of the state board of education,
but such agreements shall be subject to limitation, change or
termination by the legislature.

Section 6: The legislature shall make suitable provision for
finance of the educational interests of the state. No tuition
shall be charged for attendance at any public school to pupils
required by law to attend such school, except such fees or supplemental charges as may be authorized by law. The legislature
may authorize the state board of regents to establish tuition,
fees and charges at institutions under its supervision.

Importantly, the word *shall* remains in Article 1, making it obliga-
tory, not optional, for the legislature to provide for these broad goals.
Shall also occurs in Section 6, which gives the legislature the responsibility of providing financing for the educational interests of the state.
Importantly, the newly proposed structure gives responsibility for
determining those educational interests to a newly created branch of
Kansas government, with separately elected public officials: the Kansas
State Board of Education, which is assigned the constitutional duty for
"general supervision" of schools, subsequently assigning local opera-
tions and supervision to local boards of education. This unique distribution of powers in Kansas separates the determination of the goals
of the education system from the responsibility to fund that system,
thus ensuring that the branch responsible for financing cannot simply
determine that it wants to only finance more modest or lesser goals.
This may not have been foreseen at the time for its potential to play a
major role in later school funding litigation, in which the court would
be asked to mediate disputes between these branches, each asserting
its independent constitutional authority.

These same amendments that created such progressive opportunities in later decades also had other motives behind them, including
more questionable ones. For example, *uniform* no longer appeared in
the education articles, weakening the equity requirements that had
previously been used to enforce equity between Black and white
schools before *Brown*.[25] The establishment of the state board with

constitutional authority over the general supervision of schools was, at least in part, a power grab intended to create the authority for the state to forcibly consolidate and reorganize local public schools, an issue that had plagued the state since its founding. On several occasions, the state legislature sought to consolidate small schools and districts but had been denied by state courts on the basis that no one governing agency, nor the legislature itself, possessed the authority to reorganize local jurisdictions.[26]

Immediately prior to constitutional amendment in the 1963 School Unification Act, the legislature adopted an alternative strategy of delegating oversight to the state superintendent of public instruction. Every significant procedure in the process, including ratification of local elections, required the state superintendent's decision or approval.[27] This too failed in court on the first go-around, but once the new Article 6 was adopted, creating a state board with the relevant authority, legislators were able to enact the Unification Law, and the total number of school districts in the state was reduced from approximately 1,600 to 306. While promoting efficiency and centralizing control, this control could also be used to reinforce racially segregated school district boundaries, and it provided opportunities to allocate funding to these districts in racially disparate patterns—as Preston Green and I explained in previous writings.[28] This funding needed only be *suitable*, not *uniform*. As with so much in Kansas's history, there seem to be bright and dark sides to each episode.

Another legacy of the short-lived gubernatorial term of William Avery was the School Foundation Act—the first significant state school finance formula. Put simply, that's a big freakin' deal in 1965–1966— and huge for a one-term, two-year governor. This was a relatively advanced formula for its day. Major provisions of the act included a basic allotment of $760 per pupil and included two major adjustments to that allotment: (a) an adjustment based on teacher education and experience levels; and (b) a multiplier based on each district's pupil-to-teacher ratio relative to the state average. In addition, the legislature implemented strict limits to budget growth (limits to the local taxing authority) under the act. With the School Foundation Act, the state share of school funding rose from about 23.7 percent in 1960–1961 to about 35.3 percent in 1965–1966. At this point in time, state funding was at nearly the same level as local school district funding (35.6 percent), with county-level funding making up 20 percent.[29] This balance of revenues placed Kansas at a slightly lower level of state control than the national average at that time.[30]

In a 2003 interview, Governor Avery explained: "I proposed a state aid to elementary and secondary schools and the institutions of higher learning and the taxes to support that additional assistance. And that made me a one-term Governor. It was a disappointment at the time, of course, because I got about everything I asked for and asked for quite a bit."[31] In our 2002 conversation, the former governor put it in more blunt terms, explaining that "it all worked out great, for everyone . . . except me."

Also during this period, another character who was to become a major player in public school finance in Kansas for the next half century entered the scene: Dale Dennis, who was appointed state school finance administrator in 1967, becoming the individual charged with calculating and operating the state's first significant school funding formula.[32] Dale would hold numerous related leadership roles, running the formula and providing guidance, testimony, and oversight until his retirement in 2020.

THE IMMEDIATE AFTERMATH: TESTING THE NEW CONSTITUTION

Figure 2.5 summarizes the governing structure specified by the 1966 amendments. The Kansas State Board of Education members are independently elected by districts across the state and granted constitutional authority for general supervision of schools. The legislature, the composition of which is diagrammed in figure 2.5, is charged with making "suitable provision for finance of the educational interests of the state." The legislature also may authorize the state board to take on additional responsibilities with respect to K–12 schools, raising some questions to be vetted by the courts regarding whether and to what extent the state board possesses its own "self-executing" authority. Therein lies the role of the uniquely appointed state supreme court in evaluating the unique balance of powers over education between the state board and the legislature.

FIGURE 2.5   Kansas government structure

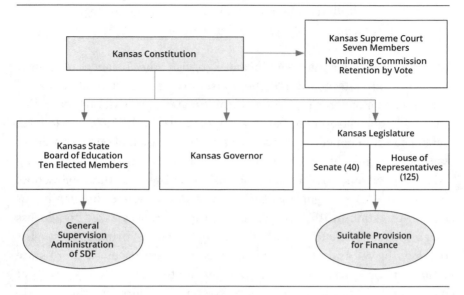

The first opportunity the state high court had to evaluate these roles was in a 1973 case involving whether the state board itself had the authority (without being given that authority by the legislature) to adopt regulations governing public school districts. That is, does the state board have "self-executing powers" under the constitution? The state's high court decided that in fact it does:

> The issue to be decided in this appeal is whether a regulation adopted by the State Board of Education relating to school conduct is or is not valid. The trial court held the regulation to be void, and its ruling has been appealed.
>
> We turn to the point first raised by the plaintiff: Is article 6, § 2 (a) self-executing as it concerns the exercise of general supervision over the public schools, educational institutions and educational interests of the state except, of course, as to functions delegated to the state board of regents? Our answer is that in the restricted sense of exercising general supervision, article 6, § 2 (a) is self-executing. In other words it is our view that the state board may exercise its constitutional power of

supervision without ancillary legislation and that its authority in that limited respect could not be thwarted by legislative failure to adopt supplementary legislation.[33]

The court wouldn't significantly revisit the balance of power between the state board and the legislature as it pertained to school funding and standards until a few decades later in the Montoy case. But the state court system did have an opportunity in the 1970s to address school funding concerns in two back-to-back cases, choosing to do so without specific reference to the new education article or its meaning with respect to school funding. Specific provisions of the 1965 School Foundation Act brought about the first round of school finance litigation in the state in 1973. In particular, the court was asked to address three major deficiencies with the school finance formula. First, districts with well-trained and experienced teachers received more state funding than districts with less experienced teachers. That is, they got more simply because they had more. Second, the pupil-to-teacher ratio multiplier placed large, urban districts at a disadvantage by placing significantly more state funding into the coffers of small, rural districts with fewer pupils per teacher.[34] Third, the index used for determining local tax efforts harmed poor school districts in rich counties because the expected contribution of a poor district was computed as equal to that of more affluent districts in the same county.[35] Another provision of the act restricted the budgetary authority of school districts. School districts were prohibited from increasing their budgets annually by more than 4 percent. This provision had the effect of codifying existing inequalities between rich and poor school districts because the provision was put into place on top of (a) provisions of the 1965 act that granted more funding to already advantaged districts and (b) disparities in local revenue raising that had existed prior to the 1965 act.

In 1972, the Johnson County District Court ruled in *Caldwell v. State* that the school finance system violated the Equal Protection Clause (not the new Article 6) to the extent that it "[made] the educational system of the child essentially the function of, and dependent on, the wealth of the district in which the child resides."[36] Interestingly, the existing School Foundation Act failed to improve equity between schools in wealthy and poor towns and counties not merely because

it failed to provide sufficient aid, but also because of the various provisions that drove aid to districts that were wealthier and had simply
spent more in the past.

Following legal challenges to the School Foundation Act, the legislature adopted the first iteration of the School District Equalization
Act (SDEA). SDEA replaced the pupil-to-teacher ratio adjustment with
different base budget amounts for districts of different sizes. SDEA
provided districts with fewer than four hundred students a base budget
of $936 per pupil and districts with more than 1,300 students a base
budget of $728 per pupil. That is, the previous mechanism was replaced
with state-defined allotments not directly associated with staffing
parameters, but ultimately replicating the inequities of the previous
version. In addition, the state established new limits on annual budget
growth and tied those limits to district size groups. Districts above
the median spending of districts in their size group could increase
their budget by 5 percent per year. Districts below the median spending of districts in their size group could increase their budget to the
lower of (a) 5 percent above the median or (b) a 15 percent increase
over the previous year. This policy led to a ratcheting effect over the
next eighteen years, wherein higher-funded enrollment categories
(small districts) significantly outpaced revenue growth of lower-funded
enrollment categories (large districts). That is, not only did the same
patterns of disparity continued to exist, but the state-defined disparities widened in dollars over time because state-controlled growth rates
were established on a percentage basis and districts could adjust their
budgets relative to others in their same size group. In effect, the legislature was micromanaging the system toward increased disparity, with
the biggest losers being the larger cities and towns that were home to
the state's minority population.

The second round of challenges to state school finance policy came
in 1976, in *Knowles v. State Board of Education* (1976). Plaintiffs chal-
lenged the constitutionality of the SDEA on the grounds that it violated the Bill of Rights of the state constitution (focusing on equitable
taxation under Article 11) and the Equal Protection Clause of the US
Constitution. The Chautaqua County District Court struck down the
SDEA because "the distribution of state funds under the formula provided in the Act resulted in unequal benefits to certain school districts

and an unequal burden of ad valorem school taxes on taxpayers in various districts with no rational classification or basis."[37] The district court also held that the SDEA's provision for school funding "was not sufficient to enable the plaintiffs to provide a fundamental education for the students within the respective districts on a rationally equally basis with students of other school districts within the state as required in the state constitution."[38]

However, the district court noted that the legislature was in session and gave the legislature time to correct the inequalities. The legislature then amended the SDEA to address the deficiencies. For example, the limitation on school budget increases was raised from 5 percent to 10 percent, and in some instances to 15 percent. That is, under pressure from the court, legislators relaxed the restrictions on budget growth they themselves had proactively implemented. *District wealth* was also redefined to be an average of the previous three years, to "soften any sharp increase or decrease in either the adjusted valuation or the taxable income within a district."[39] The district court then dismissed the case as moot because the amendments to the SDEA were substantial enough to constitute an entirely new law.

The Kansas Supreme Court, however, vacated (read, tossed out) the lower court's dismissal because "the ultimate effect of the formula depends upon the use of similar factors contained in the prior law such as district wealth, local effort, budget per pupil and sales ratio to local assessed valuations."[40] Thus the constitutional questions raised by the plaintiffs remained unsolved. The case was remanded to the Shawnee County District Court because the record was insufficient to decide on these constitutional issues. The district court upheld the SDEA in 1981, seven years after *Knowles* had been originally filed. Again, no pressure was provided by the courts to substantially alter the legislature's approach to financing schools.

REFLECTIONS ON THE 1960S REFORMS

Perhaps most importantly, this history illustrates that the current structure of Kansas's government, roles, and responsibilities, laid out in the state constitution, are not ancient artifacts that can't reasonably be interpreted and applied to modern-day Kansas. Many of the most substantial changes have in fact occurred in the last sixty years, in a time frame in which a single individual oversaw the state school finance system and the multiple major structural legislative changes to that system. Further, these changes led to a uniquely structured system of governance for elementary and secondary education, which by the end of the period discussed in this chapter had yet to be tested and fully vetted by the state's high court. Further, the state had ratified a high court appointment and retention structure that would, for decades to follow, result in deep institutional knowledge on complex issues like school finance under the unique constitutional structure of the state. Finally, perhaps the oldest unique element of Kansas governance discussed here that played an important role in shaping the school finance saga in the decades that followed was the creation of the nonpartisan Legislative Division of Post Audit.

While the 1960s reform period in particular is most often characterized as *progressive* in that it achieved a high degree of centralization of authority and provided seemingly strong language regarding the legislature's responsibility to fund public schools, there were also other sides to the story. Although the word *shall* stuck—in the legislative obligation to "encourage the promotion of intellectual, moral, scientific and agricultural improvement," and it was even added to the legislature's obligation to "make suitable provision for finance"—the word *uniform* did not. And thus equity requirements in particular were eroded, at least until the court in later decades began to unpack the term *suitable*.

Finally, it is also apparent that to a large extent, the structural reforms of the 1960s came about to provide the state the authority to regulate local public school districts, including forcing their consolidation. On the one hand, this promoted statewide organization and efficiency, but it also reinforced interdistrict segregation and funding disparities between districts that fell along racial lines. These funding disparities emerged in part because of the state's continued habit of building each iterative new school finance formula on disparities that existed in the previous iteration.

3

MOCK TRIALS

*Laying the Legislative Groundwork
for Educational Equity*

"With every good wish and with appreciation for
your splendid cooperation and professionalism."

—Terry L. Bullock, April 10, 1992

Now our narrative will usher in the modern era of Kansas education policy, still prior to my own arrival on the scene. This chapter digs into the first high drama on the high plains, in which Judge Terry Bullock arrives on the scene and orchestrates a legislative showdown, eventually resolved under the leadership of democratic governor Joan Finney and her task force with the adoption of the 1992 School District Finance and Quality Performance Accreditation Act. That formula is later evaluated and upheld in part and overturned in part by another of Kansas's strong women, District Court (now High Court Chief Justice) Judge Marla Luckert. The high court, in an opinion written by justice Kay McFarland, then upheld the formula in its entirety.

I'll introduce many of the characters who have helped to shape the modern era of Kansas school finance, from Shawnee County District Court Judge Terry Bullock to legal counsel from both sides of the aisle, district and high court judges, legislators, and political operatives along the way. Over time, many key players have moved from one position to another—from lower courts to the high court, or from representing an involved client to an appointment on the high court.

Kansas is often characterized as a populist state, and at numerous points in recent decades, the path forward has been laid by citizen task forces. The 1960s constitutional revisions began with a task force. The 1990s in Kansas began and ended with task forces laying the groundwork for future school finance reforms. The late 1990s and early 2000s ushered in the modern era of school funding legal challenges and introduced the first evaluation of the cost of meeting the state's constitutional obligation, on recommendation from the governor's (Governor Graves) Vision 21st Century task force. The task force's study, completed in 2002 and initially ignored, would become a lightning rod for political debate and judicial evaluation of the legislature's responsibilities to fund Kansas schools.

THE ROAD TO *MOCK*

When we last left our fearless heroes of the Kansas legislature, they had escaped an adverse ruling in the *Knowles* case, making minor adjustments to the tax side of the School District Equalization Act (SDEA). SDEA remained largely in place. The courts had thus far only focused on equity concerns under the equal protection clause and under the taxpayer equity provisions of Article 11 of the Kansas Constitution. And SDEA remained largely based on funding formula factors that were determined by prior spending behavior of local public school districts—including, and most notably, spending differences by district size. That is, if you spent more previously, when the formula was set, you were given more subsequently. But this was not uncommon at the time. Few policy analysts or researchers had figured out how to determine well the "costs" of what was actually needed separately from evaluating expenditures as they were presently distributed. To top it off, the limits on spending growth rates in the formula were proportionate to spending. And the *Knowles* decision had led to a relaxation of these growth caps, providing the opportunity for significant disparities to emerge over the next decade. And so the formulae drifted forward for a decade, with gradually increasing disparities.

Figure 3.1 shows that total per capita revenues grew through the 1980s, driven by modest increases in sales tax revenues. As revenues flattened from 1988 to 1991, local school districts began to feel the pinch. Governor Joan Finney, though a democrat, ran partly on a platform of tax cuts and reduced state aid to schools by $19 million in 1990, the "sharpest decrease in funding since the SDEA's enactment."[1] In 1989, statewide reappraisal of property values also put the squeeze on some districts more than others, especially those districts that were large enough to have started at the bottom of the distribution and lacked the local property tax base to continue to max out their local revenue growth options year after year. In the end, forty-two separate districts across the state found some gripe with SDEA, including Wichita,

FIGURE 3.1   Kansas state and local revenue by source, from *Knowles* to *Mock*

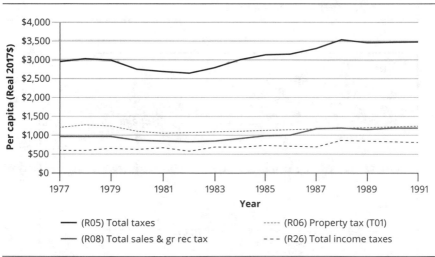

── (R05) Total taxes   ····· (R06) Property tax (T01)

── (R08) Total sales & gr rec tax   – – – (R26) Total income taxes

Data source: US Census Bureau, Annual Surveys of State and Local Government Finances, 1977–2017 (compiled by the Urban Institute via State and Local Finance Data: Exploring the Census of Governments; accessed October 26, 2020), https://state-local-finance-data .taxpolicycenter.org.

which felt shorted by a total-dollar rather than per-pupil amount cap on *hold harmless* aid; and seven mid-sized town districts that received less aid than either their larger or smaller peers, had weaker tax bases than the state's larger cities, and were facing increasingly changing student population needs.

A tour of Kansas, with my own crude picture (figure 3.2), is in order here for those unfamiliar with the lay of the land. For Kansans, I just hope you aren't too offended by this representation. The area I focused on previously in chapter 2 is in the northeastern corner of the state, adjacent to Kansas City, Missouri, and is characterized by the high poverty urban fringe (fringe of Kansas City, Missouri) city of Kansas City, Kansas—also referred to as KCK—in Wyandotte County—also referred to as the Dot. KCK is home to a large black population and, over the decades, a growing Latinx population. Johnson County (JoCo) is the county where racially restricted housing development first grew, in its northeastern corner, with sprawling single-family homes built from the 1940s through the 1970s largely retaining their racial purity and many racially restrictive covenants

FIGURE 3.2   Kansas: The lay of the land

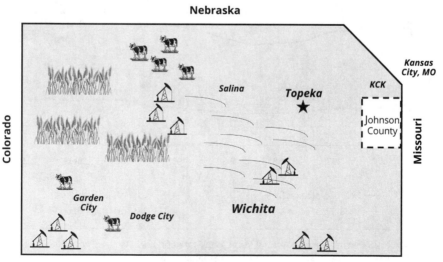

being introduced into home deeds through HOAs well into the 1960s, long after they were no longer permissible or enforceable. The school district serving the northeastern corner of Johnson County had grown to over thirty thousand students—mostly white—by the 1990s and was the second-largest district in the state, second to Wichita, which enrolled over forty thousand, and larger than KCK, which enrolled around twenty thousand.

Enrollments over time for the state's largest districts are shown in figure 3.3. By the late 1980s, the northeastern corner of Johnson County was built out, and Shawnee Mission enrollments had maxed out. The sprawl would continue to grow south and west to fill out much of the rest of the county and the school districts of Blue Valley (Unified School District [USD] 229) and Olathe. As the county built out further south and west, larger homes (in some cases on larger plots) and more country clubs were developed, and the area retained its almost entirely white demographic through collective practices of the local real estate industry and its agents. Wichita and KCK enrollments remained largely stagnant, though some internal demographic shifts occurred.

FIGURE 3.3   Kansas: Large district enrollments

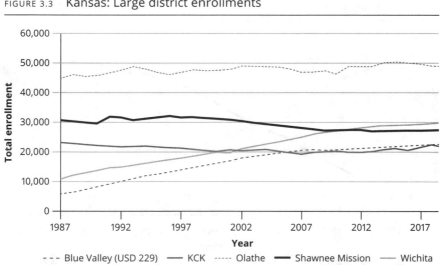

Data Source: School Finance Indicators Data System, district-level data panel.

Changes in the agriculture industry from the postwar period on, but especially beginning in the late 1980s, led to substantial reshaping of the demography of other regions of Kansas. Much of the high plains of Western Kansas had previously been, and to some extent remained, home to wheat farming and, in some cases, oil and natural gas. Small towns sitting on oil and natural gas in particular had a huge advantage in raising local tax revenues for schools. These include some towns in the Flint Hills region near Wichita and a handful of tiny towns in the southwest corner of the state. Beef feedlots expanded in southwest Kansas, along with major meat-processing plants, leading to significant immigration of low-wage labor.[2] Dodge City, Kansas, perceived by us coastal elites as some remote outpost of classic Western lore, was an epicenter of this change, along with its lesser-known neighbor to the west, Garden City. These towns and others, including Salina, Newton, and Emporia, fell into the group of "midsized" districts that received the least funding because they were neither large and wealthy nor small.

Figure 3.4 shows the racial demographics of Dodge City from the years just prior to *Mock* through 2019. By 1988, Dodge City had already

FIGURE 3.4   Dodge City, Kansas

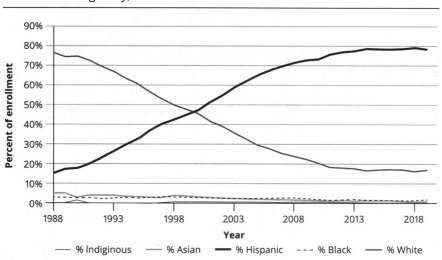

Source: School Finance Indicators Data System, district-level data panel.

risen to about an 18 percent Hispanic population in a town where the teacher workforce consisted largely of middle-aged white women, who themselves had grown up in a town that had looked much different, and where finding bilingual educators was not an easy task. By the late 1990s—which we'll reach by the end of this chapter—Dodge City had climbed to a 50 percent Hispanic enrollment. Even by the time that the *USD 229* case was resolved in 1994, Dodge City's Hispanic enrollment had doubled from the years leading up to *Mock*, which set in place the reforms upheld in *USD 229* (denying USD 229's claims). In short, Dodge and towns like it in the run up to *Mock* were starting to see a change, experiencing new needs and costs and caught in the squeeze of a formula that provided them fewer resources than other districts while their own local capacity to raise more was waning.

THE *MOCK* DRAMA

Enter Judge Terry Bullock! Bullock was district court judge in Shawnee County, which is home to the state capitol of Topeka. Suits brought against the state legislature would typically be tried in the district court of the county that is home to the capitol. And that was Terry Bullock's territory. One of Bullock's first actions was to consolidate the various challenges brought by the forty-two districts against the state. Each had its own unique claims about how it was disadvantaged by the state school finance system, which had come to a head with Finney's tax cuts and reductions to state aid. Bullock had reviewed the claims and decided that collectively they revealed systemic problems with the school finance system. Bullock summarized the claims brought as follows:

> The various plaintiffs in these consolidated cases, in the aggregate, challenge the constitutionality of the entire scheme of financing the public schools (grades kindergarten through twelve) of Kansas. They raise various arguments in support of their claims of unconstitutionality, including three key claims:
>
> 1. The financing scheme violates the requirements of the education article of the Kansas constitution.

2. The financing scheme violates the equal protection clauses of the Kansas and United States constitutions.

3. The system of taxation used to finance public schools violates the "uniform laws" clause of the Kansas constitution.[3]

Typically, the way the process would go from here is that the district court would hold a trial in which experts and practitioners representing the districts and the legislature would testify for days on end. The district court judge would summarize the facts (findings of fact) and rule on the legal questions—constitutional violations (or not)—that were argued. More often than not, because these trials are a lot of work and time-consuming, a district court judge will initially dismiss the claims on one basis or another, such that plaintiffs appeal to a higher court to evaluate whether the case should move forward. While this step can drag out the process, when a higher court remands the case to a lower court to be heard, the lower court judge at least has more confidence that his or her decision might be taken more seriously when the case is eventually appealed back to the higher court.

But Judge Bullock wasn't particularly interested in playing these games and dragging things out. That's not really his style, as described by many, including himself. What Bullock wanted was to *encourage* the legislature to fix the problems with the school finance system without the hassle of a trial, an appeal, and what could be a five-year-plus process. Instead, Bullock drafted a "preruling," in which he offered what would most likely be his opinion *if* the case were to go to trial. Then he set up a conference for all the parties involved, which has been described in academic writing and to me personally by those in attendance as quite the spectacle. Bullock reserved the chamber of the State Supreme Court for this event. Further description is best left to an email exchange with John Robb, attorney for the midsized district plaintiff group in attendance that day:

> Judge Bullock's most famous letter/order was not in the Montoy case, it was in the Mock case in 1992. You will recall that October 14, 1991 he had issued his Mock opinion in advance of trial on the law that would be controlling in the trial of the case. This was done with much fanfare. He decided that

his courtroom was not large enough for the event so he "borrowed" the Supreme Courtroom for the reading of his opinion. He invited the Governor, the Senate President, Speaker of the House, Chairs and ranking minority members of House and Senate Education, Ways and Means and Appropriation committees, the Attorney General, the State Board of Education, Commissioner of Education and . . . oh yes. . . . the parties also. We even had a "pre-reading" conference of all the attorneys and clients to aid him in assigning seats in the Supreme Courtroom for the show.

With TV cameras rolling it was a contest of wills between Governor Finney, a Democrat, and Attorney General Stephan, a Republican, as to who would grandly enter the courtroom last. Every seat in the courtroom was assigned seating and was filled. Neither the governor nor the attorney general would budge from the hallway. Both waiting to make the grand final entrance for the cameras and assembled group. The assembled courtroom and invitees waited about 10 minutes and finally General Stephan gave in and let the Governor enter last. She did and we began. The Chief Justice of the Supreme Court introduced lowly trial Judge Bullock to the assembled audience with high praise as to Judge Bullock's qualifications as a jurist. Judge Bullock then read his opinion to the group which left no misunderstanding that he indeed intended to declare the entire school finance system unconstitutional after the useless step of a trial. He then asked the assembled legislators and governor if they wanted him to proceed to trial or if they wanted a legislative session to fix things. The politicos caucused then informed him that they wanted a session to fix it. The spectacle was adjourned and the case was continued until after the 1992 legislative session. A performance truly worthy of an Academy Award.[4]

In his article titled "Equity without Adjudication," Charles Berger explains that the goal of the conference was "deceptively simple": "The Court wanted the answer to a single question: "Did they [the

Governor, legislative leaders, and State Board of Education] want the Court to review school finance legislation as it then existed or did they want to overhaul the state's educational funding plan before the Court reviewed it?"[5]

After Bullock had read his preruling, those in attendance heard from Dale Dennis of the state board's finance department. He illustrated the vast disparities both in per-pupil spending and in adopted tax rates across Kansas districts at the time. By this point, Dale was already a veteran with over twenty years' experience as the lead on any and all issues pertaining to the state school finance formula (SDEA). Dale's presentation was followed by a presentation from a former Kansas legislator and school finance advisor from the National Conference of State Legislators, John Myers. The same John Myers would eventually conduct the 2002 cost study (as part of the Augenblick & Myers consulting firm). Myers presented on what other states were doing to improve equity in school funding. The basic conclusion of the expert presentations was that there were huge inequities and little or no relationship between the rate of taxation and education spending. As Berger explained: "Fortunate enough to have a power plant in their district, the Burlington school board, with the lowest levy in the state, had enough funds left over to build an Olympic-sized indoor swimming pool for their high school."[6]

Also in attendance that day was Dan Biles, in his role as attorney for the state board of education. While the legislature was charged with adopting the taxes and providing the funding for the formula, the state board was charged with its operation. Dale himself was charged with running the numbers. And Dan Biles was charged with defending the formula, along with the attorney general's office. As Berger described it: "Faced with the uncomfortable prospect of defending such a law, Dan Biles, attorney for the State Board of Education, was more relieved than anything else when Judge Bullock issued his opinion on points of law before trial, which cast serious doubt on the constitutionality of the SDEA. 'I just did you a big favor,' confided Judge Bullock to him afterwards."[7] The next task was to get to work on coming up with a solution to the plethora of problems and constitutional violates laid out by Bullock.

THE GRAND BARGAIN: SDF-QPA

In the fall of 1991, in advance of the 1992 legislative session, democratic governor Joan Finney created a task force to continue seeking expert advisement and provide a reform framework to guide the work of the 1992 legislature. The task force consisted of eight members of the legislature and eight appointees of the governor: her chief of staff, appointments secretary, legislative liaison, education advisor, and secretary of revenue, two budget division officials, and the chairperson of the state board of education. The group met four times during November 1991.[8] To Finney's advantage (as an advocate for tax cuts), the resulting proposals included establishing a statewide minimum property tax rate that would, in effect, result in lower local property taxes for many school districts, though for a few it would lead to increases. The proposed mill levy (a property tax rate expressed in thousandths, rather than as a percent) of thirty-two mills (3.2 percent) was lower than the statewide median at the time.[9]

During the spring session of 1992, a bill based on the task force proposals passed in the Kansas House relatively easily but stalled in the Senate. The idea of a statewide minimum property tax, which significantly raised property taxes in some of those small, mineral-rich Southwest Kansas towns was a contentious issue, leading to counter-proposals being discussed in the Senate and divisions along political ideological lines. More libertarian minded leaders in Southwest Kansas went so far as to propose secession, a movement that would escalate after the eventual passage of the new school finance law.[10] Senate republicans were unable to round up support for any one alternative plan by the close of the regular session, and everything ground to a halt. As John Robb described it:

> The 1992 session was a rocky session from the start with no agreement from the Senate Republicans as to the appropriate fix. The session ended with no support in the Senate for any fix. It appeared that Bullock's plan of a legislated fix to end the case was about to crash. But he still had hopes for the veto session. He then sent his April 10, 1992 letter to counsel. We

later found out that he sent it to the press before he sent it to counsel. I attach that letter for your review. In it he orders the attorneys to research what would be needed to shut down the entire tax gathering system of the state with an injunction to be served upon the state, all county treasurers, all school districts and the like. He also ordered us to have process servers on hand to serve the proposed injunction on all these parties.

The media carried the pronouncement statewide. Five days later the Supreme Court Office of Judicial Administration issued a follow up "clarification" letter that I also attach. It said: "Judge Bullock asked me to pass along . . . to the media . . . to advise . . . that the memo was designed to aid the attorneys in their research, and nothing more. The judge did not intend to convey any messages to anyone. . . . "[11]

Bullock responded to the gridlock with a letter (shown in figure 3.5) and subsequent clarification (shown in figure 3.6).

In any case, the ensuing chaos seemed to result in some action and eventual agreement in the veto session that followed (commencing April 29, 1992). During that session, Senate Majority Leader Sheila Frahm (who would later take Bob Dole's US Senate seat as he ran for the presidency) played a central role in pushing the plan through the Senate. Frahm's district covered several small rural districts in the northwestern part of the state. And as it turned out, the House plan, which proposed the objectional (to some) statewide minimum property tax, also included a significant weight that would yield additional support for small rural districts: the *low enrollment weight*. With Frahm's support, the plan eventually passed by the end of the veto session.

Reflecting on that year, John Robb wrote: "Only a Judge Bullock could have or would have done this. It got us SDFQPA in the 1992 session. Bullock was invited to Governor Finney's signing ceremony for the bill and she gave him the bill signing pen. He had it framed in his court chambers along with a copy of the bill and a picture with the governor. After he retired from the bench, Alan and I had dinner with him to discuss old times. As I told this story at dinner, he just beamed."[12]

FIGURE 3.5 Bullock's letter

Shawnee County, Kansas

Chambers of
Terry L. Bullock
Judge of the District Court
Division No. Six
Shawnee County Courthouse
Topeka, Kansas 66603-3922

Officers:
Joseph R. Martinez
Official Reporter
Nina H. Robinson
Administrative Assistant

April 10, 1992

TO: Counsel of Record and Friends (Hamill and Goodell)

RE: School Finance Litigation

Greetings:

An additional point which may take some research and preparation in the event an injunction is ultimately required in these cases concerns the question of upon whom the injunction would need to be served. In order to halt all illegal tax gathering and spending, it may be necessary to enjoin not only the state but county treasurers, school districts, and the like. In the event we get this far in the litigation I hope you will have done your homework on this point and we will have the names and addresses needed, as well as process servers on hand, in the event that is required.

In addition, because capital improvements are a part of this case and because time will not permit the Court to visit all the necessary facilities, perhaps some photographs of existing school facilities for comparative purposes would be useful for our purpose and for appeal if that becomes necessary. I would appreciate your thoughts on this matter as well.

With every good wish and with appreciation for your splendid cooperation and professionalism, I am

Sincerely,

Terry L. Bullock

TLB:nr

Basic Elements of the School District Finance and Quality Performance Accreditation Act

The main thing that can be said about the SDF-QPA is that it signified a sharp shift in control over taxation, financing, and accountability, toward the state and away from local districts. The key elements of the finance side of the formula included the statewide base, property tax, or base mill levy of thirty-two mills, raised in the first few years to thirty-five mills (by 1994). The formula itself had two tiers. The first tier guaranteed that all districts, for their thirty-two-mill levies, would

FIGURE 3.6 Bullock's follow-up clarification letter

State of Kansas

Office of Judicial Administration

Kansas Judicial Center
301 West 10th
Topeka, Kansas 66612-1507   (913) 296-2256

April 15, 1992

To: Statehouse News Media

From: Ron Keefover
        Education-Information Officer

Re: School Finance Litigation

        Judge Bullock asked me to pass along the attached to any
media interested and to advise you that the memo was designed
to aid the attorneys in their research, and nothing more.

        The judge did not intend to convey any messages to anyone
with the memorandum, but wrote it merely as an addendum to last
week's pretrial hearing. He said he viewed the information in
the memo as necessary only in the event of a finding of
unconstitutionality. Of course, no such finding has been made
to date because it is not clear which statute will be subject
to court review.

        He remains optimistic that the legislature will solve
the matter without court intervention.

RK:pd
Attachment

be provided with base funding of $3,600 per pupil, and that base funding would have several adjustments applied to it:

1. An additional 10 percent for each child from a low-income family, identified as qualifying for free lunch under the national school lunch program (130 percent of the poverty income threshold)

2. An additional 20 percent per full-time-equivalent (FTE) child in bilingual education programs (where typically one FTE resulted from approximately three non-English-speaking children receiving services)

3. A small district, or low enrollment, weight, which provided 2.14 times the base level for districts enrolling one hundred or fewer students and 1.58 times the base level for districts enrolling three hundred or fewer students, declining to the base funding level for districts with 1,800 or more pupils (see figure 3.7)

FIGURE 3.7 **Low enrollment weight.**

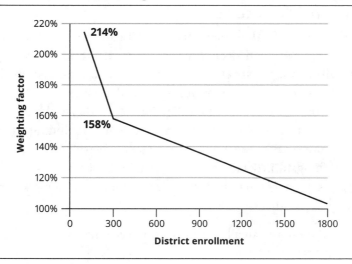

Source: Author representation (from 1999 class notes).

This last one, the low enrollment weight, was the big one. Taken together, these weights would lead to general fund budgets for some districts around $4,000 per pupil, and for other, mostly small rural districts, over $8,000 per pupil.

One political trade-off added was a second tier that permitted districts to raise additional revenue, up to 25 percent above their adjusted basic funding, by adopting additional local property taxes. That is, if your *general fund budget* per pupil was $4,000, you could raise an additional $1,000 per pupil, and if your general fund budget was $8,000, you could raise an additional $2,000 per pupil. To ensure that this *local option budget* (LOB) or *supplemental fund budget* didn't exacerbate inequities, the state would provide matching aid to districts such that all would have the ability to raise the amount of revenue that would be raised if the district had the seventy-fifth percentile of taxable property wealth per pupil. The LOB was adopted to appease those concerned with the loss of local control, but it was equalized with state aid and capped to preserve equity in compliance with Judge Bullock's order.

The Secession Movement and Legal Challenges to the School District Finance Act

Overall, the school funding plan made significant strides in disrupting the relationship between taxable property wealth and district spending, especially among districts of similar size. The plan also made significant strides in the first few years toward raising spending levels in the previously lowest spending districts. And these changes led to measurably positive effects on student outcomes, including improved graduation rates.[13] But the plan, like almost any school finance plan that shakes things up to such a degree, was not without its detractors. Three groups in particular had significant concerns, some expressed more loudly than others.

- *Group 1:* Remote, small, natural resource–rich towns in Southwest Kansas
- *Group 2:* Affluent growing suburban (white) districts wishing to spend more on their schools (and receiving low general fund budgets)
- *Group 3:* Towns caught in the middle, which saw improvements under the formula, but still fell at the bottom of the curve

Group 1 was perhaps the most vocal and defiant. Group 2 rallied lawyers and sued the state, challenging various features of the formula as lead plaintiffs. Group 3 joined in some concerns raised by group 2—notably, that the low enrollment weighting was distorted and not based on real evidence of cost differences, providing too much to very small districts and too little to districts enrolling over 1,800 pupils. Groups 1 and 2 together were particularly peeved about their loss of local control over raising additional revenues, with group 1 especially upset about being required to also raise a minimum levy well above what some of the oil- and natural gas–rich towns had previously levied. In a 1995 article in *Great Plains Quarterly* on the Kansas secession movement, Peter McCormack explained: "The effects in the southwest were drastic. Many districts there, accustomed to setting their own tax rates and to retaining all monies collected, spent upward of $5000 per student on tax levies below 20 mills. With the new formula, taxes collected from the 32 mills in excess of the $3600 per-student limit would have to be released to the state for disbursement."[14]

Group 1 also was geographically remote from the state's center of power—Topeka, or the Kansas City area. The group felt put upon by the actions of both the state court and the legislature in passing the act, even though the act passed with, if not because of, the support of Sheila Frahm, who herself represented a portion of rural Western Kansas. All of this led to a boisterous, albeit short-lived push for a new fifty-first state covering a slice of Western Kansas and Eastern Colorado's high plains, extending southward into the Oklahoma and Texas panhandles and Northeastern New Mexico. McCormack further explains:

> In the heart of southwest Kansas petitions signed by hundreds reached county commissioners within a matter of days after the proposal of the school tax plan. Kearny Countians, numbering just 4000 total, produced more than 500 valid signatures advocating secession. Headlines in local weekly papers talked of the tax, its implications, and the secession movement throughout the early months of 1992. Larger regional papers, such as the Garden City Telegram and The Hutchinson News, echoed the same refrain. The sign "To Hell With Topeka, Let's Secede" welcomed travelers on US Highway 50 at Lakin's Ken Ark Motel. The idea was widely supported, as reflected in the Kearny County petitions and similar petitions in Stevens and Morton counties.[15]

The group carried on, from a contentious *airing of grievances* gathering at the Garde City Hilton in March 1992, to their own constitutional convention in September of 1992, focused mainly on the grievance that tax dollars of these towns would in effect be going to support the education of children in the state's larger cities and towns. Taxpayer dollars in Kansas would be flowing west to east, with less representation provided to the west in the process. After failing to convince towns in neighboring states to join the effort, the secession movement quickly faded, but it was followed by legal challenges to the School District Finance Act. In light of the fact that Kansas as a state has provided a more robustly funded education system than neighboring states in particular, towns involved in the secession movement may be quite lucky in retrospect that their efforts failed.

Meanwhile, a mind-numbing six-hour drive to the east, in the sprawling white suburbs of Johnson County in the Blue Valley school district, lawyers, including John Vratil, were framing up their legal challenges to the newly imposed revenue limits and tax structure, as well as features of the formula they felt didn't accurately reflect costs, like the low enrollment weight. By this point in Johnson County, the older suburbs like Fairway, Prairie Village, and Old Leawood consisted of two- to three-bedroom, 1,500-square-foot postwar homes of the 1940s, and three- to four-bedroom, 2,000-square-foot ranch homes built in the 1960s and 1970s. Northeast Johnson County also includes Mission Hills, a neighborhood of stately mansions developed in the 1920s by J. C. Nichols as part of his Country Club District of Kansas City, Missouri—conveniently across the state line.

By the 1990s, the sprawl went on for miles and continued to grow like ragweed, with 3,000- to 5000-plus-square-foot homes popping up on quarter-acre, neatly manicured lots. Families flocked to shiny new school buildings and favored even more school spending than was allowed under the new law. USD 229, represented by John Vratil, became the lead plaintiff in this next legal challenge to school funding in Kansas, and USD 229 was joined in the challenge by two districts from group 1—Burlington (home to a high-value hydroelectric plant) and Rolla (home to high-value natural resources—and a district from group 3—Newton, the quintessential midsized Kansas town, caught in the middle of it all. Newton was represented by local lawyer John Robb and by Alan Rupe from Wichita. The state was again represented primarily by Dan Biles, legal counsel for the state board. The case was heard in Shawnee County district court by Judge Marla Luckert (who would later sit on the high court and eventually become chief justice).

In her district court opinion, Luckert largely upheld the taxing structure imposed by the new law, but she raised concerns about the rather extreme low enrollment weight, noting that while such an adjustment could be permissible in theory, the current adjustment was not built on any rational basis. That is, it had not been determined by figuring out the actual differences in costs of providing equitable programs, but rather, like previous formulas, had been built based on average spending differences before 1992, thus perpetuating historical disparities. However, the state supreme court unanimously upheld all parts of the statute, perhaps not wanting to push the issue further given all the state had been through. This would be the first time the state high court had chimed in on a school finance formula, applying the 1966 education article to evaluate the legislation, and thus it would become the precedent on which future cases would rest. This showed a downside to the fact that Judge Bullock's original ruling in *Mock* was not a ruling, and thus that case—the original challenge to SDEA—was never vetted by the state's highest court.

Rounding out the Decade

Within the first few years, the School District Finance Act faced troubles. The base state aid per pupil (BSAPP) stayed at $3,600 for the first three years, and by 1998–1999 it had only crept up to $3,720. During the first few years, the base mill levy was increased from thirty-two to thirty-five mills, increasing the amount of the formula paid for with local property taxes, but in the years that followed, the base mill levy was slashed first to twenty-seven mills in 1997 and then down to twenty mills in 1998. This pulled a significant amount of property tax revenue out of the system, costing the state more from sales and income taxes. It was these cuts to the base mill levy that led to further stagnation in the growth of the BSAPP. The state simply didn't have, or chose not to raise through income and sales taxes, the additional money needed to replace the property tax cuts. Again, districts at the bottom of the curve were unhappy. And while Judge Marla Luckert had opined in 1994 that the low enrollment weight wasn't necessarily rationally derived, it had been upheld by the highest court in the state.

In an article I wrote with University of Kansas colleague Mickey Imber back in 1999, we showed just how problematic, and not so rational, that low enrollment weighting was—largely due to classically Kansas quirks in the distribution of property wealth.[16] Table 3.1 breaks down the problem. The analysis behind the weight used district spending data from 1991 for districts in the categories in the table. It found that the average spending in districts with 75 to 125 students was about 2.14 times that of districts with over 1,900 students and that the average spending of districts with 200 to 400 students was about 1.58 times the average spending of larger districts. They then took the midpoint of these categories, assigned those weights, and connected them with straight lines.

TABLE 3.1   Data underlying the original low enrollment weight calculation

Enrollment	Median General Fund Expenditures per Pupil 1991 (ratio to >1,900)	Median Assessed Valuation per Pupil 1991 (ratio to >1,900)
75–125	$7,337 (214%)	$75,718 (325%)
200–400	$5,406 (158%)	$41,007 (176%)
> 1,900	$3,426	$23,292

Data source: Bruce Baker and Michael Imber, "'Rational Educational Explanation' or Politics as Usual? Evaluating the Outcome of Educational Finance Litigation in Kansas," Journal of Education Finance 25, no. 1 (1999): 121–139.

The problem is that Kansas's very small districts, including those oil-rich southwest Kansas towns, had 3.25 times the average property wealth per pupil, and the middle group had 1.76 times the average property wealth per pupil of larger districts. They weren't necessarily spending more because they were small and lacked economies of scale—although, sure, that was part of it—but they were spending more because they could. They had the tax base to raise and spend more even with much lower tax rates. This not-so-small problem had not come to light in deliberations in the *USD 229* case. While this may have reinforced Luckert's concern over the rationality of the weight, it may not have influenced the high court, which seemed to want the turmoil over and done with at the time. If not empirically, at least some suspected instinctively that problems with using prior spending data led to problems with the low enrollment weight.

With the end of the decade approaching, and with continued rumblings about problems with the School District Finance Act, moderate republican governor Bill Graves followed in the footsteps of Governor William Avery and Governor Joan Finney. He convened a series of citizen task forces across wide-ranging topics regarding the future of Kansas. These Vision 21st Century task forces included one on the financing of the state's public education system, to be headed by then state securities commissioner David Brant. I believe it was by recommendation of one of my colleagues at the University of Kansas (KU) that I was appointed to this task force, but to this day I remain unsure. The full list of members is shown in figure 3.8.

FIGURE 3.8   Vision 21st Century Task Force membership

VISION 21st CENTURY INITIATIVE
K-12 EDUCATION: FINANCING FOR RESULTS
TASK FORCE MEMBERS

David Brant (Chair)	Topeka	Kansas Securities Commissioner
Susan Roenbaugh (Vice Chair)	Kinsley	Former State Representative
Dr. Bruce Baker	Fairway	Assistant Professor of Teaching and Leadership, The University of Kansas
Rep. Barbara Ballard	Lawrence	Associate Vice Chancellor for Student Affairs, The University of Kansas and State Representative
Lew Ferguson	Topeka	Retired Associated Press Statehouse Correspondent
Sheila Frahm	Colby	Executive Director, Association of Community College Trustees and Former U.S. Senator and Lt. Governor
Dennis Jones	Lakin	Kearny County Attorney
Myrne Roe	Lindsborg	Retired Journalist and Former Teacher
Keith Roe	Mankato	Farmer and Former State Representative
Edward Roitz	Pittsburg	President, Fleming Petroleum, Inc. and Former State Senator
Sen. John Vratil	Leawood	Attorney and State Senator
Jerome Williams	Wichita	Director of Business Ethics and Compliance, Raytheon Aircraft and Former School Board Member
Mary Yewell	Emporia	Market President, Intrust Bank

Notable members of this task force included former senate majority leader (and former US senator) Sheila Frahm, who had negotiated the passage of the School District Finance Act. John Vratil, who had represented USD 229, challenging the formula, had been elected to the Kansas Senate in 1998 and was also appointed, as was attorney Dennis Jones of Kearny County (one of the secessionist counties). Jones in particular was a character, and his views closely aligned with my earlier New Hampshire–styled, *live free or die* libertarian views, which had shifted slightly by this time. Assigned as the liaison from Governor

Grave's office was a young staffer named Ed O'Malley, who would later attend my school finance classes at KU, on his own time and not for credit, and eventually be appointed and reelected to a seat in the Kansas legislature as a republican representing an older section of Northeast Johnson County.

Like any citizen task force, each participant came with their own local interests and historical perspectives. I had already come to some conclusions of my own, drawn from the academic article I had just completed with my colleague at KU, titled "'Rational Educational Explanation?' Or Politics as Usual?" In that article, we critiqued the school district finance act, and low enrollment weight in particular. It was quite the learning experience to dive in at this level in only my second full year in the state. The charge to our task force was as follows:

> The task force should review the current school finance formula and the School District Equalization Act that preceded it to understand the most recent models used to finance public schools in Kansas. The task force should also review school finance models in other states. Analysis should be undertaken of the difficulties facing schools with declining enrollments and those with rapid growth. Also the challenges of schools that are currently at the maximum local option budget should be reviewed. Efforts should be directed to determine alternative-funding formulas that reward schools for superior performance. Finally, the number of school districts and school attendance centers should be reviewed to ensure we maximize the results of school finance. In meeting the goal of funding for results, equity and fairness must be components. The task force should make priority policy recommendations to address the findings it makes and submit its report on or before December 1.[17]

From the beginning to end of the task force timeline, during the spring and summer of 2000, our group met across the state, in towns from Emporia (home to the National Teachers Hall of Fame) to Lindsborg, a surprisingly Swedish town in Western Kansas, to the Kearny County seat—center of the great rebellion—of Lakin in the southwest corner of the state. I still have my souvenir coffee mugs from a few of these excursions.

As the resident school finance "expert" on the task force, my role was to help inform on technical matters, share the latest research, and, to an extent, play a role similar to that of John Myers in the *Mock* conference and discuss how other states were addressing similar issues. Wyoming, for example, had recently engaged in the task of costing out, piece by piece, the required elements of a constitutionally adequate education system. What I share from my time on the task force is based on my best recollections, which I hope are sufficiently accurate and representative. Senator Vratil, with the wounds of the *USD 229* case still fresh, now in a position in which he wielded legislative influence, seemed very tuned in on finding ways to make the Kansas system more rational and more cost-based.

I had discussed two recent books with the group, which had been published by the National Research Council and included discussions of the Wyoming approach.[18] I believe that Senator Vratil in particular expected that better cost analysis might find two things: (1) that the basic cost of education is somewhat, if not significantly, higher than the original $3,600 base and (2) that the additional costs of small districts, while they do exist, are not as big as the current low enrollment weight. Both of these findings would serve his constituents in Johnson County. Other states were beginning to look at costs, estimating basic costs and how costs vary for different children and in different settings. But methods and models for doing so, while they had existed in academic work for some time, had not made their way into the mainstream of directly influencing state policies.

Nonetheless, our group agreed, with little arm-twisting, that proposing that the state consider studying "costs" once and for all as the basis for determining how the formula should be structured, rather than simply relying on previous spending, was the way to go. It was always my feeling on that task force that Sheila Frahm kept us in check. At least to me, for all her kindness, she was still an intimidating force to be reckoned with, and she had put in a lot of effort and spent significant political capital to achieve the reform we were now pecking away at. I recall playing a significant role in drafting the following recommendation, primarily in editorial collaboration with Senator Vratil and our committee chair David Brandt on the first cut. Writing with the senator (much like writing with my KU colleague Mickey Imber) taught me just how bad a writer I was at the time, with bad word selection, limited vocabulary (Senator Vratil would often correct me publicly), and poor punctuation. Our task force deliberated most extensively on which of the following bullet points for our conclusions should end in a colon and which a semicolon:

1. Kansas must re-evaluate the 1992 school finance formula to address inadequacies and inequities in the current system. The state needs to determine the cost of a "suitable" education to enable students to reach high standards.
    a. The state should conduct a professional evaluation to be initiated in January, 2001, and completed by December 1, 2001, with the following objectives:
        i. Determine funding needed to provide a suitable education in typical K-12 schools of various sizes and locations;
        ii. Determine additional support needed for special education, at-risk, limited English proficient students and other special circumstances;
        iii. Determine funding adjustments to ensure comparable purchasing power for all districts, regardless of size or location; and
        iv. Determine an appropriate annual adjustment for inflation.
    b. The Governor and the Legislature should create an on-going "School Finance Council" to conduct the evaluation of the cost of a suitable education and then to annually monitor and make recommendations regarding school funding.[19]

Our report set the stage for an analysis that would, like the 1995 Wyoming analysis, identify the various inputs needed to provide an adequate—or more specifically, *suitable*—education for all Kansas children. I, as the resident "expert," was still concerned at the time about a methodology that used existing spending data to model and project costs tied to specific outcome measures. Look where analysis of prior spending data had gotten Kansas so far! I would later not only warm to this idea, but strongly prefer it, as methods and models improved. We also set the stage for any analysis that would be done to determine costs, ensuring they would look very specifically at costs for schools and districts of different sizes, which had not been done in previous studies. Figuring out the size-related differences in costs was perhaps the main issue to be dealt with in reforming the existing formula.

REFLECTING ON THE ERA

Charles Berger's manifesto on Judge Bullock, the *Mock* case, adoption of SDF-QPA, and affirmation of the act's constitutionality in USD 229 is titled "Equity Without Adjudication."[20] It was based on the premise that Judge Bullock's creative process led to an expedited legislative solution to the state's equity woes. Not foreseen were some of the problems that might result from a lack of formal adjudication by Judge Bullock. Bullock himself had the first shot at offering a formal inter-pretation—an official ruling—on the constitutional requirements and applying that interpretation to SDEA. But the decision he offered came without a trial and a full vetting of the facts. It did lead to expedited reform, and that reform was vetted by a lower court that offered some scrutiny into the rationality of SDF. But the high court at the time, given the turmoil of the past few years, was not willing to advance that critique under the circumstances. All of this is of course hindsight. But the early 1990s, though they provided the state with a new school finance structure, also left the state with a new structure built on the underlying disparities of the old structure and a high court ruling that upheld that structure and offered no detailed framework for critiquing it against the constitutional requirements as the next rounds of legal challenges approached. In short, there was in fact adjudication, but there was little improvement to equity. Although constitutional stan-dards remained unclear, the state was about to be provided with its first reference point of empirical estimates of the *costs* associated with meeting those constitutional standards.

4

"THAT DOG WON'T HUNT
IN DODGE CITY!"

*Proving That Money Matters
in Education*

This case, of course, is about the rest
of those children.

—Terry L. Bullock, December 19, 2003

Now we'll move to the modern era of school finance litigation in Kansas, the increased role of the courts, and the soap opera–like reshuffling of characters that would occur over the next two major rounds of judicial battles: the *Montoy* and *Gannon* cases. Of particular interest is how legal arguments pertaining to the independent roles of the state board of education and legislature evolve during the course of *Montoy v. Kansas*, as well as how those evolving legal arguments, advanced by specific individuals, shape the next round of empirical analyses pursued by the legislature, under the watchful eye of the court.

This chapter explores in detail the legal theories advanced by involved parties and the language and analysis applied by district court judge Terry Bullock and by the high court. This chapter explores specifically the *Montoy* period, in which the framework for subsequent analysis in *Gannon* is established. (We return to *Gannon* in chapter 5, as the *Gannon* case arises from the great recession and drastic cuts imposed by the Brownback administration.) This chapter also sorts through the defiant rhetoric of Kansas legislators, coupled with their largely compliant responses to judicial orders. Ultimately in each round of litigation, majority wisdom and level-headedness largely prevailed. When necessary, Kansas voters have stepped in to rebalance that majority wisdom. Throughout this period, the 1966 constitutional amendments have withstood attempts to gut, alter, or otherwise neuter the legislature's obligation. But conservative pushback has led to some changes—including changes to the rules of litigation specific to cases involving school funding, adding waiting periods and trial by a three-judge panel.

EMERGENCE OF *MONTOY* AND *ROBINSON*

During the spring and summer of 2000, our task force was touring the state, hearing testimony from local school officials, lawyers and consultants, crafting the recommendations laid out at the end of the previous chapter. Around that same time, Wichita lawyer Alan Rupe and Newton lawyer John Robb were evaluating their next moves, understanding that the previous waves of legal challenges, while yielding some improvements, still largely codified the inequities of the past. The districts and children they served were being disadvantaged by the state school finance system. Many districts were experiencing dramatic demographic changes and increased needs and costs, and the legislature was cutting the base mill levy that provided the foundation for the formula. Base funding was stagnant, and suburban legislators like John Vratil had decided that the short-term solution would be to tweak SDF to their own advantage, finding ways to allow their constituents to raise more local taxes and sneaking in "cost adjustments" that increased general funds in the suburbs.

During this time, large districts had achieved a 6.32 percent increase to their base, chipping away at the low enrollment weight with a new counterbalancing factor called the *correlation weight*. What *correlation* was supposed to mean in this context I could never discern, other than a form of "you got yours, we want ours." Midsized districts would also benefit from this weight, down to enrollments of 1,725 pupils, at which point the low enrollment weight would kick in. Districts in rapidly growing Johnson County were given a 25 percent increase per child attending a new school facility for the first two years of operation. This weight would apply to large numbers of children in Blue Valley, Olathe, and DeSoto during this period, and with continued growth and new facilities popping up for the next several years, the revenue generated by this weight would not soon fade. Eventually the legislators would also add an adjustment to the local option budget caps to expand revenue-raising ability for districts with children in new facilities, called the *ancillary new facilities weight*. Collectively, in the Johnson County suburbs, these weights would generate more per-pupil revenue than at-risk and bilingual weightings combined in the nearby, much poorer KCK, despite conventional wisdom in school finance that the latter requires far more attention than the former.

The Schools for Fair Funding advocacy organization[1] was founded in 1997 as a small collection of mainly midsized districts from Central and Western Kansas, many of which were serving increasingly diverse student populations. This alliance of local public school districts would provide support for the next several rounds of litigation, and it still exists to this day, with about forty member districts. The legal team of Alan Rupe and John Robb was engaged by Schools for Fair Funding to evaluate the feasibility of bringing legal challenges against the School District Finance Act in order to fix the stuff that had gone unfixed—stuff that had unfortunately now been upheld by the state's high court as *fixed enough*.

This is where things got a bit creative, in ways that I've not seen in most other cases of this kind since. A great deal of planning was done on the front end to identify a handful of different litigation strategies, the cleverest of which was to challenge the inequities of the school funding system in federal court as the state court might decide that the SDF had already been established as meeting state constitutional standards (*USD 229*). The federal approach would be two-pronged, arguing that the inequities created by the weighting system—most notably, the low enrollment weight, but also new facilities weightings—created a pattern of disparities that specifically deprived districts serving the state's minority student populations, including Black students in Wichita, Topeka, and KCK—but also increasingly in some cases majority Latino districts like Dodge City. Two similar cases were brought in Pennsylvania[2] and New York[3] around that same time. But also at this time (two years after the case was filed), the US Supreme Court ruled that such cases could only succeed if it could be shown that the state intended to create disparities based on race, not merely that racial disparities arose for some other cause or reason but resulted in racially disparate effects.[4]

Rupe and Robb also argued that the racial disparities resulting from the weighting system violated the equal protection clause of the Fourteenth Amendment. The apparent major barrier to this challenge arose back in the 1970s, in the well-known, but often misinterpreted, San Antonio Independent School Dist. v. Rodriguez.[5] The US Supreme Court had ruled that disparities in school funding in Texas, which resulted from the state relying heavily on local control over property taxes, did not violate the equal protection clause. That is, the court decided it was rational for Texas to permit local control, leading to such disparities, and that those disparities didn't warrant heightened scrutiny by the federal courts because they resulted in differences in resources based on local taxable property wealth. But there were two important differences in the Kansas argument. First, these weren't disparities that simply emerged by allowing greater local control. They were disparities baked into the state school finance system itself, as weights to drive more money to some and less to others. Second, the disparities were linked to race and built on historical patterns, policies, and actions that codified racial boundaries and racial disparities in funding.

Eventually, the tenth circuit in 2002 agreed that the types of disparities presented were in fact different than in Rodriguez and could be heard in federal court. But the fact that the disparities fell along racial lines, but not clearly with racially discriminatory intent, meant that they did not warrant heightened scrutiny.[6] By the time the federal courts were beginning to address these concerns, the state case appeared to be moving forward.

Rupe and Robb filed *Robinson* and *Montoy* in 1999, a year before the task force began meeting. But these things move slowly. Judge Bullock from the *Mock* case was assigned the state case. Bullock of course knew that in the *USD 229* challenge, district court judge Marla Luckert raised significant concerns about the weighting system in SDF, much like the concerns raised in the new legal challenge. But the high court had overturned Luckert's ruling. Bullock wanted to be sure that if he put the time in for a trial, his decision, if he ruled against that same formula, would be taken seriously by the high court. More specifically, he wanted to be sure that there were specific legal questions, including changes to the law, that the high court thought required going through the arduous process of a months-long trial.

In November 2001, Bullock dismissed the *Montoy* case, asserting that the school funding formula had a presumption of constitutionality, based on *USD 229*. But in January 2003, the state supreme court ordered that the case be heard by Judge Bullock: "We do not believe that the plaintiffs' factual allegations are a sham, frivolous, or so unsubstantial that it would be futile to try the case we now consider. The issues raised in this case require the district court to determine either on the basis of uncontroverted facts or on facts [*155] determined by trial whether the school financing provisions complained of are now constitutional."[7] The pattern was similar, and concurrent, in federal court. The case had been filed in 1999, but the federal district court had simply determined that the equal protection challenge was governed by Rodriguez and thus not justiciable. But the Tenth Circuit Court of Appeals ruled in 2002 that the challenge could be heard. That trial, however, was postponed until the state case could be heard because these types of issues tend to be more easily and more comprehensively addressed in state courts, under state constitutional requirements.

All of this was going on while our task force was meeting, and we were aware of but relatively unconcerned by these new challenges. If I recall correctly, my first encounter with Alan Rupe and John Robb was when they attended a meeting of the task force to present the current status of their legal challenges. By the end of my time on the task force, neither case had gone to trial. Both were essentially waiting appeal to determine whether they would go to trial. At the conclusion of my time on the task force, I spoke to Rupe and Robb and they offered a unique proposition: pick a handful of the top experts I could think of and invite them for a two-day meeting in Kansas City to discuss the claims presented in the federal and state cases, then consider data and empirical methods that might be useful for providing evidence related to those causes of action.

We met in the Country Club Plaza district of Kansas City (much of it named for renowned segregationist J. C. Nichols) at the Sheraton Suites Hotel, locked in a conference room for two days. I had invited Leanna Stiefel, coauthor of the original book on measuring equity in school finance,[8] and Bill Duncombe, who I had met on a few occasions at conferences and who was among the most helpful, supportive, and kind individuals in the field (along with Leanna), as well as being simply brilliant when it came to statistical analysis of school finance. Bill had also written a piece on Kansas school finance with then University of Kansas professor Jocelyn Johnston, with whom Bill had attended graduate school (at Syracuse).[9] And for an impressively creative thinker on the legal side, I invited my graduate school peer Preston Green.

We spent two solid days digging through data on Kansas school funding, viewing maps, regression output in Stata (version 7 at the time, for those who care), and graphs of the relationships between spending disparities, district racial composition, income, and wealth, all in an effort to test the theories presented by Rupe and Robb in their legal challenges. Mainly, they theorized that the state school finance system, and specifically the design of the weighting system, (a) merely replicated past disparities rooted in property wealth and (b) adversely affected the state's Black and Latino populations, which were concentrated in KCK, Wichita, and Topeka, as well as towns like Dodge City, Garden City, Salina, and Emporia.

In March 2019, the annual meeting of the Association for Education Finance and Policy (AEFP) was held in Kansas City, Missouri. I traveled with my son, and we ran into Leanna Stiefel on our flight from Newark to Kansas City and offered her a ride to the conference hotel. I opted to stay in a different part of town, where we had held that planning meeting. We reminisced briefly about that meeting at the Sheraton. Leanna brought up how Bill seemed to sit quietly and observantly for much of the first day and then came out the second day with a list of elegant solutions to every question and problem we had encountered the day before—illustrating step by step how to decompose the racial disparities caused by the weights while still considering the idea that some relevant cost adjustment might be warranted.

In the federal case, Rupe and Robb were leaning heavily on the racially disparate impact claim: that the weighting system, while not intentionally based on race, led to racial disparities and that the weighting system was not sufficiently based on any sufficient rationale or analysis to justify the disparities. Even then, Preston Green and I thought a stronger argument might be made that there was in fact some racially discriminatory intent behind many features of the weighting system, from the low enrollment weight to the new facilities weight, rooted in the state's history of policies treating cities with Black residents differently from outlying rural areas and in the state's preferential treatment of the Johnson County suburbs, which had been built on racial restrictions in real estate ownership.[10]

Some of our conversations would soon be reflected in my own expert testimony provided for both the *Robinson* and *Montoy* cases, in reports submitted in February (*Robinson*) and July (*Montoy*). Table 4.1, for example, takes the state's weighting scheme and converts it into a

TABLE 4.1 Average general fund aid (by weighting ratio calculation) by race (2000–2001)

	N(a)	Mean Weighting Ratio	Std. Dev.	General Fund per Pupil	% Below White
White	368,830	1.285	0.217	$ 4,909	
Indian	6,112	1.244	0.182	$ 4,752	3.2%
Hispanic	41,499	1.215	0.158	$ 4,641	5.4%
Asian	10,278	1.172	0.093	$ 4,477	8.8%
Black	41,615	1.163	0.073	$ 4,443	9.5%

Data source: Author's testimony.

Note: Mean weighting ratios by race were created by using district minority populations as weights. So as not to deflate standard deviations on the false assumption that all students in a given district have access to the exact same amount of revenue per pupil, analytic weights were used in place of frequency weights in Stata version 7.0. Analytic weights assume that a value applied to multiple cases represents a mean value for those cases. As such, standard deviations in this table are conservative.

weighting ratio for every district in the state. A very small district, by low enrollment weight alone, might have a weighting ratio of over 2.0, yielding a general fund budget double that of a larger district. Table 4.1 shows the enrollment-weighted averages of the weighting ratio by student race. The average white student in the state in 2000–2001 was in a district with a weighted adjustment of nearly 30 percent over base funding. By contrast, the average Black student attended a district with nearly 10 percent lower cost- and need-weighted adjustment. This was despite the fact that many of these districts likely faced the greatest costs and needs due to high, concentrated child poverty rates.

More to the point of the broader state constitutional challenge in *Montoy*, table 4.2 shows that within the adjacent counties of Johnson and Wyandotte in the Kansas City metro area, differences in weights intended to reflect differences in needs, and costs were not logically associated with needs and costs. This was largely a function of the magnitude of the new facilities weights and, to a lesser extent, a function of the low enrollment weight. The Piper district was a relatively small, somewhat rural, mostly white district carved out of the boundaries of KCK. Turner was also carved out of the boundaries of KCK and had fewer minorities and higher income and housing values than KCK. There was significant racial and economic segregation in Wyandotte County itself and among districts carved out of Kansas City, Kansas. And then there were the much richer and whiter districts in Johnson County immediately to the south. Taking the School District Finance Act as representing costs and needs, one would be led to believe from table 4.2 that the highest cost district in which to meet the state's constitutional mandate was Piper, at 31 percent above basic costs, followed closely by Blue Valley and De Soto, which receive substantial new facilities adjustments. KCK, with the lowest family income and housing values and adult population education levels, was presumed to need 10 percent less need-/cost-based adjustment than Piper or Blue Valley. This is exactly what Tony Ortega was ridiculing in his article in the *Pitch* titled "Funny Math."[11] It seemed obvious, even to a casual outside observer.

TABLE 4.2 SDF makes no significant adjustment among large districts to accommodate socioeconomic differences

District	County	Median Family Income	Median Housing Unit Value	Percent HS Graduate	Percent BA Graduate	Adjusted FTE Enrollment	General Fund Weighting Ratio1	General Fund per Pupil
Piper/KC	Wyandotte	$67,822	$123,600	91%	23%	1,266.30	1.31	$5,061
Blue Valley	Johnson	$90,709	$229,600	98%	64%	17,129.50	1.29	$4,983
Desoto	Johnson	$69,517	$160,900	94%	40%	3,473.10	1.26	$4,867
Turner/KC	Wyandotte	$40,155	$61,800	79%	9%	3,432.80	1.23	$4,751
Spring Hill	Johnson	$58,860	$130,200	90%	23%	1,483.40	1.23	$4,751
Kansas City	Wyandotte	$30,845	$47,800	72%	12%	19,808.10	1.20	$4,636
Bonner Springs	Wyandotte	$44,012	$77,600	81%	16%	2,175.80	1.19	$4,597
Gardner-Edgerton	Johnson	$52,059	$111,500	90%	20%	2,944.00	1.17	$4,520
Olathe	Johnson	$62,633	$143,400	94%	43%	20,312.00	1.17	$4,520
Shawnee Mission	Johnson	$54,383	$136,700	95%	47%	29,677.40	1.13	$4,365

Data source: Author's testimony.

[1] Calculated by dividing weighted pupil count for 2003 (excluding special education) by fall 2002 enrollment (excluding four-year at-risk and declining-enrollment adjustment).

TABLE 4.3 Problem with the district size weighting

Group	SDF	Curve Fit, No Controls (wgt1)	Demand Controls (wgt2)	Less Admin. (wgt3)	Less Trans (wgt3)	Combined (wgt4)
75 to 125	2.12	2.20	1.99	1.82	1.93	1.75
200 to 400	1.62	1.59	1.52	1.44	1.48	1.39
400 to 600	1.51	1.41	1.38	1.31	1.33	1.27
600 to 1000	1.41	1.28	1.27	1.22	1.23	1.19
1000 to 1400	1.27	1.19	1.19	1.16	1.16	1.13
1400 to 1800	1.13	1.14	1.14	1.12	1.11	1.09
>1725	1.06	1.05	1.06	1.05	1.05	1.04

Data source: Author's testimony.
Note: Unweighted means for districts in each enrollment group, district unit of analysis.

Finally, table 4.3 dissects the original problem with the low enrollment weight, based on Bill Duncombe's second-day recommendations, in which we acknowledge that, yes, there is a legitimate reason to think that very small districts operate at higher per-pupil costs, but the analysis behind SDF really messed up when it failed to consider that the very small districts in Kansas in many cases were sitting on oil and natural gas fields and may have been spending so much more not because they needed to, but because they could. Table 4.3 starts with the original weight (SDF) and then peels that weight back, first by estimating what that weight would have looked like if the analysis corrected for (equalized) the income and property wealth of the districts and if it had, instead of drawing straight lines between the points, been represented as a smooth curve. The very smallest districts would drop from a weight of 2.12 to 1.99 and many in the middle ranges by similar amounts. Given that transportation expenses were provided for separately in the formula, we also determined that excluding transportation expenses would further chip away at that low enrollment weight. As one chips away at the low enrollment weight, one also chips away at the racial disparities, many of which were greatest between large, racially diverse towns like Dodge City and nearby rural districts receiving inappropriately large low enrollment adjustments.

But these analyses and representations of the problems with the expenditure analysis that had caused so many problems with SDF would also be supplemented with the 2002 release of the cost study report that had been recommended by the task force, and that report would also shed new light on (a) cost differences between smaller and larger schools and districts based on determining the inputs needed to run those schools and (b) cost differences for providing the necessary programs and services to low-income and non-English-speaking students with the goal of meeting the state's prescribed curricular and outcome standards.

THE AUGENBLICK AND MYERS STUDY

Our task force had made its recommendation in November 2000: that the legislature should once and for all conduct a study of the costs of providing a suitable education. (Chapter 7 will discuss in much greater detail the particulars of the three cost studies that were conducted over time.) While consultants working for states had come up with a handful of different names for their approaches to estimating costs, they really boiled down to two different approaches: one that involved identifying all of the ingredients (teachers, administrators, support staff, materials, supplies, and equipment) needed to meet the constitutional standards and another that used data on spending along with data on outcomes achieved with existing spending to attempt to identify spending levels sufficient to achieve the desired outcomes. In the 1990s and early 2000s, the emphasis was increasingly on outcome goals. Because so many of the problems that had time and time again been replicated in the Kansas school funding formulas were due to reliance on prior spending behavior, our task force expressed a preference for costing out the system from the bottom up, focusing on its ingredients. We also pushed back on consultants when they visited our task force, asking how they would determine the differences in costs facing smaller versus larger districts. No previous study of this type had actually looked separately at districts of different sizes. Most instead had relied on costing out a single prototype school and district of a specific size and then used prior spending data to apply adjustments after the fact.

Augenblick, Myers, and their associates at the Augenblick & Meyers (A&M) firm were contracted by the Legislative Coordinating Council (LCC) in the fall of 2001. At many points in later litigation, their study would be referred to as the legislature's own study, representing the costs of what the legislature itself had established as meeting the definition of "suitable provision for finance of the educational interests of the state." The Legislative Coordinating Council then delegated direct oversight of the work to the Legislative Education Planning Committee (LEPC), which, among their most important tasks, assisted Augenblick and Myers (A&M) in developing an operational definition of the suitability requirements of Article 6 of the constitution. This, in particular, was something that hadn't previously been attempted. LEPC and A&M looked, in part, at curricular requirements that had been laid out in the Quality Performance Accreditation (QPA) side of the 1992 School District Finance Act. They also looked at specific benchmarks for achievement on state assessments laid out in QPA.

The suitability definition would serve to guide two sets of analyses to be conducted by the A&M team. On the one hand, both the input requirements and outcome goals would be used with focus groups of education professionals (called *professional judgment panels*) to guide their exercise in determining the various inputs needed to meet these goals and standards. And in a second analysis, A&M would study the average spending of districts that achieved the state testing outcome benchmarks (which they called *successful schools analysis*). Only the former, the professional judgment panels, would address the issue of differences in costs associated with differences in school size, ideally correcting the error that had been carried over from the original school finance act to SDEA and then to SDF by relying time and time again on prior spending of smaller and larger districts. Both methods would be used together to figure out just how much spending overall would be needed to achieve the suitability definitions provided.

A&M conducted its focus group exercises by developing prototypical resource profiles for *very small, small, moderate,* and *large* districts, as shown in Figure 4.1.

FIGURE 4.1   Prototype school and district characteristics

	Very Small	Small	Moderate	Large
Range in Enrollment	<324	325–555	556–3,600	>3,600
Size of Prototype District	200	430	1,300	11,200
Size of Prototype School				
Elementary	140	150	200	430
Middle	—	—	300	430
High School	60	130	400	1,150

Source: J. Augenblick, J. Myers, J. Silverstein, and A. Barkis, *Calculation of the Cost of a Suitable Education in Kansas in 2000-2001 Using Two Different Analytic Approaches* (Topeka: Legislative Coordinating Council, State of Kansas, 2002), IV2.

A&M developed tabulations of inputs and the costs of those inputs for districts serving 200, 430, 1,300, and 11,200 pupils, producing four points of cost estimates across district size ranges. Like the previous expenditure analyses that had been done, A&M connected these dots with straight lines to determine what adjustment should be provided for all sizes in between and beyond both ends.

At the time, the SDF base funding was $3,820. In its focus group–based, input-oriented method, A&M found that the basic education costs for a large district were $5,811. The average spending analysis of districts meeting the suitable outcome targets produced a lower number, $4,650—but both were much higher than $3,820. Aligning the A&M district size weight findings with the SDF inflection points, we get the data in table 4.4 (from my *Montoy* testimony). Rather than needing 2.14 times the basic funding level, the smallest districts were estimated to need only 1.43 times that level. The next group needed 1.24 instead of 1.58. These were substantial reductions to the small district cost weight, even more so than the reductions I had estimated by attempting to correct the prior spending data.

The other big differences included providing significantly more funding (a larger weight) for at-risk children, identified as being from low-income families. Where SDF provided a 10 percent adjustment (times the $3,820 base), A&M's analyses suggested a 33 percent

TABLE 4.4   A&M scale component using base of $4,650 (2000–2001 data)

Enrollment	Budget per Pupil (Scale Adjustment Only)
75–125	7,536 (1.43)
200–400	6,524 (1.24)
1900	5,257
>11,200	4,650

Source: Simulation of A&M findings by author prepared for testimony.

adjustment in small districts and 56 percent adjustment in larger districts, which also would be multiplied times a larger base value (either $4,650 or $5,811). In total, raising existing general fund budgets per pupil to the A&M estimated needs (using the lower base figure) would increase statewide general fund spending by over $1 billion, above the current total spending of $3.87 billion. But this report, which was released in May 2002, was largely ignored by the legislature. For example, base funding was raised in 2001–2002 by only $50 per pupil, to $3,870 but was actually cut in 2002–2003 to $3,863 when state revenues came up short.

MONTOY TRIAL AND BULLOCK RULING

The case went to trial in the fall of 2003, for eight days in Judge Bullock's Topeka courtroom. Alan Rupe and John Robb had set up their war room at the Capitol Plaza Hotel a few miles down the road—a conference room filled with large foam board exhibits and boxes and boxes of documents. Rupe and Robb would present the case on behalf of plaintiffs. Defending the state were Dan Biles, the attorney for the state board of education who had represented the state in earlier rounds; and an attorney hired from the outside, representing the attorney general's office, Ken Weltz (of the same Kansas City firm at which John Vratil practiced law). Weltz was a grandstanding trial attorney with little to no background in school finance and seemingly little interest in learning. Meanwhile, Rupe, Robb, Biles, and Judge Bullock had been around this block for over a decade.

The claim in the state case, reduced to its simplest form, was that the system of school funding was inadequate and that those inadequacies were handed out inequitably. It was inadequate in the sense that the funding available did not "make suitable provision for finance of the educational interests of the state" (Article 6, Section 6). And the system was far less adequate for some than others, focusing specifically on the inadequacy of funding, programs, and services and the related educational outcomes of children in districts like Dodge City. The system did not necessarily have to be inadequate for all for the system to be depriving some children of their rights under Article 6. For good measure, Rupe and Robb also advanced their claims in state court that the system violated equal protection and produced a racially disparate impact on the state's Black and Latino populations.

I recall one moment in the trial when Weltz's grandstanding style got the best of him. I was being cross-examined by Weltz about the racial disparities I had laid out in my reports. From a legal standpoint, it did indeed matter whether those disparities were intentionally based on race. So, from a defense standpoint, it would be relevant to get me to admit on the stand that these were merely patterns of racial disparity and not some intended form of discrimination. But my opinion on this question had continued to evolve as I learned more and started writing on the topic. Weltz built up to his dramatic moment by first having me walk through the racial disparities I had found, one by one. He then turned his back and paused. Next, he abruptly turned, got right in my face (I was on the stand, sitting about three feet to Judge Bullock's left), and said loudly and dramatically, "You don't think those disparities are intentional, *do you?*" I paused, shocked by his rather dramatic move (with him now *right in my face*), and also thinking, "I can't believe he just asked me that in front of the judge." I responded, "Well, actually . . . I do." He immediately attempted to change the topic, but Judge Bullock was intrigued, and asked him to stop, saying, "No, I want to hear this." At this point, I walked Bullock through much of the history I've laid out previously herein, explaining how Kansas legislators had taken specific steps in the school funding policy to accommodate school districts serving neighborhoods that those legislators knew had been developed on racially restrictive covenants. (The record of public statements and adopted policies in this regard actually became more damning in the years after this trial.)

While Bullock was intrigued by the explanation, in the end he didn't find it sufficiently compelling to declare the school funding system *intentionally* racially discriminatory (a high legal bar to meet). To summarize Bullock's ruling, issued December 2, 2003, he found that the School District Finance Act did not meet the standards of Article 6 of the Kansas Constitution but was not intentionally racially discriminatory. It did also violate equal protection in his view, however, and he agreed that there was racially disparate impact, triggering equal protection concerns. The formula was, in his view, "troublesome" and "wholly lacking," and a "cruel hoax" that could leave some Kansans "diabolically frustrated."[12] Regarding the unevenness of the school funding system, and the disparities in outcomes for low-income and minority students, Judge Bullock noted:

> Even more troublesome is Defendants' well-phrased and superficially attractive argument that even if one chooses to examine alarming student failure rates of Kansas minorities, poor, disabled, and limited English, one finds these failure rates compare "favorably" with similar failure rates for such persons elsewhere. Reduced to its simplest and clearest terms, this argument suggests that there is "no problem" in Kansas since our vulnerable and/or protected students aren't performing any worse than such students are performing elsewhere. This argument seems to the Court to be on a par with the following statement: "Persons of color should be comforted by the fact that lynchings in Kansas are no more frequent than lynchings in many other states."[13]

A few weeks later, Bullock would offer a more concise paraphrase: "The Court will never forget Mr. Weltz's statement in closing argument in this case when he said, *in haec verba*, 'Our education system is strong and is producing meaningful results for most children.' This case, of course, is about the rest of those children. The Court's message is in Movants' own words: 'JUST GO FIX IT!'"[14]

Bullock was equally impatient with the state's assertions that there was plenty of money available to school districts to meet the state standards and that they just needed to use that money more wisely and that having a judge step in to require the legislature to increase funding really wouldn't help—that money really wasn't a major driver of the quality of programs and services a school or district could provide. This is a rather common line of defense in such cases, advanced by a common set of hired gun expert witnesses. Bullock explained:

> Perhaps one example from the evidence will suffice as an illustration of this factual conclusion for present purposes: Last year, Jacque Feist, principal of Dodge City High School and Kathy Taylor, principal of Dodge City Middle School, applied for and received a short-term federal grant. With this grant, they doubled their teachers, cut their middle school classes in half, and added special training for their teachers in how to teach children with reading problems. In one year, they raised their middle school reading proficiency from 44 percent to 70 percent in a school with a makeup of 74 percent minority (Hispanic), 67 percent impoverished, 13 percent disabled, 47 percent ESL, and 25 percent LEP and all in a district where the bilingual teacher-pupil ratio is one to a hundred, where two hundred summer school applicants were denied admission for lack of funds, and where 120 wait on the waiting list for the after school tutoring program.
>
> "Money doesn't matter?" *That dog won't hunt in Dodge City!*[15]

Bullock also had opportunity to review the A&M study as evidence of what it might actually cost the state to meet the "suitability" standard of Article 6. Bullock explained: "Finally, as previously observed, the Augenblick & Myers' cost study, commissioned by the State Board and the Legislature, found current funding levels dramatically short of that necessary to provide a suitable education by the Legislature's own standards. That is the issue at bar and on this overarching point the evidence is uncontroverted."[16] A few things mattered here. First, while not contracted and overseen by the full legislature, the A&M study was a legislatively sponsored one, in which legislators had guided the operational definition of *suitability* and overseen the estimation of related costs. It was also the only evidence of costs on the table. Bullock noted: "When asked whether there was anything the Court could consider other than the Augenblick & Myers report in deciding what a suitable education would cost and how that figure compared to current funding, the State Commissioner of Education, Defendant Dr. Andy Tompkins, testified unequivocally there was nothing."[17] Of course, the news headline read, "$1 Billion School Fix Ordered."[18] As Bullock pointed out to Joe Miller in "You Got Schooled": "'I read these headlines: "Judge orders $1 billion." I didn't write that.'" Miller explained: "The order does mention a billion dollars. But that's the *Legislature's* number, not Bullock's."[19]

State politicians on both sides of the political aisle seemed to take aim at Bullock specifically. In the December 4, 2003, *Johnson County Sun* article, Senator Vratil argued: "I think Judge Bullock has in mind trying to influence the Legislature during the next legislative session. That will be extremely unethical for him to do because he's not supposed to be lobbying the Legislature on issues that are pending before him in a case," going on to suggest that Bullock was attempting to do what he had done back in 1991 in *Mock*. Joe Miller quotes Kathleen Sebelius' response from an earlier *Wichita Eagle* article: "'For taxpayers, that can be a very dangerous proposal to have a court essentially make decisions based not on knowing the situation or having responsibility for raising taxes, but just making mandates that shut down the schools unless you come up with a certain funding amount.'"[20] In short, there wasn't a whole lot of love in the air for Judge Bullock, and there most certainly would be an appeal to the state supreme court.

In response to the lack of any substantive action taken to revise SDF during the 2004 legislative session, Judge Bullock issued an order on May 11 that schools would be closed until the legislature responded to his original ruling. Proposals for increased funding had been offered by the governor and summarily dismissed by legislators. Multiple smaller efforts followed and also failed, as Bullock explained: "To paraphrase Aesop: The mountain labored and brought forth nothing at all. In fact, rather than attack the problem, the Legislature chose instead to attack the Court."[21] The supreme court would take the appeal and issue its first ruling on January 3, 2005. It had now been nearly six years since the case was filed, three since the state had been provided with evidence of what it would cost to meet its constitutional obligations. Base funding still sat at $3,863 for a third straight year.

BATTLE BETWEEN THE KANSAS STATE SUPREME COURT AND THE LEGISLATURE

In the weeks before the start of the 2005 legislative session, on January 3, the Kansas Supreme Court (KSSC) issued its ruling on the appeal of Judge Bullock's ruling of just over a year earlier. To summarize:

- KSSC reversed the district court's holding that SDFQPA's financing formula is a violation of equal protection.
- KSSC also reversed the district court's holding that the SDFQPA financing formula has an unconstitutional disparate impact on minorities and/or other classes. In order to establish an equal protection violation on this basis, one must show not only that there is a disparate impact, but also that the impact can be traced to a discriminatory purpose.
- KSSC affirmed the district court's holding that the legislature has failed to meet its burden as imposed by Art. 6, § 6 of the Kansas Constitution to "make suitable provision for finance" of the public schools.[22]

That is, the high court narrowed the scope of the legal claims to focus entirely on the requirements of the 1966 education article, setting aside other claims that might have more implications in the end for cases beyond the education system.

The legislature attempted at least to appear responsive to the state supreme court, which it could not as easily paint as an unreasonable adversary. During the spring session of 2005, the legislature advanced HB2247, which would provide modest increases and minor changes to the SDF. HB2247 also proposed to conduct a new cost study—one that would estimate the costs of providing only the bare-bones inputs to public schooling, in compliance with the basic curricular components laid out in the state standards. It was ultimately this proposal by the legislature, in the context of this bill, that would lead to the state's high court clarifying the balance of powers between the legislature and state board as laid out in the 1966 amendments.

On May 11, 2005, parties convened for oral arguments at the state supreme court. By this time, Marla Luckert was on the court, along with Carol Beier. These oral arguments, which I attended in person, involved multiple layers of drama—and one especially important shift in legal positioning. On the one hand, these were the high court oral arguments in which Justice Beier in particular grew impatient with the state's hired outside counsel Ken Weltz, who offered little substance in defense of HB2247 (leading to the Crowson cartoon in chapter 1, figure 1.2). More importantly, when it was time for Dan Biles to argue on behalf of the state board of education, Biles explained to the court that the legislature's new proposed cost study would not meet the constitutional demands and why—because it ignored the state board's self-executing authority to establish outcome standards that, in effect, represent the educational interests of the state. That is, the legislature's responsibility is to "make suitable provision for finance" of the "educational interests," where the state board has authority over establishing those interests and determining outcome metrics to evaluate whether those interests have been met. The smaller point, in context at this juncture, was that for any cost study conducted by the legislature to validly represent the constitutional obligation, that study would have to take into account the outcome standards established by the state board—Mr. Biles's client.

The court was faced with three competing arguments:

1. From the plaintiffs' attorneys Alan Rupe and John Robb: that HB2247 failed to comply with the court's January order, and the court should continue to rely on the A&M study as the only available benchmark.
2. From the state's perspective (representing the attorney general's office): that the court shouldn't be involved with such things to begin with, that HB2247 itself was sufficiently compliant, and that the legislature had the authority to determine the costs of providing only the bare-bones inputs to schooling and subsequent obligation to fund only those costs.
3. From the state board's perspective, as presented by Dan Biles: that HB2247 was a step forward, albeit an insufficient one, but that the court should await the results of additional cost analysis, where any future cost analysis used to guide the state formula must take into account the outcomes and full array of standards established by the state board. Biles also took issue (as did plaintiffs) with HB2247's raising of the cap on local option funding.

Within a month (on June 3), the supreme court ruled, finding in favor of plaintiffs that HB2247 had not gone far enough toward fixing the deficiencies of SDF. It further adopted the reasoning advanced by Dan Biles regarding the independent roles of the legislature and state board under Article 6. In short, the court found that HB2247 did not comply either with the equity or adequacy concerns of its January order. With respect to the proposed cost study, and consistent with Bile's oral arguments, the court noted: "It also appears that the study contemplated by H.B. 2247 is deficient because it will examine only what it costs for education 'inputs'—the cost of delivering kindergarten through grade 12 curriculum, related services, and other programs 'mandated by state statute in accredited schools.' It does not appear to demand consideration of the costs of 'outputs'—achievement of measurable standards of student proficiency."[23]

It was now June 2005, and the legislature needed a fix that would be acceptable to the court before the start of the next school year (mid-August in Kansas). Governor Sebelius called the legislature back to Topeka for a special summer session to address the court's concerns. I recall going on local KCUR radio host Steve Kraske's *Up to Date* show on the eve of that session, along with Ed O'Malley—a moderate Republican and education supporter, who was now a member of the Kansas legislature—and a more conservative legislator from southern Johnson County.

The special session began on June 22, with legislators facing a suggested funding increase for the coming year of around $285 million. Legislators proposed modifications to HB2247, some good and some in fact bad (from an equity standpoint). Overall, legislators proposed to increase base funding in the coming year. This, however, is also when legislators retained (from HB2247) the "cost of living" adjustment to local option budget caps for the seventeen districts with the highest housing prices, arguing that this adjustment was needed to recruit and retain teachers. The legislature also increased local taxing and spending authority. The new plan took into account Biles's argument and the high court order that the new cost study to be completed by the start of the 2006 session would both look at basic input costs and consider the costs associated with meeting the state board's outcome standards.

But passage of the bill in that summer session ground to a halt over Republican demands that the new funding be linked to a constitutional amendment that would, in effect, grant full authority to the legislature over determination of education funding and related tax policy. Democrats in the legislature refused a vote on the proposal until the constitutional amendment was removed. Legislative democrats won this battle, even though their governor, Kathleen Sebelius, refused to take their side on the issue. The legislature missed its original July 2 deadline to avoid having schools closed by the courts. But by July 6, after dropping the constitutional amendment, the legislature passed a bill that increased funding by approximately $290 million (or up to $400 million, depending on how increases were counted).

Oral arguments were held less than two days later. The court permitted the school year to move forward and funding to flow, but retained jurisdiction, in part to await the findings of the newly commissioned cost study to be conducted under the supervision of the Legislative Division of Post Audit and to be produced by January 2006.

POST AUDIT COST STUDY: JANUARY 2006

The new study (to be discussed more extensively in chapter 7) was adopted as legislation and handed off to the legislature's own research arm: the Legislative Division of Post Audit, which at the time was headed by Post Auditor Barbara Hinton; her chief in-house analyst at the time was Scott Frank. The in-house staff seemed sufficiently comfortable taking on the charge of collecting data from the state department of education to calculate the costs of providing the basic programs and services mandated by the state (the input-based cost analysis), focusing on bare-bones inputs. But Hinton and Frank had questions on how they might approach the task or who they might contract externally to work with them specifically on calculating the costs of meeting the outcome standards adopted by the board.

At the time, only a few researchers were really working on approaches to estimate costs associated with specific outcomes, using actual data for spending outcomes, student populations, and other characteristics, as well as methods designed to sort out *costs* from merely *what was being spent.* This is a far more complex endeavor, for example, than the analysis done by A&M that simply took into account average spending data from districts meeting state standards. Doing this right required figuring out how much more or less spending was associated with achieving those outcomes in higher and lower poverty settings, in smaller and larger districts, and in different regions of the state, using a method known as *cost function modeling.* I had been collaborating with Lori Taylor, an economist from Texas A&M University at the time on similar projects, and I was also doing more work with Bill Duncombe, who had participated in the *Montoy* and *Robinson* planning meeting. After discussing minor differences in methods, Hinton and Frank agreed to reach out to Bill, who, with his Syracuse colleague John Yinger, would provide cost model estimates associated with the state board outcome measures.

The eventual Legislative Division of Post Audit report, released in January 2006, would include three layers of analysis. First, the report included the input-based analysis the legislature had originally proposed. Second, the LDPA report included, albeit as a technical appendix only, the cost model estimates produced by Duncombe and Yinger (provided a month earlier, in December 2005). Third, LDPA staff had developed a funding formula model that made use of the Duncombe and Yinger estimates and added back in costs outside of those estimates, including transportation costs, but then subtracted from the state responsibility the role of existing federal aid.

The bottom line was that this study yielded results that were substantially similar to the previous one, both in terms of the total additional funding needed and in terms of which districts faced the greatest additional needs and costs. On January 10, 2006, the front page of the *Topeka Capitol Journal* read: "Sobering Report: Audit Says Schools Need Additional $399 Million."

THE END OF THE *MONTOY* ERA

New study in hand, the legislature was somewhat responsive during the 2006 session, pushing through SB549, which increased base aid from $4,257 to $4,316 in 2006–2007; to $4,374 in 2007–2008; and to $4,433 in 2008–2009. At-risk weighting was increased to 0.278 for 2006–2007,

0.378 for 2007–2008, and 0.456 for 2008–2009. Bilingual weighting held at .395. Also, in response to a unique feature of the Duncombe and Yinger cost model, the legislature included an additional adjustment for population-dense, high-poverty districts. The changes certainly did not comport fully with the LDPA cost estimates, but by this point the high court seemed to be looking for a way out—perhaps especially Chief Justice Kay McFarland, who was nearing retirement. On July 28, 2006, McFarland wrote:

> Our prior orders have made it clear that we were concerned that the then existing financing formula was distorted and provided disparate funding because it was based on former spending levels with little or no consideration of the actual costs and present funding needs of Kansas public education. The legislature has responded to this concern. The legislature has undertaken the responsibility to consider actual costs in providing a suitable system of school finance by commissioning the LPA to conduct an extensive cost study, creating the 2010 Commission to conduct extensive monitoring and oversight of the school finance system, and creating the School District Audit Team within LPA to conduct annual performance audits and monitor school district funding as directed by the 2010 Commission. In addition, the new legislation contains numerous provisions designed to improve reporting of costs, expenditures, and needs.
>
> These new components provide the fundamental framework for a cost-based funding scheme in which the legislature will be regularly provided with the relevant, accurate information necessary to meet its constitutional obligation to provide and maintain a suitable system of financing of Kansas public schools.[24]

The court, having retained jurisdiction at the appellate level to this point, was not in a position to offer opinions about (a) features of the law that were new or (b) the LDPA cost study because neither had been vetted at trial by a lower court. Of course, the high court could have chosen at that time to remand the case back to a lower court to address the issues, but it did not. Justice Beier makes this point in her dissent, joined by Justice Luckert:

> I respectfully dissent from the majority's decision to dismiss this action, leaving for another day in a future lawsuit the determination of whether S.B. 549 meets the standard of Article 6, § 6 of the Kansas Constitution. That issue is alive in this action. Constitutionality has always been and remains squarely presented. . . .
>
> The soundness of the methodology and conclusions of the Legislative Division of Post Audit (LPA) cost study have not been tested by a typical adversary process. No evidence has been admitted on the ways in which the members of the legislature considered actual and necessary costs or equity. Without testimony and documentary evidence in the record to evaluate on these matters, this court simply cannot conclude the State has carried the burden placed upon it last year to demonstrate that the legislature's actions brought Kansas' school finance system into compliance with the state constitution. The appropriate way to respond is not to throw the plaintiffs out of court. It is to retain jurisdiction, acknowledge the factual deficiencies of the record, and remand to the district court for further proceedings focused on the constitutionality of the finance system, as altered by S.B. 549.[25]

Particularly offensive features of the new formula remained in place, even though the court expressed concern over their rationality. About the "cost of living weight," the court opined: "We held that the new cost-of-living property tax provision was not based on any evidence that there was any link between high housing costs and higher education costs or that the 17 districts that would benefit from the provision pay higher teacher salaries. We noted that the evidence at trial demonstrated the opposite—that the districts with high-poverty, high at-risk student populations are the ones that need help attracting and retaining teachers."[26] Vetting the cost of living adjustment or the application of the new cost study to the suitability standard would have to wait for another day and another trial. And as the Kansas economy collapsed and revenues dried up in the great recession, before the third-year implementation of SB549, that too would come to pass. Of course, in its usual style, the Kansas legislature had slipped in a few rule changes to attempt to tip the scales in its favor for the next round. First, any litigation involving challenges to the state school finance system would have to go through a waiting period; second, such challenges would need to be heard by a specially assigned three-judge panel for trial, with judges representing different regions of the state. The stage was set and the new rules determined.

5

THE BROWNBACK YEARS
AND BEYOND

Steering Through the Laffer Curve

"'Republicans want to replicate these policies on a
national level, but even when you buy couch cleaner
they tell you to try it on a small patch of fabric
first,'" he said. 'That's what happened here—
Kansas was the small patch of fabric. Not only did
the cleaner not work, the couch exploded.'"

—Seth Meyers, *Late Night with Seth Meyers:*
A Closer Look, March 22, 2016

Kansas tax cuts under Governor Brownback gained significant national
attention when they occurred, and again a few years later when President Donald Trump and the Republican Congress espoused a comparable ideology to advance a federal tax cut plan. Kansas has often been
caricatured in national media as an extreme illustration of conservative
economic and social policy. While the Brownback tax cuts were among
the largest in any state and had negative ripple effects through the

Kansas economy, and on school budgets, it's important to acknowledge that because Kansas school funding was in so much better position than surrounding states at the time of the cuts, even after those cuts, Kansas remained in relatively good position. Yes, the cuts hurt. A lot. But the longer-term pressures in place that have kept Kansas in balance over time also kept those cuts from being completely disastrous, as they have been in other states, including Arizona, Oklahoma, and Colorado. And those longer-term pressures, government structures, judicial oversight, and informed voters set the stage for a recovery.

In July 2013, the three-judge trial court panel issued its ruling criticizing the state's assertion that cuts cause no harm and pointing out that some Kansas children had already had a third of their education adversely affected by those cuts. By 2017, moderate Republicans had retaken the Kansas legislature and voted to reverse the Brownback tax cuts.[1] We'll explore the temporary disconnects among statewide tax policy, conservative reverence to the oft-debunked Laffer curve, the actual fallout of the Kansas tax cuts, and the trial court's view of the evidence on school spending, school quality, and student outcomes.

First, let's introduce Arthur Laffer, who was recruited as an advisor for the Brownback tax plan. His most notable work, the Laffer curve, advocated the facile premise that beyond a certain level of taxation, higher taxes thwart economic growth. That is, taxation for public goods and services yields little or no economic benefit and in fact causes economic harm. Those who believe in this ideology also generally believe that the US as a whole and all US states individually presently tax well above any optimal level. As such, according to this premise, cuts can only ever make things better and tax increases can only make things worse. Subscribing to this ideology, Brownback had promoted his tax cut plan as a shot of adrenaline for the Kansas economy. The fallout was far more like an overdose of sedative.

GOVERNOR BROWNBACK'S SHOT OF SEDATIVE TO THE KANSAS ECONOMY

Kansas, like its waving fields of wheat, has had the tendency to sway back and forth with the political winds, but it's often remained moderate at the top—in the governor's office. Kansas politics are largely ruled by the Republican Party of the state, and the most significant ideological split in the state—which largely ends up controlling public policy—is that between the conservative and moderate wings of the Republican Party. Recall that I migrated to Kansas as a registered independent, born and raised a Vermont Republican. I learned early in my time in Kansas that all political influence was wielded through the Republican Party. Often, Democrats would switch parties to vote in primaries just to make sure that the Republican candidate at the top of the ballot was more moderate—and, perhaps more importantly, that moderates won the down-ballot primaries for senate and house seats. Those were the races least likely to be won by an actual Democrat. At least at the top of ticket, if the Republican candidate for the general election was too extreme, a moderate Democrat would likely win, but that was a risky prospect to bet on. I resided in Kansas for the latter part of moderate Republican governor Bill Graves's rule and witnessed the election and reelection of moderate Democrat Kathleen Sebelius. I left right before the election of Sam Brownback, who would end up being more extreme than any Kansas governor of the past few decades. It was often those looking to make their name on the national stage, with middle "'merica" as their home base, that were the most extreme, whether on the economy, religion, or immigration. During and after my time in Kansas, Kris Kobach successfully became secretary of state, but he was too extreme even for Kansans in a number of subsequent attempts, including losses in primaries for the US Senate, the gubernatorial race, and the third Congressional district.[2]

In the run-up to Brownback's election, Democrat Mark Parkinson had stepped in to replace Kathleen Sebelius when she took a position in the Obama administration. Parkinson stepped in at the onset (2009) of the budgetary aftermath of the great recession, which coincided with the time the legislature had promised to phase in increased funding for schools to comply with the final order in *Montoy*. In fact, it was this promise that led the court to dismiss *Montoy*. To offset some of the cuts that had already begun, the legislature approved increases to the sales tax for three years (from 5.3 to 6.3 percent), with the intent that those rates would revert to 5.7 percent down the road.

Sam Brownback was elected governor in 2010, and by a wide margin (over 63 percent of the vote). He was reelected by a similar margin in 2014. Brownback was perhaps better known in the run-up to his election for his conservative religious and social policy views. But he decided (or others decided for him) that he would make his name on the national stage on economic policy. In his first state of the state address, Brownback promised to "reset our tax code, particularly with an eye toward lowering income tax rates."[3] It appeared that by late 2011, the Kansas budget had seen its bottom and was beginning to rebound. Brownback had not yet had time to follow through on any tax policy proposals.

Brownback pushed forward on dramatic cuts to income taxes again in his 2012 state of the state, soon thereafter calling in "celebrity supply-side pitchman Arthur Laffer to Topeka to sell his program to legislative tax committees."[4] In chapter 7, I'll summarize how Kansas legislators, at times seemingly despite themselves, have produced a string of three major studies of the cost of providing a suitable education, each time producing studies that were independently conducted even if politically overseen, applied reasonable methods—among the most rigorous used in any state—and produced thoughtful, reliable, and valid policy recommendations. I have written elsewhere how other states, like Arizona and Colorado, have been more likely to be sucked in by quick-fix, off-the-shelf schemes—but not Kansas.[5] Kansas has typically stayed the course and taken a more measured approach—but not this time. As reported in the *Wichita Eagle* in the summer of 2012: "Brownback gave Laffer a $75,000 contract to consult with the state on tax reform efforts earlier this year, and Laffer tried to rally support for a massive tax-cutting plan at legislative hearings during the legislative session. The plan called for reduction of individual income taxes, the phasing out of income taxes on businesses and the elimination of more than a dozen tax credits and deductions, including several popular ones such as the home mortgage deduction and the earned income tax credit that benefits the working poor."[6] Also from the *Eagle*: "Laffer told more than 200 people at a small-business forum at Johnson County Community College that there is a war among states over tax policy and that nowhere is that revolution more powerful than in Kansas. He said Kansas' tax cuts and political shifts will produce 'enormous prosperity' for the state. 'It's not a left-wing, right-wing thing,' Laffer said. 'It's economics.'"[7]

Let's take a quick look at what Laffer offers as his basis for the notion that it's always better to cut taxes, cut taxes more, cut taxes as far as you can, to the bone, if possible. Laffer is purported to have sketched on a napkin one day the brilliant revelation portrayed in figure 5.1 (my rendering, not his). The idea here is that up to a certain point, raising tax rates will generate more revenue. But at some point, additional increases in tax rates will lead to a slowing of economic activity and revenues will plummet. The premise is not altogether that absurd. It seems reasonable that a government could adopt such high taxes that it becomes unbearable to operate under that government any longer, so business and individuals seek tax refuge elsewhere.

What is absurd is Laffer's conclusion that therefore, the only way to ever increase revenue—in any circumstance, in any state in the US, in any nation of the world—is to lower taxes. Assuming any validity to the Laffer curve, the only way for lower taxes to increase revenue is if our initial point on the curve is either D or E (I've added these for reference). If, however, we are sitting at A, B, or C, then cutting taxes is going to lead to a backslide in revenues. The curve also ignores that these revenues collected in taxes themselves promote some degree—a

FIGURE 5.1   The Laffer curve

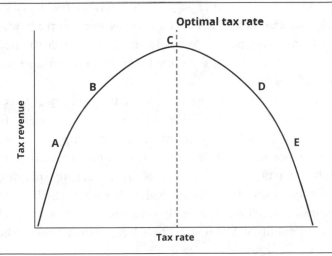

significant degree—of economic activity, from improving the quality of schools to increased employment from public infrastructure projects.

Somehow, Brownback—with Laffer as his expert—was able to convince a significant share of Kansas legislators that cutting taxes could only make things better. Either that, or a significant share of legislators at the time really just didn't care that much about what would follow and simply had a distaste for taxes. Having listened to Kansas legislators ask insightful technical questions about the variables used to distill the relative efficiency of school districts, in the context of Lori Taylor's 2018 cost model analysis, I have difficulty believing most Kansas legislators couldn't see through the Laffer curve. Rather, it was a convenient excuse to do something many of them—the more conservative Republic legislators who came to power in the same election cycle as Brownback—wanted to do at the time, regardless of evidence.

Competing plans were offered in the house and senate during 2012. By May 21, 2012, Brownback had coerced the Senate to pass a plan adopted by the House, which he then signed on May 22. He declared: "Today's legislation will create tens of thousands of new jobs and help make Kansas the best place in America to start and grow a small business."[8] In perhaps his best-known quote on the expected effects of the proposed tax cuts, on July 29, 2012, he said: *"Our new pro-growth tax policy will be like a shot of adrenaline into the heart of the Kansas economy. It will pave the way to the creation of tens of thousands of new jobs."*[9] By the end of the 2013 legislative session, the legislature and Brownback had cut individual income taxes even further and scaled back deductions. The plan also made most of the 2010 income tax increase permanent, keeping the rate at 6.15 percent rather than letting it revert to 5.7 percent.

Revenues started to plummet, and a credit downgrade was enacted by Moody's Investors Service, declaring Kansas's recovery from the recession to be a "relatively sluggish recovery compared to its peers" and noting the problem of "revenue reductions (resulting from tax cuts) which have not been fully offset by recurring spending cuts." Other credit agencies also reduced Kansas's ratings. Still, in the 2014 election, Kansans decided to give Brownback a chance to see his plan through to its eventual bitter end. Not long thereafter, in the fall of

2014, Kansas's revenue projections were on pace to fall $1 billion short of expenses for 2015 and 2016.[10]

Kansas, as a result, became a focal point for national ridicule, both in popular media and in various public policy–oriented media and think tank outlets. This was in part because the collapse of the Kansas experiment came right before the Trump administration also chose to publicly rely on Art Laffer and propose a plan of deep tax cuts built on Laffer's claims. It was all too easy for the national media and policy think tanks to use Kansas as an example of just how flawed this approach might be. As described in great detail, in a six-minute segment called "A Closer Look" from late-night host Seth Meyers, the Brownback tax cuts were an experiment that went horribly wrong.[11]

Michael Linden of Business Insider explained that the Kansas tax cuts failed on the specific measures by which Brownback and his advisors claimed they would reap the greatest benefits: job growth, population growth, and income growth: "Nick Jordan, the state's revenue secretary, said the administration ultimately imagines the creation of 22,000 more jobs over 'normal growth' and 35,000 more people moving into the state over the next five years. And he expects the tax changes to expand disposable income by $2 billion over the same period."[12] Alexandra Thornton and Galen Hendricks of the Center for American Progress also explained that state revenues declined sharply, government programs suffered brutal cuts, and, between 2013 and 2016, Kansas's "real gross domestic product only grew by 3.8 percent, while national GDP growth was nearly double that at 7 percent."[13] Further: "Employment growth in Kansas has also lagged far behind the rest of the nation. Since the tax cuts took effect in 2013, total employment rose just 2.6 percent, compared with the 6.5 percent average increase experienced by the rest of the nation. And the story for private sector employment was similar, with Kansas' 3.5 percent growth falling far behind the national growth rate of 7.6 percent."[14]

Other national outlets took their shots at the great Kansas tax experiment as well.[15] And few, even among the most libertarian of think tanks, stepped up to defend the plan. The libertarian Cato Institute last addressed the Brownback tax plan in 2014, claiming that the plan was not doing well as it should, leading to credit downgrades primarily because the legislature was unwilling to make sufficient programmatic cuts to counterbalance the revenue losses.[16] The Reason Foundation, of similar policy preferences, seems not to have addressed the Kansas "experiment" since about 2013, still reiterating assertions that the plan would lead to significant economic growth.[17]

IMPLICATIONS FOR KANSAS REVENUES

The Brownback tax cuts certainly inflicted harm on state revenues, funding for public programs and services, and the state's economic recovery from the recession. If one benefit came from the national interest in the Brownback tax cut experiment, it was the folly of Laffer and his curve as serious economic policy. With a shift in the Kansas legislature in 2016, those cuts were reversed in 2017. The tax cuts had their major impact on Kansas revenues from about 2013 to 2017. On the upside, when it came to Kansas school funding, Kansas was relatively well positioned, at least regionally, and on the path to increasing school funding and targeting it toward those with greatest needs from 2007 to 2009 in the wake of the *Montoy* case. The downside was that school funding and state revenues had already started to take a hit from 2009 to 2011. This was the great recession dip. And while most other states would follow that dip with a flattening or rebound, Kansas would follow it with a Brownback dip.

Figure 5.2 shows Kansas's revenues, per capita, in constant (2017) dollars over time. Total revenues experienced flattening and dips during the late 1980s and early 1990s economic slowdown (run-up to *Mock*) and during the 2001 post-9/11 slowdown (run-up to *Montoy*). Total revenues experienced a much larger dip from 2008 to 2010 from the great recession, much of the decline coming from declining income tax revenues. This was in the years immediately prior to Brownback's election. Total revenues, as a function of sales tax revenue increases, started to rebound a bit from 2010 to 2012 as income tax revenues temporarily stabilized. Income tax revenues took an additional hit with the Brownback cuts, flattening out what might have been a stronger recovery.

Figure 5.3 compares income tax revenues per capita for Kansas and its neighbors. Among its Great Plains peers, Kansas sat around

FIGURE 5.2   State revenue by source in Kansas

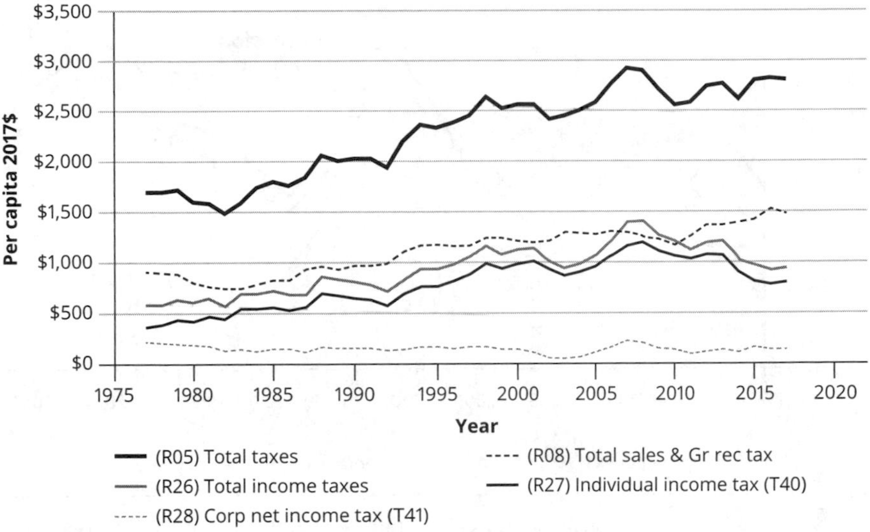

Data Source: US Census Bureau Annual Survey of State and Local Government Finances, 1977–2017 (compiled by the Urban Institute via State and Local Finance Data: Exploring the Census of Governments; accessed April 27, 2020), https://state-local-finance-data. taxpolicycenter.org.

the middle of the pack in income tax revenue per capita until around 2003, when income tax revenues increased substantially, bringing Kansas above the national average and all of its neighbors. So this was at least a good starting point from which to absorb the pending recession and Brownback shocks. Picture, if you will, Colorado or Oklahoma suffering a secondary shock after the recessionary shock, given their very low starting points. After the recessionary shock, Kansas was back in line with but still on the upper margin of income tax revenue per capita. The secondary shock of the Brownback tax cuts was almost as large as the shock of the recession, bringing Kansas down to the income tax revenue levels of Colorado and Oklahoma. By contrast, Nebraska flourished during the same period. (Some of the graphs throughout this book make me wonder whether I should have perhaps written about Nebraska instead.)

Aside from the sharp secondary dip in income tax revenues— which did indeed blow a hole in Kansas's budget and made it nearly

FIGURE 5.3   Total income tax revenues by state

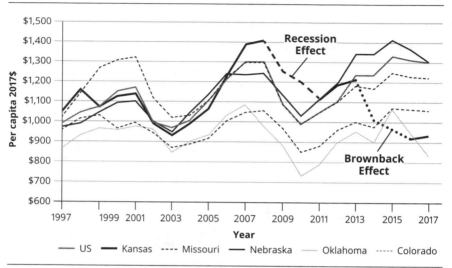

Data Source: US Census Bureau Annual Survey of State and Local Government Finances, 1977-2017 (compiled by the Urban Institute via State and Local Finance Data: Exploring the Census of Governments; accessed April 27, 2020), https://state-local-finance-data. taxpolicycenter.org.

impossible to get back on track with implementing post-*Montoy* funding reforms—the overall tax picture for Kansas remained more moderate. For example, figure 5.4 shows total taxes as a share of personal income for Kansas and neighboring states. By around 2006, Kansas had climbed near the top of the pack. Taxes as a share of income tend to decline more as incomes rebound during economic recovery periods, not during recessions themselves, when incomes decline. Even after the tax cuts, Kansas and Nebraska remained nearer the top than the bottom of the distribution among neighboring states. It would take much deeper cuts over a more sustained time frame to bring Kansas to the depths of economic and educational deprivation of states like Oklahoma or Colorado.

Looking specifically at revenue for elementary and secondary education as a share of personal income, the biggest hit was from the recession itself. As incomes dropped (the denominator), education spending as a share of income spiked. But as incomes rebounded and/

FIGURE 5.4   Total taxes as a percent of personal income

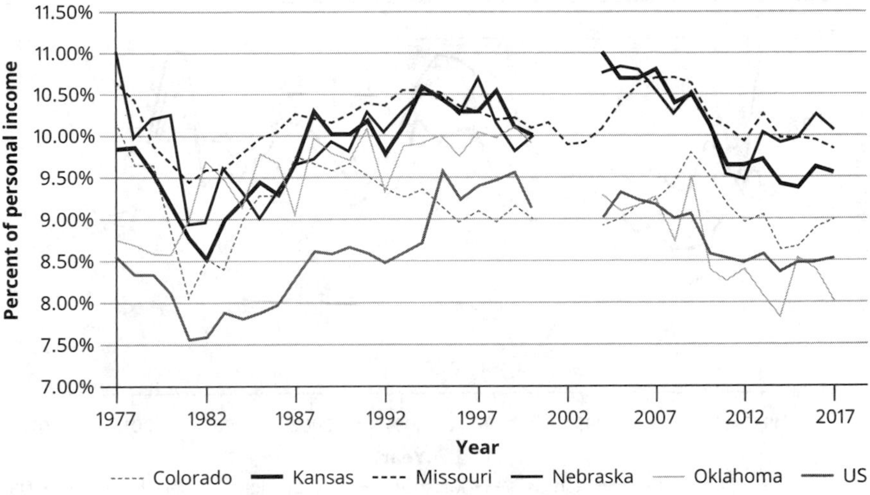

Data Source: US Census Bureau Annual Survey of State and Local Government Finances, 1977-2017 (compiled by the Urban Institute via State and Local Finance Data: Exploring the Census of Governments; accessed April 27, 2020), https://state-local-finance-data. taxpolicycenter.org.

or stabilized from 2011 to 2012, education spending as a share of those incomes dropped sharply, and to levels below prerecession levels. From 2013 to 2017, education spending as a share of income started to climb back out of the hole, with Kansas staying well ahead of Colorado and Oklahoma and trailing only Nebraska. Some of this growth in education spending as a share of income in Kansas may be a function of income growth itself being relatively stagnant through this period.

Michael Leachman of the Center on Budget and Policy Priorities has written extensively on the effects of both the recession generally and the Kansas tax cuts specifically on public education spending in Kansas and elsewhere.[18] Figure 5.6 uses data from the School Finance Indicators Database (SFID) to calculate the change in inflation-adjusted per-pupil spending from immediately prior to the recessionary impact to the most recent available year of data—2018. Kansas experienced the tenth largest decline over this time period.

FIGURE 5.5   Elementary and secondary education direct expenditures as a percentage of personal income

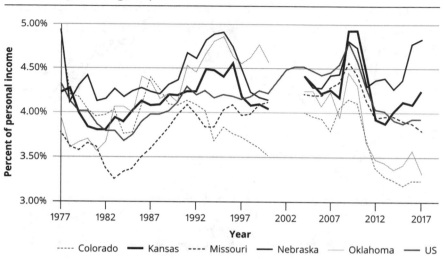

Data Source: US Census Bureau Annual Survey of State and Local Government Finances, 1977-2017 (compiled by the Urban Institute via State and Local Finance Data: Exploring the Census of Governments; accessed April 27, 2020), https://state-local-finance-data. taxpolicycenter.org.

Figure 5.7 shows the distribution of funding by poverty quintile for Kansas school districts through the periods discussed in this book thus far, in inflation-adjusted dollars. So when the bars go up, that means that the actual value of the dollars spent on schools is going up. From just before *USD 229 v. State* to 2008, the second year of *Montoy* remedies, spending levels increased for Kansas schools and spending levels for the districts in higher-poverty quintiles went up, making the system more progressive and more in line with what the two available cost studies up to that point had recommended.

The recession itself dumped Kansas school spending roughly back to where it had been in the 1990s by 2013. The highest-poverty districts in particular fell backward. By 2018, the highest-poverty districts had fallen even further backward, and the system sat stagnant overall during the five-year period from 2013 to 2018, less robustly or

FIGURE 5.6   Current expenditure per pupil change from 2008 to 2018

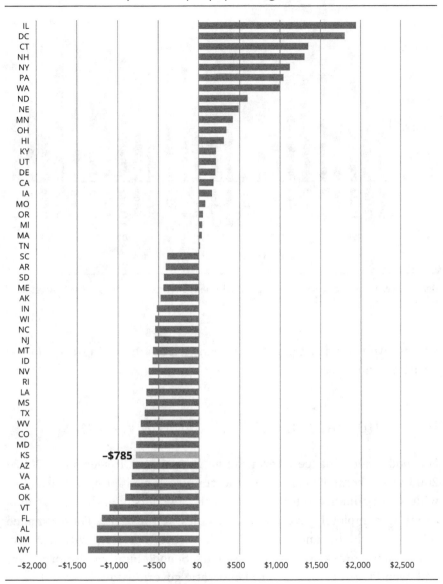

Data Source: Author's calculations using School Finance Indictors Database, district-level panel.

FIGURE 5.7   Kansas school district revenues by poverty quintile

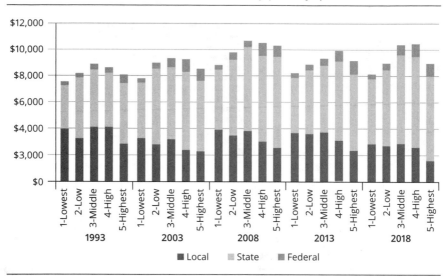

Data Source: Author's calculations using School Finance Indictors Database, district-level panel.

progressively funded than it had been in 2008 following the *Montoy* decisions and reforms.

JUDICIAL CORRECTION: *GANNON V. KANSAS*

No good school finance reform can go unpunished. It seems like 2007–2008 was a banner year across the country for adopting major state-wide school finance reforms, with both New Jersey and Pennsylvania adopting completely overhauled formulas at the time. These finance reforms would be undermined by the great recession within a few years. New Jersey had just passed its School Funding Reform Act, and even Pennsylvania under Democratic governor Rendell had finally adopted a state school finance formula that would start to resolve that state's worst-in-the-nation (well, tied with Illinois) school funding disparities. Kansas was in the process of a significant phase-in of remedies, based in part on findings from the post audit cost study and driven by the court orders in *Montoy*. Then the great recession came and crushed all of these efforts. Pennsylvania under its next governor, Corbett, would disband its formula altogether, and New Jersey under its next governor, Christie, would choose not to fund the formula for years to follow. The same would occur in Kansas, even before Governor Brownback came to office.

Constitutional rights don't pause for economic downturns. It may to some feel illogical to bring a legal challenge to cuts to school funding in the context of an economic recession, when state revenues are collapsing, family incomes are dropping, and home foreclosures are rising. But these are actually the very times when courts and legislatures most need reminding of their obligations to protect the rights of those most in need. Further, as evidenced in previous rounds, these things take years to resolve, so in all likelihood judicial orders and legislative responses were at least three to five years down the line.

In January 2010, the next round of legal challenges to the state school finance system was set to begin, with an announcement from Alan Rupe and John Robb. Rupe and Robb's initial plan was to convince the court to reopen the *Montoy* case, as it would be both quicker and cheaper than requiring plaintiffs to file an entirely new legal challenge. As described by Justin Kendall in the *Pitch*:

> If they don't, awesomely mustached attorney John Robb told the *Eagle*, then a new lawsuit will be filed.
>
> "If they re-open Montoy, it's going to be a lot quicker and cheaper," Robb said.
>
> The attorneys for Schools for Fair Funding have said that education funding cuts have killed the gains made in the Montoy case and violated the state Supreme Court's ruling as well as the Kansas Constitution.[19]

Eventually, Rupe and Robb were forced to file a new case, *Gannon v. Kansas*. A few things had changed, including some of the rules.

First, toward the end of the *Montoy* litigation, the Kansas legislature had passed statutes that (a) required a waiting period between the filing of a legal challenge regarding school funding and the advancement of legal proceedings in that case and (b) required that district court proceedings be handled by a three-judge panel with judges from different regions across the state. The second of these conditions seemed focused specifically on avoiding a single judge, Bullock, being assigned the case.

Also, in 2009, Dan Biles had been appointed to the state supreme court. First, this meant that the former state board attorney who had advanced the framing of the balancing roles of the state board of education and legislature with regard to education obligations would now sit in judgment of arguments which might be framed to the contrary. Second, and perhaps equally important, this meant that the state would no longer have on its side the depth of knowledge and institutional history Dan Biles offered. This arguably left a gaping hole in the competence of the state's defense, even though Biles himself had chosen a middle ground in the later rounds of *Montoy*. Biles had still preferred judicial deference to the legislature and state board to resolve issues pertaining to school funding and quality standards.

The *Gannon* trial proceeded in the fall of 2011 in front of a three-judge panel. The promised base funding increases from *Montoy* hadn't materialized, and in fact, base aid was cut from 2008–2009, when it had hit $4,400, to 2011–2012, when it had been lowered to $3,780. All of this was before the Brownback tax cuts. Figure 5.8 shows what was labeled Exhibit 237 at the trial. It illustrated that whatever your starting point and whatever your source of "cost" projection—be it simply inflating the 1992 base, adopting and inflating the lower of the two A&M base figures ($4,650 in 2001), or adopting and inflating the post audit base from 2006—the current and projected base figures were well below those targets and falling further and further behind each year.

Interestingly, or perhaps disturbingly—it's a matter of perspective—a central theory of the state's defense, advanced by its own experts, was that the cuts were kind of like an experiment. An experiment to show that dramatic cuts to education spending would not cause harm to students' outcomes but would instead improve the operational efficiency of schools. Experimenting was the thing to do in those unprecedented economic times! Schools would learn to do more with less, and all would be better for it—both taxpayers and students. After all, as the experts opined, there was no clear evidence of any connection between the amount of resources available to schools and the quality of education they could provide. Thus, if funding was increased

FIGURE 5.8 **Plaintiff's exhibit no. 237**

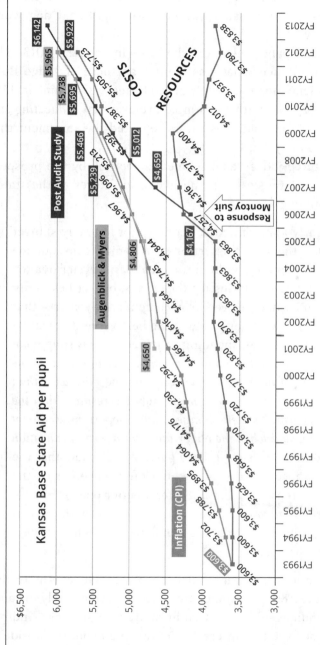

Actual base: from Kansas Fiscal Facts (LEG003707) & SB294

Inflation (CPI): from U.S. Department of Labor—All Urban Consumers—Kansas City, MO–KS—All items, base of 3600 adjusted for inflation each year (BLS000001-4)

Augenblick & Myers: from May 2002 Study (LEG001414), June 2005 Update (LEG003516), October 2011 Update (EXP-MYERS000073), all amounts direct from reports, except 2012 adjusted for inflation

Post Audit Study: from January 2006 Cost Study (USD443 001586), January 17, 2006 Memo (LEG003410), all amounts direct from reports, 2007 through 2012 amounts are in 2007 dollars

Source: Somers, Robb & Robb Gannon Exhibit Archive.

and quality didn't improve, then if funding was decreased, quality would not decline. Or so they opined, despite Judge Bullock's previous proclamation regarding this same line of reasoning: "That dog won't hunt in Dodge City."

The three-judge panel ruled on the case in January 2013. The judges' writings were somewhat less blunt than those of Judge Bullock, but their patience for the state's central theory was similar. Like Bullock, the court agreed with the simple premise that "*educating students costs money.* Several administrators repeated the sentiment that 'everything costs money.'"[20]

Further, the three-judge panel seemed concerned by the prospect of experimenting at large scale on the lives and futures of the state's schoolchildren, opining:

> Here, it is clearly apparent, and, actually, not arguably subject to dispute, that the state's assertion of a benign consequence of cutting school funding without a factual basis, either quantitatively or qualitatively, to justify the cuts is, but, at best, only based on an inference derived from defendant's experts that such costs may possibly not produce the best value that can be achieved from the level of spending provided. *This is simply not only a weak and factually tenuous premise, but one that seems likely to produce, if accepted, what could not be otherwise than characterized as sanctioning an unconscionable result within the context of the education system. Simply, school opportunities do not repeat themselves and when the opportunity for a formal education passes, then for most, it is most likely gone.* We all know that the struggle for an income very often—too often—overcomes the time needed to prepare intellectually for a better one.
>
> *If the position advanced here is the State's full position, it is experimenting with our children which have no recourse from a failure of the experiment.*[21]

The legislature a decade earlier had gone to great lengths to distance itself from the A&M study and attempted to preemptively distance itself from any findings of the post audit study in case those findings would turn out not to suit its interests. On the one hand, the upside of all of this is that the legislature really didn't try to directly meddle in the study. It left the study to the Division of Post Audit, which worked with Bill Duncombe and John Yinger to conduct a methodologically sound, independent analysis. But it did know that doing so came with risk and tried to mitigate that risk. Again, the three-judge panel simply wasn't buying the argument that the statue it passed gave carte blanche to ignore evidence (which it had sponsored) when setting school finance policy:

> Hence, the Legislature's enactment in 2005 of K.S.A. 46-1226 (a), which statute still stands, that states "(a) Any cost study analysis, audit or other study commissioned or funded by the legislature and any conclusions or recommendations thereof shall not be binding upon the legislature. The legislature may reject, at any time, any such analysis, audit or study and any conclusions and recommendations thereof." is, without rational justification, no more than a misplaced, however, sincere, declaration of either desire or displeasure, while, yet, surely being a suspect marker of non-compliance, if followed, with the requirements of Article 6, § 6(b) as declared in *Montoy*.[22]

The High Court Revisits the Balance of Powers in Kansas

As with *Montoy*, it would take an appeal to the state's high court to move the legislature into action. It would also take replacing a significant share of legislators in 2016 and a repeal of the Brownback tax cuts. The Kansas Supreme Court, with Dan Biles now sitting on the court, issued its first ruling in the *Gannon* case in March 2014. This timing was a bit different than previous lower and high court rulings, which often came in December or January, immediately in advance of the legislative session. Those release times often gave an appearance that the rulings and their timings were intended to immediately influence the legislative session. This was portrayed as the court being political. But then what's the court to do? The only way the plaintiffs' claims could be resolved was through legislation, enacted on by the legislature, which would most likely occur during the legislative session.

Perhaps most importantly, the high court affirmed in even clearer language in *Gannon* the balancing roles and responsibilities of the legislature and state board, explaining: "As for the constitutional relationship between the legislature and the State Board of Education, this court has made clear that the general supervisory powers of the board under Article 6, Section 2(a) are 'self-executing,' i.e., not requiring empowerment by the legislature."[23] The court's March 2014 ruling was otherwise a mixed bag for the plaintiffs who brought the case, but a mixed bag was better than nothing. The court concluded that the state had failed to meet its obligation to mitigate inequities by providing state matching aid for capital outlay.[24] But the high court took issue with the way in which the three-judge panel arrived at its judgment regarding the adequacy of funding and remanded the case back to the lower court to apply the original standards set forth in earlier rounds of the *Montoy* case.[25]

Eventually, when the case finally made it back to the high court in March 2017, the court concluded: "Accordingly, we conclude the state's public education financing system, through its structure and implementation, is not *reasonably calculated to have all Kansas public education students meet or exceed the minimum constitutional standards of adequacy.*"[26] By this point, a significant share of conservative Republican legislators in Kansas had been displaced either by moderate challengers in primaries or by democrats in the general election. The tax cuts had inflicted even more pain on the state's public services, including schools, and Kansans seemed ready for a change.

POLITICAL SELF-CORRECTION UNDER JUDICIAL COVER

Kansans had given Brownback his second term, waiting to see the eventual effects of his shot of adrenaline to the heart of the state's economy. But, as discussed earlier, the patient lay motionless on the gurney. Even worse, the patient's vitals were declining rapidly. The next round of midterm elections would result in a significant shift in legislative balance—not entirely along partisan lines, but most certainly along lines of supporting or not supporting (a) Brownback's tax cut plan and (b) education funding. A major platform issue for Kansas legislators running for office in nearly any cycle is their view on school funding. It's as important, if not more so, than many of the national political litmus test issues superimposed on Kansas's political leaders.

And in Kansas, there exist moderate Republicans who are strong advocates for a combination of responsible fiscal policy and robust education funding, as well as Democrats who favor robust education funding. And both the moderate Republicans and Democrats in the state exhibit a healthy respect for and responsiveness to the state's high court in this regard. The midterm elections of 2016 created just enough shift on these issues to start the healing process.

During the 2017 legislative session, both houses of the Kansas legislature passed plans that would repeal the Brownback tax cuts, which had blown a massive hole in the current year's budget in Kansas. But Brownback quickly vetoed the plan, significantly raising the count of how many additional Republican legislators in each house would be required to push the plan through and override the veto. As described in the *Topeka Capitol Journal* in June 2017:

> The Senate, which contains 31 GOP members and nine Democrats, voted 27-13 for the two-thirds majority necessary to reverse the governor's action. The threshold was attained when Sen. Rick Wilborn, R-McPherson, agreed to support the override after previously voting against the tax bill.
>
> "The Legislature has the power to override the veto. I see no other path," said Senate Vice President Jeff Longbine, R-Emporia.
>
> The House put together a coalition to complete an override of the governor's veto, striking that bell by a modest four-vote margin—88–31. The GOP dominates the House numerically 85–40 over Democrats. More than two dozen representatives who voted against the tax bill one day earlier fell in line behind the override.
>
> "This wasn't an easy vote," said Rep. Troy Waymaster, a Bunker Hill Republican and chairman of the House Appropriations Committee. "This does move the state of Kansas forward."[27]

Brownback would leave before the end of his term, after being appointed US ambassador-at-large for international religious freedom in the Trump administration.

With the tax cuts repealed and the potential for the revenue bleeding to stop, Kansas legislators' next task was to refocus their efforts on school funding, which had taken a substantial hit in two waves, first from the great recession and then from the Brownback tax cuts during the first few years of recovery. In March 2017, the state supreme court had determined that these cuts left the system not only in violation of equity requirements per its earlier order, but also in violation of the broader adequacy requirements under Article 6.

By this time, the cost analyses that had guided the *Montoy* reforms were nearly twelve years old and the A&M study that much older. Although the legislature at this point had shifted in favor of public school funding, it was still in its interest to try to get the court to adopt a lower bar for adequacy, which is exactly what its counsel did in oral arguments before the court in the summer of 2017, on July 18. In their oral arguments, the state's lawyers offered calculations by the Kansas Legislative Research Department (KLRD) of the average spending of forty-one districts it had identified as successful. It divided that spending by weighted pupils to back a required base of $4,080—a base figure that was certainly a bit higher than the present base but was much lower than either the prior post audit or A&M base figures, even before inflation adjustment.

I recall listening to the oral arguments that day. In an email to a colleague in Kansas the next day, I noted that Biles was on fire in those arguments, specifically in his dissecting of the proposed base and the analysis behind it. Among other things, he referred to the analyses as a "calculation" and not a "model," delineating by contrast that what the Division of Post Audit had contracted Bill Duncombe and John Yinger to create in 2006 *was* a model. By this point, Dan Biles had been through twenty-plus years and two more rigorous studies of costs, as well as having shaped the constitutional requirements that inform the basic empirical requirements of those studies in the Kansas context. The Duncombe and Yinger cost model component of the post audit study, linking spending to the state board's outcome standards and accounting for other factors affecting the costs of meeting those standards, was a direct response to Biles's own arguments to the court in May 2005.

The Kansas Supreme Court ruled on October 2 regarding the current legislation and the analysis and adequacy standards offered to the court over the summer: "As explained below, we agree based on the record before us that these 41 selected school districts have not been shown by the State to be appropriate candidates from which to extrapolate the costs of achieving the educational outcomes set out in *Gannon I,* 298 Kan. 1165-70. Simply put, merely performing 'better than expected'—while perhaps a test for efficiency—is not our Kansas test for constitutional adequacy."[28] The court continued: "Consistent with the complexity of such studies, after the LPA study expressly rejected the successful schools model in favor of the cost function approach, it 'hired consultants to perform *the sophisticated statistical techniques* involved in a cost function analysis that would estimate the cost of meeting the performance outcome standards adopted by the State Board of Education.' (Emphasis added.)"[29] The court provided the legislature with specific methodological marching orders at this point. Rather than resist, the legislature largely complied, funding a new cost study to be released in the spring of 2018 and adopting the more thorough and complex methods laid out in the October 2 ruling.

As with the 2006 post audit "redo" cost study, there was certainly plenty of suspicion that the primary intent of the legislature was to seek a lower estimate of its obligation. After all, that's what its own back-of-the-napkin estimates provided in testimony had done. Legislators had tried harder, by running "calculations" rather than models through the Legislative Research Department, to maintain control over those estimates. Even the newly proposed cost study would not be run by the Legislative Division of Post Audit but rather would be coordinated through a political consultant and former legislator. That person would identify external consultants to conduct the study and additional external consultants to review and critique the study's methods once complete and would compare the methods and findings to prior studies. Credibility, under the scrutiny of the court, remained important to the legislature, even though what some really seemed to want were politically palatable results.

At this point, legislators and their headhunter were seeking outside consultants for both roles, and the easiest explanation for who was eventually selected for each role is that lots of people were asking around. Plaintiffs' attorneys were asking around, watching who the legislature might pick. Former legislators, current legislators, and friends of legislators were all asking around about names being tossed into the ring both to conduct and to review the study. Bill Duncombe had passed away in 2013 at the age of fifty-seven—a huge loss to all of us, especially those who had benefited from interacting with him personally and professionally and learning from him over the years (my book *Educational Inequality and School Finance*, published in 2018, was dedicated to Bill).[30] Few others continued to work with and advance the art of education cost functions—which brings us back to Lori Taylor of Texas A&M, with whom I had worked on several related and unrelated projects. Lori was a native Kansan, born and raised in Salina, and a graduate of the University of Kansas. Lori's PhD advisor in economics was none other than Eric Hanushek, the state's go-to expert who had advanced claims that more money wouldn't matter anyway. I'm not sure which aspects of Lori's background were ultimately most appealing to the legislature, but she got the gig to conduct the new study, and as a peer, colleague, and collaborator, she received my endorsement as well—all of which served only to confuse parties on all sides. Still, some remained skeptical, including Kansas's Democratic leadership.[31]

Eventually, my colleague and frequent collaborator Jesse Levin was hired as the outside consultant to review Lori Taylor's work, along with the post audit and A&M studies, on behalf of the legislature. I was hired by Alan Rupe and John Robb to provide a review of both Jesse Levin's review and Lori Taylor's report, which was conducted with Jason Willis and colleagues at the education policy consulting firm WestEd. All three of us—Jesse, Lori, and I—had collaborated on numerous occasions.[32] And on one occasion, Lori had consulted with opposing counsel (for the state of Texas), closely advising an attorney about what questions to ask me at deposition and trial as I worked for the plaintiffs. Previous rounds of litigation had involved Alan Rupe deposing his own ex-wife, Carol Rupe, as a member of the state board of education. So why not have three frequent coauthors review and critique each other's work?

Taylor's study was produced on March 15, 2018, to much fanfare and to big headlines: "Kansas School Funding Report Blows a Hole in Conservative Doctrine." That *conservative doctrine* was the commonly stated argument that there exists little if any relationship between access to funding and the quality of schooling that can be provided. This in fact was the career-making argument of Dr. Taylor's own doctoral advisor!

The study came back with an initial cost estimate that was even higher than the previous two studies, adjusted for context and time—and requiring an increase of $2.1 billion![33] Taylor explained that the high-end $2.1 billion dollar figure was based on setting a very high outcome standard—but the lower-end estimate was still approximately $1.5 billion. Kansas lawmakers got some additional national attention for these efforts. Comedian Wyatt Cenac, in his deep policy dive HBO series, *Problem Areas*, explained: "Republican lawmakers in Kansas . . . they responded to that school funding court ruling . . . by hiring their own outside consultants. Presumably hoping to support the view that greater funding doesn't lead to better outcomes. And their own consultant . . . the person that they hired . . . revealed the opposite."[34] The screen then showed a quote from a *New York Times* piece from July 4, 2018: "Their handpicked consultant's report tied increased funding to improved outcomes."[35]

But again, the national caricature of Kansas wasn't entirely in line with the reality on the ground in Kansas. Yes, there were legislators looking for a lowball estimate, just as they had argued to the court the summer before. But just as they had done on *two previous occasions*, those same legislators included safeguards ensuring that the study would be conducted independently and this time would even be reviewed independently. Further, any experts involved in this process would at least have an air of independence and outside expert credibility. They also knew that any study they pursued and used as a basis for addressing their constitutional requirements would be scrutinized by a state supreme court that knew its stuff!

It is rarely normal to end a chapter with a graph. But figure 5.9 shows the proposed and adopted response to the *Gannon* court's final rulings and the legislature's 2018 cost study. Unfortunately, much like the immediate post-*Montoy* era, these proposed reforms would be undermined by economic collapse—this time, from the onset of the COVID-19 pandemic.

FIGURE 5.9   Base state aid per pupil

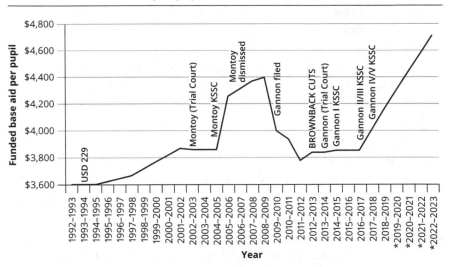

Data source: Kansas School Finance System, Kansas Legislative Research Department, January 18, 2019.

In school years 2002–2003, 2003–2004, and 2004–2005, the statutory base was $3,890; however, $3,863 was funded.

In school year 2009–2010, the statutory base was $4,492. After the 2009 legislative session ended, the governor enacted two separate allotments that decreased the base to $4,012.

During school years 2015–2016 and 2016–2017, the state operated on a block grant funding system. There was no official base, but total funding was approximately the equivalent of a base of $3,852.

*Planned increases to the statutory base.

SECTION
II

Insights and Lessons

6

WOMEN OF THE
HIGH PLAINS

Gender, Politics, and Leadership

"Women will have achieved true equality
when men share with them the responsibility
of bringing up the next generation."

—Ruth Bader Ginsberg, *in a 2001 interview
with the New York City Bar Association*

For the past several decades in Kansas, women have frequently led the way on matters of educating future generations of Kansans. When national media focuses on outspoken Kansas women, it's usually with the purpose of advancing caricatures akin to Dana Carvey's church lady from *Saturday Night Live*—like Kansas State Board of Education antievolution antagonist Connie Morris,[1] outspoken antiabortion state legislator and senate president Susan Wagle,[2] or Westboro Baptist Church heiress Meghan Phelps Roeper. But Kansas has had more women governors than most other states, with three since the 1990s, all of whom were Democrats.[3] Kansas has also had a significant share of women as state supreme court justices, including two chief justices.[4] And Kansas has had a significant share of women in the state legislature for decades, though those numbers peaked in the mid-2000s. So let's explore the recent history of key women in Kansas, with particular emphasis on their roles in the school funding story.

Gender plays a unique role in politics and political leadership. A significant body of academic literature finds that the gender balance among elected officials is associated with support for and expenditure on programs that serve families and children, like public schools.[5] Also, public schools are large employers in states, and the majority of their employees, who are teachers, are women. Perceptions and treatment of women in the workforce—specifically, public employees—differ among male and female political leaders in ways that shape public policy. I recall learning upon my arrival in Kansas in 1997 that many Kansas school districts did not offer their teachers health insurance because it was perceived (by male leaders) that most were women, second-income earners, in families in which the *man of the house* likely carried insurance for the family.

During my time living in Kansas from 1997 through 2008, throughout the *Montoy* litigation, Kansas had a woman as governor from 2003 to 2009; had three women as justices on the state supreme court, including Chief Justice Kay McFarland (on the court from 1977 to 2009 and chief justice as of 1995); women made up approximately one-third of state legislators; and the legislative post auditor, the head of the legislature's research arm tasked with conducting numerous studies of Kansas school districts and the state school finance system, was a woman. Since my time in Kansas, the share of women in the legislature declined (during the Brownback era) and Chief Justice Kay McFarland was replaced by Lawton Nuss, who has since announced his retirement—but Kansas has elected another woman governor, Laura Kelly (D), and Marla Luckert was appointed as chief justice to replace Nuss.

Here, I'll focus specifically on the words and deeds of a few major players in the Kansas school finance saga. Specifically, I begin with Kansas's first woman governor, Joan Finney, who presided over the onset of the modern era of Kansas school finance: the *Mock* case, Judge Bullock's negotiated agreement, and eventual adoption and upholding of the School District Finance and Quality Performance Accreditation

Act. The framework behind the act was established by a task force created under Governor Finney in response to Bullock's ruling in *Mock*. That formula was ultimately upheld by the state's high court after being partially upheld by lower court judge Marla Luckert, who was later appointed to the high court.

Justice Luckert brought an impressive institutional history and knowledge pertaining to school finance to the state's high court and was joined on the high court by Carol Beier. Throughout the *Montoy* and *Gannon* litigations, the two would eventually become a formidable tag team in high court oral arguments. Recall the cartoon in chapter 1 showing the state's legal counsel reporting back to then attorney general Phill Kline, with his head under his arm. That "beheading" occurred at the hands of Justices Luckert and Beier in particular. One exchange from oral arguments that day (May 11, 2005) was summarized in the *Lawrence Journal World*: "In one exchange Justice Carol Beier asked Weltz how the Legislature determined the increase in base state aid per pupil. 'Honestly, I can't tell you how that was arrived at,' he answered. Then Justice Marla Luckert asked whether the increase was adequate from a constitutional standpoint. Weltz answered 'yes,' which prompted Beier to ask, 'How would you know if you don't know how you got there?'"[6] Beier would ultimately pen an impressive essay in the form of a concurring opinion, in which she explained that in fact, historically, contextually, and literally, the Kansas Constitution does create a fundamental right for individual access to education. In more recent years, a cadre of organized and informed women in the legislature, both Democrats and Republicans, helped to push through tax increases (restoration of the Brownback cuts) to support renewed school funding.[7]

WOMEN IN STATE LEADERSHIP

Kansas is tied with Arizona in terms of states with the most *elected* women governors, with three. Our nation's first three women governors were elected or appointed as surrogates for their husbands, who were either deceased or could not seek an additional term in office (Wyoming, Texas, and Alabama), between the 1920s and 1968.[8] Ella

Grasso of Connecticut became the first woman governor elected in her own right in 1975, and Madeline Kunin of Vermont, a governor of my own childhood, became the first woman to serve three terms as governor. Connecticut has had one other woman governor, Republican Jodi Rell, the named defendant in that state's most recent legal challenge to the state's school funding formula. Vermont has not had another woman governor since Kunin.

New Hampshire, like Kansas, has had three women governors, the first of whom served for only seven days between 1982 and 1983 when the governor passed away. Texas has had two, but the first was a surrogate for her husband. Texas's first elected woman governor, Ann Richards, presided over that state's significant school finance reforms in the early 1990s. In total, Arizona has had four women governors, three of whom were elected.[9] Overall, more women governors have been Democrats (twenty-six) than Republicans (eighteen). As of the time of writing, nine states had women governors, three of whom were Republicans.

Among the states neighboring Kansas, Colorado and Missouri have never had a women governor. Oklahoma had a women governor from 2011 to 2019 and Nebraska from 1987 to 1991. Kansas, Republican stronghold that it is, has had three Democrat women governors: Joan Finney, from 1991 to 1995; Kathleen Sebelius, from 2003 to 2009; and Laura Kelly, from 2019 to the present. One might argue that in each case, these governors came into office positioned to clean up school funding messes left behind by male predecessors, with the political cover of judicial orders to do so. But recall that Finney's mess was in part a function of Finney's own promises to cut taxes. Still, she in particular was a major player in what I characterize here and elsewhere as the *grand bargain*. Sebelius steps into the governor's office in the buildup to Judge Bullock's order in *Montoy*. Laura Kelly comes into office as the legislature has begun the process of cleaning up after Brownback's tax cut mess and with remedies to *Gannon v. Kansas* to be maintained.

Women in State Legislatures

The broader academic literature on state and local politics and preferences for spending on public programs and services points to a number of characteristics of state legislatures as significant determinants. On average, more liberal state legislatures are more likely to favor additional spending on programs and services like public schooling. They are also more likely to favor redistribution, including raising taxes to target more state aid to local school districts with less capacity to raise their own and those districts serving populations with greater needs, which are often the same.[10] A multitude of studies have also shown that demographic differences between adult voting-aged populations in states and children served by the public schooling system drive school spending decisions. Put bluntly, aging white voters tend not to favor increased spending on public schools serving increasingly Black and Brown student populations.[11] It's also the case that the gender balance in state legislatures matters. State legislatures with larger shares of women are generally more likely to support additional expenditure for services associated with education and childcare, above and beyond political affiliation. That said, it's also generally true that the share of legislators who are women tends to be higher in more liberal states, on average. Kansas would appear to buck that trend.

Starting in 1990 in particular, Kansas was among the top ten states in terms of the share of legislators that were women, as shown in figure 6.1. The 2002 election cycle was not good for women in Kansas, but in 2004, along with the election of Kathleen Sebelius as governor, women rebounded. However, from 2006 on, the tide shifted and fewer women held positions in the Kansas legislature as shares increased in other states. The 2016 election cycle, amid the disastrous Brownback tax cuts, saw a rebound. Kansas did not, however, see the dramatic shift that occurred in nearly every other state in 2018. So though Kansas had been near the top of the nation in terms of women in the legislature from the 1990s through the mid-2000s, Kansas now sits near the middle of the pack—but partly because of progress elsewhere.

Figure 6.2 focuses on Kansas and its neighboring states. Kansas and Colorado together led the pack from 1990 to about 2005, when shares of women legislators began to decline in Kansas and started to climb in Colorado. Colorado and Oklahoma in particular saw significant increases in women legislators in the 2018 election cycle. In the spring of 2018, Oklahoma was among states that had gained some notoriety nationally for their very low school spending and teacher pay,

FIGURE 6.1   Percent of state legislators who are female (all states)

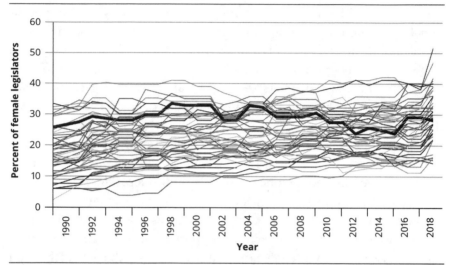

Data source: Marty P. Jordan and Matt Grossmann, *The Correlates of State Policy Project v.2.1* (East Lansing, MI: Institute for Public Policy and Social Research, 2020), http://ippsr.msu.edu/public-policy/correlates-state-policy.

with national news stories covering the second, third, and other odd jobs Oklahoma teachers were forced to take just to get by. The teaching workforce in Oklahoma and nationally remains largely a workforce of women. Across the country in the spring of 2018, low teacher pay became a focal point of national media attention, with teacher uprisings in West Virginia, Arizona, Oklahoma, Colorado, the city of Los Angeles, and elsewhere.[12] In the fall of 2018, 177 teachers ran for state legislative offices, 94 of whom were women.[13] Notably, the share of these educators who were women was significantly less than the overall share of educators who are women. Forty-three educators—twenty-one women and twenty-two men—won their general elections. Six were from Oklahoma. When expanded to include any current or former Oklahoma school employees, the total count elected to the state house or senate was sixteen.[14]

Figure 6.3 shows the relationship between the political ideology (x-axis) and gender balance (y-axis) of state legislatures at two points in time: first in the mid-2000s, when Kansas was at its peak; and second

FIGURE 6.2 Percent of state legislators who are female (Kansas and neighbors)

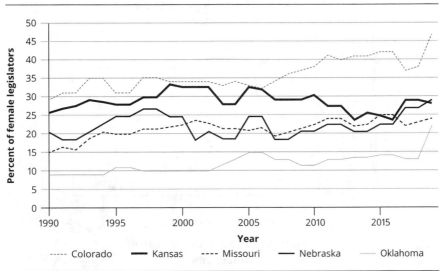

Data source: Jordan and Grossmann, *The Correlates of State Policy Project v.2.1.*

in the most recent year for these data, 2016, when Kansas had slipped back to about average on gender balance. State houses of representatives and senates in the figure that are further to the left are in fact further *left* by the political ideology measure as well. They're bluer. More liberal. Certainly, the average share of women is higher in liberal versus more conservative state legislatures. Or is it that state legislatures with more women tend to be more liberal on average? Really, it's that these things are simultaneously determined by a voting population: more liberal voting populations elect more liberal representatives, which also happen to include more women.

But that's not uniformly the case! Kansas stands out in the 2005 figures by having female representation in its state legislature similar to that of California, Connecticut, or New Jersey, but political ideology more aligned with South Carolina. Kansas is not alone here. Arizona is even further to the right ideologically and has an even higher share of female representation in both its house and senate. Arizona also manages to blow a hole in the central theory presented here that

FIGURE 6.3 Gender and ideology by state (houses and senates, 2005 and 2016)

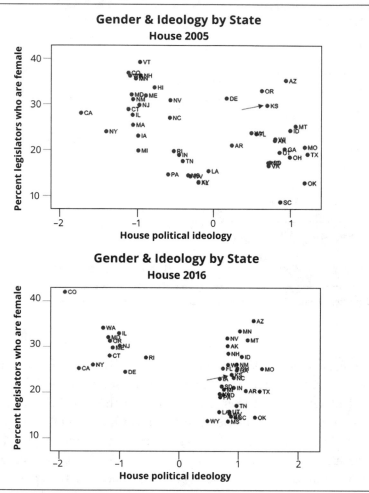

Data source: Jordan and Grossmann, *The Correlates of State Policy Project v.2.1.*

having more women in leadership roles can be a major driving force in achieving and maintaining more equitable and adequate school funding. Arizona is consistently among the least well-funded state education systems in the nation, spending much less and having less competitive teacher wages than nearly any other state.[15] The state's women governors have done little to support public schools, and Arizona's legislature

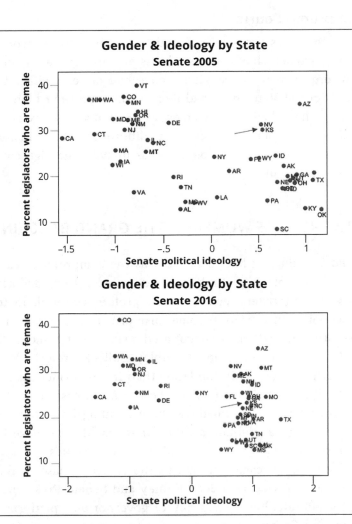

Gender & Ideology by State
Senate 2005

Gender & Ideology by State
Senate 2016

has failed to come through time and time again. The state's high court has failed to take a stand in past challenges. Finally, in 2020, by direct voter referendum, Arizonans voted to increases taxes to spend more on public schools.[16] Put simply, having women in leadership alone does not ensure equitable and adequate school funding will follow, though it still may be an important element of a much larger, more complex puzzle.

State Supreme Courts

To date, Kansas has had five high court justices who are women and has had two women chief justices. This is one area in state politics and policy where women, across states, have had more significant representation. Several states have had more women on their high courts.[17] Other states have had more women as chief justices. Sixteen states have had majority female high courts at different points in history, and in one case, for a special session in Texas in 1925, the high court was entirely composed of women.[18]

THE ROLE OF WOMEN IN THE GRAND BARGAIN

The *grand bargain*, as I like to call it, was the compromise reached in the wake of the (not really a) ruling issued by Judge Terry Bullock in the *Mock* case. Other writers seem to have a preference for characterizing Kansas school finance trials as some form of manly gunfight in Dodge or some brilliant settlement negotiated primarily by Judge Bullock himself.[19] One certainly cannot downplay Bullock's role in *Mock* and *Montoy*, perhaps more so in the latter than in the former. As I've said previously, Bullock's choice to not take the *Mock* case to trial and to attempt to orchestrate a remedy without a ruling ultimately led to a trial and a ruling—a trial and a ruling that would later make it more difficult for plaintiffs to seek more substantive remedies.

Two key players came through in the remedy phase to Bullock's ruling that wasn't: Governor Joan Finney and Senate President Sheila Frahm. To reiterate, Finney had run for governor on a platform of cutting taxes, and Frahm was a Republican from rural Kansas. Certainly, it's unlikely they'd have collaborated to push through a major school finance reform without some external pressure. The pressure was created by the plaintiffs' lawsuit and Bullock's creative intervention. But it still took their efforts to get the job done.

Governor Joan Finney

Finney was Kansas's first woman governor, and the state's forty-second governor, from 1991 to 1995. Finney had been active in Kansas politics since 1975 as state treasurer and was the first woman to hold that office. She was a Kansas native, born in Topeka, and graduated from high school in the college town of Manhattan (the Little Apple) in 1942. She attended Washburn University in Topeka, graduating in 1978. I never had the opportunity to meet Joan Finney, who passed away in 2001, prior to the summit of former governors held at KU, at which I had opportunity to meet three past governors (Carlin, Hayden, and Avery).

Senator Sheila Frahm

Sheila Frahm is a native Kansan, from Colby, in the northwestern part of the state. For context, that's just over a four-hour drive west of Topeka along I-70, and apparently home to a well-known billboard called the "Wheat-Jesus Billboard," viewable from I-70—a part of the state that, for an East Coaster, is unnervingly flat and expansive. Scientifically, in fact, it's flatter than a pancake.[20] Frahm was appointed to fill a vacant seat on the state board of education in 1985 and was elected in 1986, then later appointed vice president of the state board (in 1988). Her stint in the Kansas State Senate ran from 1989 to 1995, in which she was the first woman to become majority leader in 1993. Frahm was lieutenant governor from 1995 to 1996, when she was appointed to the US Senate by Governor Bill Graves to fill the seat of Bob Dole, who resigned to pursue a presidential campaign. Frahm was displaced by Sam Brownback in the Republican primary, and Brownback went on to be the next US senator from Kansas later in the same year (1996). Despite being replaced by a more conservative Republican, Frahm was a reliable Republican vote and seemed consistently liked and admired by centrist and moderate Kansas Republicans. This is probably why she was frequently appointed by her party to fill leadership roles at the highest levels.

Frahm was also appointed to the governor's task force, which is where we met. To be quite honest, as much as Senator Vratil at the time put me in my place on issues pertaining to Kansas's school funding details, vocabulary, and punctuation, it was Frahm who I found far more intimidating. Although she spoke less than Vratil, she clearly understood the substance of the issues at hand, the political context and history that brought us to that juncture, as well as anyone in the room. At the time, I had no idea about her role in negotiating the existing statute, which we as a group were now proposing to reshape, if not dismantle. As evidenced by my article on the 1992 reforms, labeling them *politics as usual*, I was a strong critic of those reforms, not realizing the political storm through which they emerged.[21] Frahm, as I recall, played a significant role in keeping the tone of our task force report balanced and respectful of what had been accomplished, while helping to pave a productive path forward.

Marla Luckert

Marla Luckert, who in the fall of 2019 became the chief justice of the Kansas Supreme Court, is also a native Kansan, born in 1955 in Goodland, which is actually about forty minutes west of Colby. One thing I learned in my time in Kansas was that the pathway to legal and political prominence in the state was often paved through Washburn University in the state's capitol, Topeka. This was something that Alan Rupe, who had received his law degree from Washburn, mentioned often. John Robb also attended Washburn. Luckert received both her undergraduate degree (1977) and her law degree (1980) from Washburn, and she went into private legal practice in Topeka.

It was Governor Joan Finney who would eventually appoint Luckert to the Third Judicial District Court in 1992, only two years before Luckert would be called upon to rule on the constitutionality of the state school finance system. Luckert was eventually appointed to the state supreme court in November 2002 by outgoing governor Bill Graves, not long before that court was called upon to respond to Judge Terry Bullock's lower court order in *Montoy*.

Recall that Kansas's high court appointments occur by a largely apolitical process, wherein a nonpartisan nominating commission is established to forward qualified names to the governor, who then appoints from a short list of three. Luckert, like all the others, made her way to the state's high court through this process and was appointed by a moderate Republican governor. Kansas Supreme Court justices are, however, subjected to periodic retention votes, in which the public gets to decide whether a high court judge gets to keep their position. Despite being targeted by conservative groups for removal from the court, Luckert has survived retention votes by healthy margins.[22]

Kay McFarland

Former chief justice Kay McFarland's life and career in the legal community in Kansas spanned thirty-five years and vastly different eras of Kansas's history and constitutional law. McFarland was born in 1935 in Coffeyville, Kansas, in the southeast corner of the state, near the Oklahoma border—about two hours and forty minutes south of Topeka and almost a seven-hour drive from Goodland in the opposite corner. Like Luckert and Frahm, and even Finney to a lesser extent, all were from relatively small towns not near any major city. Like Luckert, but decades before, McFarland graduated from Washburn University both as an undergraduate (1957) and from law school (1964) soon after the state's judicial structure itself was reconstituted.

While writing this book, I've come to wonder about the importance of Washburn University itself—its law school and its pipeline to political leadership in the state and the role of women in Kansas politics. Men and women of Washburn have made their way over time into positions of political leadership in Kansas, and Washburn has maintained a tradition of serving Kansans. But Washburn has also had a tradition of educating women, including at its law school, meaning that women in Kansas may have had more access to political leadership than women in other states. I pose this largely as a question or hypothesis at this point, one worth exploring further in later writing and analysis. McFarland, for example, was only two years younger than former US Supreme Court Justice Ruth Bader Ginsberg, who entered Harvard Law School in 1956 and graduated from Columbia Law School in 1959. Women were first admitted to Harvard Law in 1950. Meanwhile, at Washburn, women were admitted from the year of the law school's founding in 1903. The theme of the April 2009 issue of *The Washburn Lawyer*, Washburn's magazine, was Women at Washburn. In its pages, Charlene Smith explained: "Washburn University School of Law can proudly say it is in the forefront of legal education for women. From the school's inception in 1903, women have been welcome. Compared to other law schools, this is remarkable. For example, Columbia Law School—one of the oldest American law schools at 200 plus years—has admitted women only since 1927."[23]

McFarland broke numerous gender barriers in Kansas. She was the first female elected to a judgeship in Shawnee County, the first appointed to the state supreme court, and the first chief justice of the state supreme court. On completing law school in 1964, McFarland was admitted to the Kansas Bar Association. In 1971, she was elected a judge of the probate and juvenile courts of Shawnee County, becoming the first woman to hold a judgeship in the county. In 1973, she was elected a judge of the newly created Fifth Division of the District Court in Topeka, and in 1977 she was appointed to the Kansas Supreme Court by Republican governor Robert F. Bennett, becoming the state's first female state supreme court justice. Finally, in September 1995, she became Kansas's first female chief justice. Notably, she had authored the 1994 opinion in *USD 229 v. State*, overturning Luckert's concerns about the School District Finance Act, just under a year earlier (December 1994). McFarland retired a few years after the high court's final ruling in *Montoy*.

The Grand Bargain

Although it was Judge Terry Bullock who brought parties to the table in 1991, it was the agreement between Governor Joan Finney and Senate President Sheila Frahm that eventually would get them excused from the table. The two women were from opposing parties but shared an interest in framing the school finance reforms in terms of tax relief. As noted on several previous occasions, Finney, a Democrat, had favored tax relief, and her own 1991 tax cuts in part precipitated Bullock's action. Frahm needed a plan to sell to her Republican colleagues and to her rural Kansas constituents in towns like Colby. Meanwhile, in the southwest corner of the state, county political leaders (mostly men) were preparing for a more gunslinging revolution and proposing secession plans for a new state on the high plains. This was despite the fact that Frahm's and her constituents' interests were roughly aligned with theirs. The reality was that a relative few, very small, natural resource–rich towns would see their taxes jump substantially under the new minimum levy while not being permitted to reap the entire gains of the additional revenue generated by those taxes.

What Frahm and enough of her colleagues realized was that there were many small towns throughout the state that would not see as large a tax increase (some perhaps none at all) but would also be able to keep most of the revenue they had previously because of the low enrollment weighting. Finding the right balance between increased state aid and setting of the local tax requirement could lead to local tax "winners" (tax cuts) that outnumbered losers, a preference of both Frahm and Finney, who were able to bypass the bluster of the recessionist movement.

As I described back in chapter 3, the whole thing wasn't some great, immediate, "Kumbaya" moment of collaborative, bipartisan effort. The effort was persistent. The effort didn't even succeed until the waning hours of the veto session. But it did succeed—and for all its problems, the effort created a new taxing structure and school finance formula that could pave the path forward to more equitable and adequate solutions down the road.

Luckert, a brand-new Shawnee County District court judge at the time, identified some of those problems early on—most notably, the questionable rationality of the low enrollment weighting. In retrospect, Luckert was right to note those problems. She could see that the new, seemingly boldly different formula found its way to replicating some past disparities. She could see those disparities weren't rooted in sufficient empirical analysis or rationality. There just wasn't sufficient evidence yet for why the low enrollment weight was so out of whack— why the expenditure analysis behind the weight was flawed. But while Luckert herself was also relatively conservative in her approach, McFarland and the rest of the high court in their decision were less willing to send Finney, Frahm, and the others back to the drawing board. At least in my view, and largely in retrospect, the formula that emerged and survived through McFarland's decision was the result of a legislative and subsequent judicial balancing act among women whose moderate political ideologies hugged the center line, while others, including the rebels of Southwest Kansas, tugged at the extremes.

This was also an era in which bipartisan solutions in state legislatures were more common. State legislative politics had not yet become as polarized as in the years that followed (see figure 6.3). During this same period, for example, the state of Texas had also adopted notable bipartisan education policies, including changes to the state school funding system and a policy that would allow any students who graduated in the top 10 percent of their high school class access to any of the state's major public universities. The latter was an effort to draw more students from predominantly low-income and minority urban schools, as well as outlying rural schools, into those colleges and universities. These policies in Texas were achieved by similar unlikely geographic alliances that crossed partisan lines.[24]

THE WOMEN OF THE *MONTOY* ERA

With the exception of the Southwest Kansas rebellion of the previous era, the *Montoy* era might be characterized as significantly more polarized and combative. The *Montoy* era required the lower and higher courts to step up and take a stronger role. Several women were key players in this process, including Carol Beier and, again, Marla Luckert, both on the high court. The governor at the time, Kathleen Sebelius, seemed more interested in sidestepping controversy and pursuing political aspirations beyond Kansas.

Carol Beier

Carol Beier was appointed to the state supreme court only months after Marla Luckert took her seat on the court. Beier was the first of these women to be from the Kansas City metropolitan area, having been born in Kansas City, Kansas, in 1958. Unlike the others, Beier pursued her undergraduate education (1981) and law degree (1985) at the University of Kansas, about halfway between the Kansas City area and Topeka.

Beier's path to judicial leadership is more like that of elite judges and politicians on the national stage. While that path wasn't through Harvard or Yale Law School, and instead the University of Kansas, it led her to a judicial clerkship with Judge James Kenneth Logan of the Tenth Circuit Court of Appeals, after which she received a fellowship to the Georgetown Law Center Woman's Law and Public Policy Fellowship Program. Beier's experiences were certainly more national and somewhat more elitist than those of her female predecessors on the court, but Beier was still a Kansan who had pursued her studies at the state's flagship public university.

Not by any means to discredit her female (or male) colleagues on the court, Beier was (and is) a legal scholar, who went to great lengths to shape the court's understanding of the constitution with respect to education rights and responsibilities, as well as more broadly with respect to individual rights. Beier was not shy, whether in shaping majority rulings or authoring dissenting opinions, about laying out her legal opinions on state constitutional law.

Beier was appointed to the Kansas court of appeals in 2000 and served on that court until her appointment to the Kansas Supreme Court in 2003 by Governor Kathleen Sebelius. Beier was perhaps a bit more of a political lightning rod than Luckert and certainly more so than McFarland, frequently ruling on matters that upset more conservative corners of Kansas politics. But Beier too survived retention votes—four times—and media attempts to cast her as partisan.[25] She announced her retirement on June 12, 2020.[26]

Governor Kathleen Sebelius

Kathleen Sebelius, governor of Kansas during the *Montoy* era, differs in many ways from the other women of Kansas addressed here. Sebelius was not a Kansan. She was from Ohio and the daughter of former Ohio governor John "Jack" Gilligan. Sebelius attended a private "country day" school in Cincinnati, Ohio, and went to college in Washington, DC, before attending the University of Kansas for her master of public administration degree. KU had (and still has) a nationally recognized program in the field at the time. She moved to Kansas in 1974.

Sebelius was first elected to the Kansas House of Representatives in 1986 and maintained terms there through the 1990s, representing the Topeka area and being part of the house during the *Mock* to *USD 229* period, though her name does not surface at any point as a major player in the development of the house plan that passed during the regular session of 1992. She made a failed run at a leadership role in 1991. In 1994, she ran for and won the office of state insurance commissioner, the first Democrat to do so in a hundred years. She held that office until 2003, when she became governor. The 2002 election cycle featured a particularly conservative Republican opponent, Treasury Secretary Tim Shallenberger, who was simply too conservative for most Kansans at that time. It seemed that the Republican party had become tired of the more measured, moderate stance of the then current governor, Bill Graves. Sebelius's win over Schallenberger was decisive—and the first significant Kansas election of my personal recollection.

By my recollection as well, while in office as a Democrat, Sebelius never took any particularly strong stand regarding the equity or adequacy of school funding. She was mostly quiet and conflict-averse as the *Montoy* case proceeded. For the most part, she didn't stand as a substantial barrier to passage of legislative responses to judicial orders throughout the period. It is rumored, however, that she attempted to coerce Democratic legislative holdouts during the heated special summer session of 2005 to just go along with Republican efforts to push through a constitutional amendment as a trade-off for adopting a school funding increase. This would have been disastrous for the state, and thankfully the Democrats in the legislature held out and won this battle. As another example, attempting to play to the public distaste for Judge Bullock, recall that Sebelius responded to his lower court order in 2003 by saying, "For taxpayers, that can be a very dangerous proposal to have a court essentially make decisions based not on knowing the situation or having responsibility for raising taxes, but just making mandates that shut down the schools unless you come up with a certain funding amount."[27]

Sebelius's aspirations seemed less about leaving a positive progressive legacy in Kansas and more about making her own move to the national stage, unlike other women addressed here. Nonetheless, she remains a significant figure worth mentioning, and a figure that may be more recognizable to non-Kansan readers of this book. She went on to become secretary of health and human services in the Obama administration, resigning as governor in 2009, and now runs a political consulting firm based in Lawrence, Kansas.[28]

Beier and Luckert on the Court

Carol Beier clearly liked to write, and did so with an impressive clarity on even the most complex constitutional issues. Beier also wasn't shy about showing her depth of knowledge and understanding of both legal and substantive issues in the heat of oral arguments. Beier had only just been appointed to the court in 2003 when she was faced with the high court's response to Bullock's ruling. In majority opinions of the court, it can be difficult to sort out who may have written what or informed which specific opinions. To me, that becomes somewhat clearer at later points. But my first experience of seeing Beier on fire was in the May 2005 oral arguments before the court. Beier's colleague on the court, Marla Luckert, often formed a tag team with Beier under these circumstances. I've mentioned this exchange previously and noted the report in the *Lawrence Journal World* of an exchange in which Beier and Luckert together took the state's lawyer Kenneth Weltz to task for his sorely lacking arguments and lack of understanding of the school finance system.[29] Luckert also often signed on to lengthy dissents written by Beier. Luckert clearly understood the history of school funding litigation in the state and the particulars of the school funding formula.

In my view, one of Beier's greatest contributions to Kansas constitutional law is a concurring opinion she wrote in the January 3, 2005, Kansas Supreme Court Ruling in *Montoy v. Kansas*. Recall that this was the ruling in which the state supreme court upheld the major elements of Judge Bullock's lower court ruling of just over a year prior. Beier's concurring opinion was not necessary at that moment because the high court had ruled the existing school funding scheme unconstitutional, setting in motion the next several steps—including the volatile summer session of 2005 and the eventual resolution over a year later. But Beier felt the need to correct and clarify past records. At issue was whether the Kansas Constitution guaranteed individuals a fundamental right to an education. Whether or not education is a fundamental right for Kansans shapes how other legal questions are addressed. Beier explained:

> I concur fully in the court's result and in the bulk of its rationale. I write separately only because I disagree with the holding of *U.S.D. No. 229 v. State*, 256 Kan. 232, 260-63, 885 P.2d 1170 (1994), that education is not a fundamental right under the Kansas Constitution. I believe it is. Thus I would not, as the court implicitly did on its way to the opinion in this case, rely on *U.S.D. No. 229* to conclude that the Kansas school financing formula under SDFQAA did not violate the Equal Protection Clauses of the federal and state Constitutions. Rather, I would take the opportunity presented by this case to overrule the *U.S.D. No. 229* holding on the status of the right to education under the Kansas Constitution.[30]

When individuals are deprived of a fundamental right, the standard of legal analysis is significantly raised, making it more likely to lead to a finding that the deprivation violates equal protection. That is, a state must provide a compelling governmental interest for permitting or creating conditions under which individuals are deprived of a fundamental right. When disparities or deprivation exist around something that is not a fundamental right, courts need only apply a lower standard, called the *rational basis test*. That is, does the government have a rational basis for permitting or creating these differences? This was exactly what the US Supreme Court had done in evaluating disparities in Texas resulting from local control of property taxes.

Others, including myself, previously had viewed the phrasing of the 1966 education article as establishing governmental obligations to provide for schooling, rather than individual rights to access schooling. The state board had the authority to establish standards for public schools, for intellectual, educational, vocational, and scientific improvement, and the legislature was obligated to "make suitable provision for finance." But, as Beier noted, there were certain key words and phrases in Article 6 that were there for a reason and clearly heightened the obligations of the legislature and state board toward the state's children. Beier explained, quoting San Antonio v. Rodriguez:

> In San Antonio School District v. Rodriguez, 411 U.S. 1, 36 L. Ed. 2d 16, 93 S. Ct. 1278, reh. denied 411 U.S. 959 (1973), the United States Supreme Court held that education is not a fundamental right under the United States Constitution. In reaching this conclusion, the Court stated: "The key to discovering whether education is 'fundamental' is not to be found in comparisons of the relative societal significance of education as opposed to subsistence or housing. Nor is it to be found by weighing whether education is as important as the right to travel. Rather, the answer lies in assessing whether there is a right to education explicitly or implicitly guaranteed by the Constitution." 411 U.S. at 33-34. Article 6, § 1 of our state constitution reads: "The legislature *shall* provide for intellectual, educational, vocational and scientific improvement by establishing

and maintaining public schools, educational institutions and related activities." (Emphasis added.) Article 6, § 6 provides: "The legislature shall make suitable provision for finance of the educational interests of the state." (Emphasis added.)[31]

Beier goes on in this opinion to review both the rationale adopted in *Rodriguez v. San Antonio* and that used in a multitude of state constitutional cases regarding conditions for establishing when and whether education rights are considered fundamental, noting that Marla Luckert in her lower court ruling in *USD 229* had reviewed much the same and that the existing case law hadn't changed much since then. Based on that case law, Luckert had decided to apply the lower standard of analysis to the disparities that existed under the formula: the rational basis test. Beier goes on to explain that just because Luckert and later the high court adopted this standard, that did not mean, by reasoning backward, that education was not a fundamental right in Kansas. If it was not, the rational basis would be the correct standard. But it did not stand to reason that simply because rational basis was applied in that case, education was not a fundamental right, and that implicit assumption that had now carried over into *Montoy*. Beier explained:

> I agree that the cases on which Justice Luckert and the Supreme Court relied remain persuasive on the wisdom of applying that standard to statutes providing for education finance in Kansas. However, I am not comfortable reasoning backward from that conclusion to say there is no fundamental right to education under our Kansas Constitution. In fact, on close reading, it is evident that Justice Luckert was also reluctant to make this backward leap of logic. It was not until the Kansas Supreme Court's opinion in *U.S.D. No. 229* that Justice Luckert's use of a rational basis standard for review of school finance legislation was equated to a conclusion that the Kansas Constitution recognizes no fundamental right to education.[32]

Beier then went on to correct the record, providing four bases on which she asserted that the Kansas Constitution does in fact establish education as a fundamental right. The first two are worth quoting in full:

First, the language of the education article is mandatory. [***33] The legislature "*shall* provide for intellectual, educational, vocational and scientific improvement" and it "*shall* make suitable provision for finance of the educational interests of the state." Kan. Const. Art. 6, §§ 1, 6. Neither the provision of progressive educational improvement nor the financing of it is optional.

Second, the education article's relationship to the constitution as a whole emphasizes its centrality to the document's overall design. Only five articles precede it. Each of the first three outlines one of the three branches of government. See Kan. Const. Arts. 1, 2, 3. The fourth and the fifth deal with elections and suffrage, without which the three branches could not be populated. See Kan. Const. Arts. 4, 5. Next comes education; once the branches are established and their seats filled, it appears education is the first thing on the agenda of the new state. See Kan. Const. Art. 6. The education article comes before those dealing with public institutions and welfare, the militia, county and township organization, apportionment of the legislature, and finance and taxation, among others. See Kan. Const. Arts. 7, 8, 9, 10, 11. Our constitution not only [***34] explicitly provides for education; it implicitly places education first among the many critical tasks of state government.[33]

Beier went on to explain that while the education article was substantially revised in 1966, even its earlier forms included obligatory language regarding the state's responsibility, and education held a prominent position in the state's constitution and its precursors.

In the March 2, 2017, opinion in the *Gannon* case, in which the high court made its final determination on the adequacy of school funding at that point in time, ruling in favor of the plaintiffs, the court cited Beier's concurring opinion in *Montoy*, specifically regarding her point that "Article 6 is preceded only by the articles creating the three branches of government, elections, and suffrage—without which the three branches could not be populated." "Once the branches are established and their seats filled, it appears education is the first thing on the agenda of the new state."[34]

WOMEN OF THE BROWNBACK ERA AND BEYOND

As I noted earlier, the prominence of women in positions of political influence in Kansas seemed to peak in the mid-2000s. Due to space constraints here, I've not been able to give all of theme their due, including the state auditor Barb Hinton, who oversaw the post audit study in 2006. The 2010 election cycle was not especially friendly to female candidates for office, and in general for next few cycles, the share of women in the legislature would decline—and even those women in legislative positions of power were less supportive of public schools and significantly more caught up in national stage, conservative platform issues, like abortion. Susan Wagle had been in the state house of representatives from 1990 to 2001 and moved to the state senate in 2001. She became the Kansas Senate president in 2012. While Wagle wasn't particularly fond of the state high court's involvement in school finance, she was even less fond of the court when they overturned her signature antiabortion bill, SB 95, in 2015.[35] She and her colleagues subsequently failed to get a proposed constitutional amendment on the ballot, which would have, in effect, negated the court's ruling.[36]

While Wagle was a persistent barrier to tax and school finance reform throughout the Brownback period, there were other rumblings within the Kansas City metropolitan area and elsewhere in the state, including significant discontent over the effects of the Brownback tax cuts on schools. It turns out that the mostly white suburbanites of Johnson County still wanted well-funded public schools. Most knew that meant supporting a statewide system of well-funded schools, though some still focused on at least being allowed to raise more taxes for their own. There was not a whole lot of "taxes are evil" and "public schools are bastions of liberal atheist propaganda that must be eliminated" rhetoric floating around in the suburbs. Yes, there was some; there always is. But the clips in figure 6.4 from the house candidate interviews on the topic of school funding are illustrative of (a) the more subtle lines across which republican and democratic candidates were split and (b) the differences in tone by gender.

Figure 6.4 shows that in 2014, of four contested races in Northeast Johnson County (older suburbs that had been built under racial

FIGURE 6.4   Legislative candidate statements on education

Fall 2014 Local Races for State House Northeast Johnson County

24 (winner)
Jarrod Ousely (D)

"My focus will be on getting education funding back to constitutionally adequate levels. If we can fund the existing formula, our schools will see an immediate and direct benefit; which may eliminate the pressure to continually raise local property taxes."

24
Brandon Hermreck (R)

"I feel it is laudable for a fellow citizen from a given school district to reach into their own pockets to help out the children of the district. However, reaching into someone else's pockets to help out the district is worthy of condemnation and it despicable."

25 Incumbent (winner)
Melissa Rooker (R)

"Our first priority is to provide adequate funding for our public schools." "The Local Option Budget was created to be an enhancement to state funding, not a replacement for state funding." "The best option is for the state to live up to its constitutional duty to provide adequate funding in the first place."

25 Challenger
Jennifer Robinson (D)

"I will support full funding of the state formula—not only because it is a legal requirement, but also the right thing to do for all of Kansas. "

21 Incumbent (winner)
Barbara Bollier (R)

"The first task for the state is to adequately fund the formula! I would be open to tweaking some parts of the formula, but bottom line, we must follow the constitution and fund it!"

21 Challenger
Amy Bell

"The key to this issue is the adequate funding. Right now the local option budget (LOB) is too often looked to as the solution to school funding when it should be supplement."

19 Incumbent (winner)
Stephanie Clayton (R)

"There is one thing that they tend to agree on when it comes to education funding, regardless of Party or ideology: that they would prefer increased local authority over education tax dollars."

19 Challenger
Patricia Stratton (D)

"While I am in favor of an increase in the L.O.B. in Johnson County, I am aware that other less affluent districts may not have the same advantage. School funding needs to be increased throughout the state."

Source: Author compiled; Dan Blom, "State Representative Candidates on the Issues: Funding for Public Schools," *Shawnee Mission Post*, October 21, 2014, https://shawneemissionpost.com/2014/10/21/state-representative-candidates-issues-funding-public-schools-33014/.

residential restrictions), three were between women candidates from opposing parties, with the fourth between two men. In all three of the races between Republican and Democrat women, candidates from both parties saw the need for additional funding for their schools in Shawnee Mission School District. In two of those three, the primary ideological split was on whether the candidate felt there was also a need for increased taxes to fund schools statewide. Republican Barbara Bollier (who later in 2018 switched parties), eventual winner in the twenty-first district, strongly stated a preference for funding the state-wide formula. Both her opponent and the Republican winner in the adjacent district, Stephanie Clayton, supported increased funding for schools—but they were less interested in statewide funding increases and more interested in having greater flexibility to raise local taxes. That is, they wanted to loosen or eliminate the caps, a more typical Republican position in Johnson County. District 25 was a bit more unique in that both candidates supported the legislature's obligation to make good on financing the statewide formula. The eventual winner (and incumbent), Melissa Rooker, was a key player throughout the Brownback/*Gannon* period as a member of the education committee and the house K–12 education budget committee. Notably in figure 6.4, it is only the male Republican candidate for district 24 who refers to any and all taxes to fund the statewide system as "despicable."

Figure 6.4 is just a snapshot of information that was easily accessible, but I've chosen it because it does seem representative of the discourse of the period. A few years later, immediately following the high court's order on adequacy (March 2017), Johnson County legislators responded true to form, though not obviously in a partisan way: "Rep. Sean Tarwater, a Stilwell Republican who sits on the House Education Committee and the House Appropriations Committee, questioned whether the court ruling requires additional funding. 'They did not put an amount. They just put the funding mechanism needs to address this,' Tarwater said. 'So it's my fear that it's going to be Johnson County funding the rest of the state again. We don't necessarily have to put more money into the school system.'"[37] And by contrast: "Rep. Melissa Rooker, a Fairway Republican on the House Education Committee and the House K-12 Education Budget Committee, struck a different chord. She said a passage in the opinion about the history of education cuts in the state had resonated with her. Rooker quoted one part of the ruling where the justices found the impact of funding losses 'endemic, systemic and statewide.' The impact is being felt everywhere, she said. 'This opinion spends a lot of time focusing on the fact that money, in fact, does matter,' Rooker said."[38] The ideological split remains the same, but here, by example, among Johnson County Republicans. I raise these issues because I suspect most outside of Kansas might assume (as I might have before living there) that Kansas republicans would never openly support putting more money into public schools, whether their own local schools or schools statewide. We've reached a point in the national rhetoric among conservative Republicans that there is never a circumstance under which additional taxes to support public school-ing is a reasonable proposition, even while empirical research tying increased education spending to improved short- and long-term out-comes for children has continued to pile up. Rooker emphasizes this very point in the quotes presented. That is, money does in fact matter!

I recall inviting my old friend and former Kansas legislator Ed O'Malley to participate in a panel discussion in 2019 on Kansas school funding at the annual academic meeting of the Association for Educa-tion Finance and Policy in Kansas City. At the last minute, Ed couldn't make it, and Melissa Rooker stepped in as a substitute. Ed also was a Republican and a supporter of public schools. I thought it would be interesting for our roomful of coastal elite academics to hear from an unlikely Kansas Republican. I spoke, followed by Lori Taylor, and then Jesse Levin. Melissa Rooker spoke last and explained how Lori's cost study was informing the Kansas legislature in the context of the judicial ruling and the legislature's obligation to make good on its own promises and constitutional obligations, supported by reasonable and fiscally responsible tax policy. I watched the nods of approval across the room, but realized at some point that I never mentioned Rooker's party affiliation. After she spoke, I asked her to reveal her party affili-ation. Surely everyone in that room at the time must have thought her to be the most liberal Democrat in Kansas. You could hear the gasps when she explained she was a Republican. Kansas on the inside isn't always as you expect from the outside.

Rooker lost her seat to a Democratic challenger in the 2018 wave that brought in a number of new female representatives and the state's third woman governor.[39] Governor Laura Kelly's chapter is yet to be written. Like Sebelius, Kelly is not a Kansan. She was born in New York (god forbid!), raised in a military family, and attended college and graduate school in Indiana (Bradley University and Indiana University). She was elected to the Kansas Senate in 2004, which should certainly give her plenty of familiarity with the Kansas school finance saga. She also played a major role in helping to expand early childhood programs in the state.[40] Like Sebelius, Kelly benefited from the Kansas Republican Party's choice of a distastefully conservative and divisive opponent to run against her in the general election: Kris Kobach. Ed O'Malley had attempted a run against Kobach in the Republican primary but simply couldn't generate enough conservative support in these increasingly polarized times.

CLOSING THOUGHTS

What this chapter presented is perhaps more hypothesis than conclusion, on a few fronts. First, broadly, there remain significant questions about gender roles in political (and legal) leadership, the respect and support for programs and services for children and families, and the demeanor required to negotiate and resolve the complex issues of tax and spending policies on these programs. Although Kansas presents somewhat of a model at key points in time of women from opposing parties collaborating on unlikely solutions to improve the quality of the state's education system, other states with even greater female presence in legislative, executive, and judicial leadership have failed to achieve the same. In fact, Arizona remains one of if not the worst-case examples. There is little question, however, that the prominent women of Kansas discussed in this chapter have significantly shaped education policy and finance in Kansas over time and have ensured that public school opportunities for Kansas children are much better than they would have been in their absence.

Second, more Kansas-specific, outsiders to Kansas often get a distorted view of the state's politics in general and the state's prominent women leaders. Us folks on the coasts are far more likely to hear of the saga of Connie Morris, the state board of education member who continuously pushed for removal of evolution from the state's science standards and inclusion of intelligent design, or of Susan Wagle's efforts to advance one of the nation's most restrictive antiabortion bills.[41] Within Kansas, there are externally oriented Kansas political leaders and internally oriented ones. The pipelines to these roles differ, and over time, Washburn University seems to have played a significant role in preparing Kansas leaders with an inward Kansas focus. But increasingly over the past decade, outward-focused leaders have played a larger role.

As I close this chapter, Carol Beier has retired from the state's high court—but for the first time ever, all finalists for the open seat are women. Marla Luckert has been appointed chief justice.[42] And voters in Wichita have elected the state's first transgender representative, a woman and a former teacher, who ran specifically on a platform of supporting increased school funding.[43]

7

WHEN EVIDENCE PREVAILS

Connecting Cost Analyses to Education Outcomes

"As I am sure you are aware, the state of Kansas
has made itself the laughingstock of the
scientific world over this issue."

—Oxford University professor Richard Dawkins in 2005,
in response to being invited to testify in the Kansas State
Board of Education hearings on intelligent design[1]

A unique aspect of the school finance saga in Kansas over the past several decades is the role of empirical evidence in informing the courts and guiding school finance reforms. This is despite the same time periods involving national ridicule over Kansas's public debates over evolution versus intelligent design, and the equally dogmatic belief in Lafferism. During the *Mock* kerfuffle of the early 1990s, Governor Finney had followed in the footsteps of Governor Avery (1965) by appointing a task force to establish the framework for moving forward. In Finney's case, she was complying with the order issued by Judge Terry

Bullock to resolve vast inequities in school district spending under the
School District Equalization Act. This time period preceded the use
of cost analysis to shape school finance reforms around constitutional
requirements and legislative mandates. Finney's task force did rely on
expert testimony regarding how other states were resolving similar
disparities and used that evidence, which was provided in part by John
Meyers of the National Conference of State Legislators (NCSL), to
guide the 1992 reforms. And Finney's task force relied on evidence of
past expenditure patterns of districts based on their size.

The modern "empirical era" of Kansas school finance reform begins
with the governor's Vision 21st Century Task Force, which was charged
with providing guidance on revisions to the school finance formula.
The Legislative Coordinating Council, which delegated the responsibility of monitoring the work to the Legislative Education Planning Committee, contracted the Colorado-based consulting firm of Augenblick
and Myers (and specifically John Myers, who had advised Finney's task
force and was a former Kansas legislator himself) to conduct the study
and produce findings by 2002. Here, we'll explore in greater detail the
specifics of the task involved, the methods employed by A&M, and
why certain requirements were imposed on the research team.

By 2005, the legislature had been forced back into a special session
to resolve inequities and inadequacies in school funding, which were in
part measured against the findings of the Augenblick and Myers study.
At this point, the legislature wanted a do-over cost analysis and originally wanted that analysis to involve only the costs of bare-bones inputs
to schooling. State board of education attorney Dan Biles objected to
this proposal and urged the court (on which, as of the time of writing,
he now sits) to rule that any new cost analysis must take into account
the outcome standards adopted under the state board's independent
constitutional authority. The court agreed, and the legislature tasked
the Legislative Division of Post Audit with conducting both versions
of the study: one for bare-bones core curricular inputs and another
for the cost of achieving the state board's outcome standards. LPA
subcontracted researchers from Syracuse University to estimate cost
models for Kansas school districts and in the end came up with overall
cost estimates (and distributions of costs) very similar to those of the
A&M study!

Because this study wasn't introduced into evidence at trial, and thus had not been vetted (as a legal technicality), it could not formally guide the court's subsequent rulings in *Montoy v. Kansas*. But later, in *Gannon v. Kansas* (a trial in 2011), this study would have its turn. In 2017, facing a high court ruling in *Gannon*, the legislature decided it needed yet another do-over. In part, the previous study was now over a decade old. But also, the costs of complying with that study remained high, and at least some legislators may have been hopeful that a new study would ultimately yield a lower estimate. In the summer of 2017, legislators offered their own set of calculations of average district spending for districts meeting specific outcome standards, which was systematically debunked by the state's high court during oral arguments that July. In response to the court's critique and subsequent order that fall, the legislature contracted Lori Taylor (a native of Salina, Kansas) of Texas A&M, in collaboration with WestEd, to conduct a new study, and Jesse Levin of the American Institutes for Research to provide external evaluation of the Taylor/WestEd report. To their surprise and perhaps dismay, the Taylor/WestEd study came in with even higher cost estimates, attached to meeting new, higher standards.

We'll explore the backstory behind each of these studies, the players involved in each of the studies, the methods chosen and reasons why, the eventual findings of these studies, and how they influence judicial analysis and eventual policy. Now, let's discuss some of the backdrop for methods used in estimating education costs and the timeline over which these methods evolved and gained popularity for informing state school finance policies.

PRIMER ON COST AND EXPENDITURE ANALYSES IN EDUCATION

From the 1990s through the present day, Kansas has been on the cutting edge of applied methods in cost analyses. This is not to suggest by any means that the cost analyses done in Kansas have always been perfect. The story of using cost analyses to inform legislators of their constitutional obligation toward funding schools, the methods used, and the researchers involved coevolved over the same time period. At each point in time along the way, Kansas has done something new and different. Early in this process, the study of cost analysis methods— and specifically, studies done for states to evaluate education costs— became a centerpiece of my own academic work when I was called upon in the early 2000s to prepare a white paper for the Texas legislature, coauthored with Lori Taylor of Texas A&M, on the state of cost analyses for these purposes.[2]

There had been a few long-forgotten, painstakingly detailed studies of the costs of providing adequate programs and services in Alaska (1984) and Illinois (1982), conducted by Jay Chambers and colleagues at the American Institutes for Research. In 1995, the Wyoming Supreme Court ordered the legislature to adopt a formula based on the actual costs of providing adequate programs and services.[3] In response, one version of the modern day "educational adequacy" study was born. The study, conducted by a group called Management Analysis and Planning Associates (MAP), involved establishing the parameters of a prototypical Wyoming school and identifying all of the resources, or ingredients, it would take for that school to provide a constitutionally adequate education in Wyoming. In other words, how many teachers it would take to provide the appropriate class sizes by grade level, how many additional support staff and administrators, and what materials supplies and equipment. Further, what wages would these people need to be paid, and how much would the other stuff cost? From the summed costs of this prototype, costs could be projected for the whole state.

Other states, under court order, were engaging in less thorough exercises at the time to convince their courts they had used cost analysis to guide their decision-making and standard setting. For example, in the late 1990s and early 2000s, state legislatures, sometimes in collaboration with consultants, would select sets of schools or districts that they considered "successful," usually by some metric of which schools or districts were meeting specific outcome standards. Those standards might include test scores, proficiency rates, graduation rates, or any number of outcome metrics. Coincidentally, the 1990s were also a period in which states began introducing and expanding the use of standardized assessments for reading and math, which became convenient tools to use in such analyses. Consultants, departments of education, or legislative research departments themselves would then calculate the average spending of these schools or districts and offer it as an "adequate" amount. Presumably, if these schools or districts had met the standards while spending only this much, that should be adequate for others.

This "successful schools" approach, unlike that used in Wyoming, at least considers outcomes in the process, whereas the approach used in Wyoming was about providing the adequate inputs to schooling. But the problem with the "average spending" of "successful schools" approach was that it really wasn't appropriate to project spending levels that might work in some schools onto what was needed in others. Further, the selection process for successful schools was easily manipulated. In our review of early studies, Lori Taylor and I pointed out that problems in Ohio tied to attempts to get numbers that suited each of their positions: "The Governor's office chose 43 districts meeting 20 of 27 1999 standards, the Senate selected 122 districts meeting 17 of 18 1996 standards, the House chose 45 districts meeting all 18 original standards in 1999, and the House again in an amended bill used 127 districts meeting 17 of 18 1996 standards in 1996 and 20 of 27 standards in 1999."[4] The approach taken by MAP in Wyoming also had its limits. Among other things, in a state with diverse sizes and locations of school districts, it can be very difficult to use a single prototype to project the costs of operating these schools. Further, when state courts have emphasized outcome goals, an approach that proposes sets of inputs to achieve those outcomes lacks direct analysis of or connection to those outcomes.

The late 1990s also saw a flurry of academic research, primarily authored by William Duncombe and John Yinger, in which they developed and advanced strategies for estimating statistical models of the relationships among school district spending, student outcomes, various population characteristics, and other drivers of education cost and efficiency. Their goal was to find a way to use spending data to isolate and project the costs associated with achieving different outcome levels, with different groups of students, and across different settings. This approach was called the *education cost function* and had been used in other areas of public finance and applied to public schooling in a handful of earlier articles. But in the late 1990s, it was largely relegated to academic outlets, including an article on Kansas School finance by Duncombe and Jocelyn Johnston.[5] In our review of studies and methods in the early 2000s, Lori Taylor and I suggested to the Texas legislature that it pursue cost modeling to inform the state school finance formula, using methods that Lori and her colleagues were developing at the time and which differed somewhat from those being used by Duncombe and Yinger.[6]

There are really two basic approaches to education cost analysis, as Lori Taylor and I explained (along with Arnold Vedlitz) in a 2008 National Research Council report: input-oriented analyses and outcome-oriented analyses.[7] In an input-oriented analysis, consultants or researchers compile the various resources or ingredients necessary to provide a specific set of programs or services (perhaps on the assumption that they lead to certain outcomes), assign prices to those ingredients, and sum them up. In an outcome-oriented analysis, researchers estimate models that link spending data to actual outcomes while considering differences in contexts (district size, location, labor market prices) and considering serving different children (low income, English language learners, children with disabilities). In effect, successful schools analysis is a crude version of the latter, lacking any consideration for how one might project the costs of a successful school onto others operating under very different conditions.

Cost studies conducted as consultancies for state legislatures were being used primarily for setting basic spending levels in the 1990s. Additional spending needed to support small districts or to provide supplemental services for low-income children were often based on simple, back-of-the-napkin add-ons, like adding a few specialist staff to the prototype in an input-based model, or referring to policies of other states, even if those other state policies had not been based on any cost analysis.[8] Over the next decade or so, it would be revealed that the best way to sort out these additional costs—how much more it costs to provide equal opportunity in a very small remote rural district, or how much more it costs in high-poverty settings than in lower-poverty ones—was through education cost modeling. I would become convinced. And apparently Dan Biles would become convinced.

AUGENBLICK & MYERS STUDY 2002

Back in 2000, I was on the Kansas governor's task force, framing the recommendations for the state's first cost study, and I was not convinced. I was convinced that simply playing around with the average spending of districts was a fraught endeavor. That's how Kansas had gotten where it was, albeit without identifying specifically which districts were "successful." I was also concerned that cost modeling, using those same expenditure data, could fully correct the problems with the low enrollment weight or fully pick up the additional costs associated with proving low-income children equal opportunity to achieve the state outcome targets. It seemed to me that Bill Duncombe and Jocelyn Johnston's article on Kansas school finance suggested the need for a similarly large weight for small districts but didn't really pick up on the higher costs of the state's high-poverty districts.[9] As a result, I was all in on the Wyoming approach—with one really big caveat that we made clear in our recommendations and that our task force made clear while questioning John Myers on the day he gave a presentation to our group.

A major point of contention leading to the task force recommendation of a cost study was that the low enrollment weighting in particular was merely an artifact of prior spending. This prior spending was distorted by differences in property wealth for districts of different size. The group (primarily Senator Vratil) and I pressed John Myers on how he would address this problem—how he and his team would determine and/or project the actual cost differences for districts of different size. For the first few go-arounds in this line of questions, Myers proposed that his team would estimate a base cost by two methods: one establishing a prototype and costing it out and the other taking the average spending of districts that met the state standards. Then they would add a weight for small districts. Repeatedly, Senator Vratil and I pressed him for answers on how that weight would be determined.

Finally, at some point (though perhaps I'm giving myself too much credit here), I suggested that they might have to try something new—like looking at multiple different prototypes, of different sizes, to see how the cost differentials play out. Perhaps from those multiple prototypes, they could generate an actual cost basis associated with the size differences—that is, a cost-based low enrollment weight. Given the games I'd seen played with analysis of so-called successful schools, I argued that this really was worth the time, but the additional effort was marginal. A&M's cost study of Kansas schools became the first study of its kind to take this multiple prototype approach to determine costs for schools and districts of different sizes. A&M was followed, nearly concurrently, with studies in Nebraska, Missouri, and Colorado.[10]

The input-oriented approach used by A&M, adapting the methods of MAP's Wyoming study, was being referred to as a *professional judgment* (PJ) *approach* because it involved convening panels—basically, focus groups—of informed professionals to populate the prototypes with the necessary resources. Consultants would then use other data sources, including existing teacher salary data, to set the wages for different types of employees in the model. PJ became a term of art for consultants using this focus group approach, but it's really all just based on methods developed decades earlier, referred to as *resource cost models* or *ingredients methods*, which can be applied to estimating costs based on existing conditions or proposed hypotheticals, as in the case discussed here.[11]

At the time, there were really only two possible competing consultants for the Kansas cost study: MAP and A&M. John Myers had been a Kansas legislator and had advised Kansas during the *Mock* drama while working with the NCSL. He had then joined with John Augenblick to consult with state legislators on education policy issues. Myers, with Augenblick, had been called to discuss his approach with our task force. He pretty much had the gig if he wanted and if he was willing to explore these issues of costs related to district size. The Legislative Coordinating Council gave A&M the contract, under the oversight of Legislative Education Planning Committee, and their work commenced in the spring of 2001, with a final report released in May 2002. A&M did build a "successful schools" alternative to determining the base cost figure into their proposal.

Figure 7.1 shows the prototypes established for the A&M analysis.[12] Four categories of district sizes were picked, based on the distribution of enrollments of actual Kansas districts. Consultants identified the typical school sizes within those district size ranges and used those

FIGURE 7.1   Prototype school and district characteristics

	Very Small	Small	Moderate	Large
Range in Enrollment	<324	325–555	556–3,600	>3,600
Size of Prototype District	200	430	1,300	11,200
Size of Prototype School				
Elementary	140	150	200	430
Middle	—	—	300	430
High School	60	130	400	1,150

Source: J. Augenblick, J. Myers, J. Silverstein, and A. Barkis, *Calculation of the Cost of a Suitable Education in Kansas in 2000-2001 Using Two Different Analytic Approaches* (Topeka: Legislative Coordinating Council, State of Kansas, 2002), IV2.

school sizes to establish their school prototypes. They worked with members of the LEPC and the state board of education to understand the curricular and programming standards that needed to be met by the prototypes, as well as the outcome standards that were expected to be achieved.

A notable feature of this focus group approach is that the problem is framed for the focus groups tasked with populating these prototypes with resources such that the objective is to populate the prototypes with resources sufficient to meet the outcome standards in question. That is, the method is not totally devoid of consideration of outcome standards, even though the calculations are based on inputs. Rather, one might reasonably characterize the approach as relying on the opinions and experiences of informed experts to propose a hypothesis (a hypothetical school) of the resources needed to achieve the outcomes put before them.

Figure 7.2 shows the end result of the input-oriented cost analysis. Consultants found that the total resource costs at the school and district levels for the large district would be $5,811 in 2001 before considering additional needs of children with disabilities, low-income children, or children who were limited in their English language proficiency. That base cost went up to $8,581 for the very small district—a 47.7 percent difference. While significant, this was a far cry from the 214 percent difference baked into the current low enrollment weight.

FIGURE 7.2 District-level costs and total costs of varying size

	Size of School District			
	Very Small	Small	Moderate	Large
(1) District Level				
Spending				
Administration	$1,019	$616	$353	$389
Plant M&O	$620	$784	$775	$417
Other	$250	$175	$56	$281
Special Need Students				
Special Ed			$269	$11,582
At-Risk			$12	$297
Bilingual	$250	$250		$315
(2) Total Spending				
Base Spending				
School Level	$6,692	$5,786	$5.,499	$4,724
District Level	$1,889	$1,575	$1,184	$1,087
Total Base Cost	$8,581	$7,361	$6,683	$5,811
Added Cost of Special Need Students				
Special Ed.	$7,403	$6,908	$7,731	$12,090
At-Risk	$1,919	$2,228	$3,392	$2,578
Bilingual	$1,217	$1,267	$5,590	$5,993

Source: Augenblick et al., Calculation of the Cost of a Suitable Education, table IV-10.

Recall that in our planning meeting for the *Montoy* and *Robinson* cases, Bill Duncombe had proposed a strategy for me to try for correcting the wealth difference problem that had skewed the low enrollment weight. Figure 7.3, drawn from my expert testimony in *Montoy*, compares that correction to the A&M weight, using alternative base figures. A&M found a lower base spending figure of $4,650 in its successful school districts analysis but had no basis in that analysis to determine costs related to size.

Figure 7.3 shows the original low enrollment weight over the 2003 actual base aid of $3,820, and then shows my weight (by Bill's suggested method) and the A&M weight, using both the $4,650 and $5,811 base. Clearly, the $5,811 base raises the levels much higher overall. But in both cases, the wealth-adjusted curve and the A&M scale weight

FIGURE 7.3 Application of scale adjustments

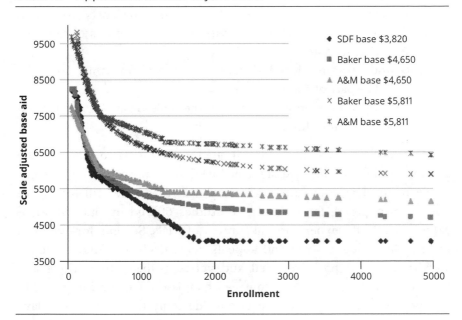

Source: Author testimony, *Montoy v. Kansas*.

are more aligned than the existing low enrollment weight, with both having a smaller top-to-bottom range than the existing weight.

Also in Figure 7.2, we have A&M's calculations of additional costs for low-income, English language learner, and special education students. The estimated cost margin in a large district for low-income children was over 44 percent, much larger than the existing weight in the formula. And the weight for English language learners was just over 100 percent. When all was said and done, even if using the lower base figure, but applying all of these new weights, the total cost of raising general fund spending per pupil to these targets would exceed $800 million. The report and its findings were immediately, summarily ignored by the legislature. This figure would serve to inform the lower court and eventually the state supreme court ruling in *Montoy*. Like Judge Bullock explained to Joe Miller of *The Pitch*, that's the legislature's number, not his own![13]

From a judicial standpoint, three things are important about the A&M study:

1. It was a study by, or at the very least on behalf of, the legislature itself, with the explicit intent of evaluating the costs associated with meeting the legislature's constitutional obligations to fund the state's K–12 schools.
2. The study was produced in advance of trial and thus could be included as part of the trial court record.
3. The study was the only evidence on the table regarding the legislature's obligation to fund schools.

On the first point, there was indeed quibbling as to whether the actions of the LCC and oversight of LEPC were necessarily representative of the legislature in its entirety. But these are still legislative bodies, as opposed, for example, to studies offered by outside advocates or plaintiff's experts in the context of trials. Second, for evidence to formally influence trial and appeals court decisions, that evidence and its use must be introduced and vetted (subject to critique and cross-examination) by a trial court—which is the fact-finding court in this process. Appellate courts may consider only the questions of law, given the facts. They may, however, remand to the trial court to address new facts that arise midprocess (during the lengthy periods of high court oversight, waiting on legislatures to respond to their orders). Third, having only the one study on the table certainly made things clearer and easier for both Bullock and the high court.

As the state supreme court explained in its June 3, 2005, ruling, setting off the chain of events that would lead to the special session:

> We now turn to this court's specific concerns about whether the actual costs of providing a constitutionally adequate education were considered as to each of the formula components and the statutory formula as a whole, and whether any unjustified funding disparities have been exacerbated rather than ameliorated by H.B. 2247. In this determination we will be guided, in large part, by the A&M study, despite the State's criticism of it and our knowledge that, at best, its conclusions are dated. We do so for several reasons.
>
> First, the A&M study is competent evidence admitted at trial and is part of the record in this appeal. See *Montoy II*, 278 Kan. at 774 (within the extensive record on appeal "there

is substantial competent evidence, including the Augenblick & Myers study, establishing that a suitable education, as that term is defined by the legislature, is not being provided").

Second, the legislature itself commissioned the study to determine the actual costs to suitably and equitably fund public school systems; it also maintained the [***26] overall authority to shape the contours of the study and to correct any A&M actions that deviated from its directions during the process. (See K.S.A. 60-460[h]). . . .

Third, the A&M study is the only analysis resembling a cost study before this court or the legislature.

Fourth, both the Board and the State Department of Education recommended that the A&M study recommendations be adopted at the time the study was completed and sent to the legislature.[14]

As the court itself explained, the A&M study provided the evidentiary framework it needed to evaluate the bill that had been put before it in the spring of 2005: HB 2247. As such, the court was willing to broadly evaluate the constitutionality of HB 2247 against the A&M study, asking whether or not it was apparent that evidence on costs had guided HB 2247, without critiquing the specific details of either the study or the bill. A deeper dive into the details would require the supreme court to remand the case back to a trial court to vet the evidence at trial.

And there was only one cost analysis on the table. The court concluded that HB 2247 did not meet the constitutional requirements it had set out in its ruling just prior to the 2005 legislative session. This was also the bill that had been argued in the May 11, 2005, oral arguments, which among other things proposed an insufficient redo of the A&M study.

LEGISLATIVE DIVISION OF POST AUDIT STUDY (2006)

By the spring of 2005, I'd reviewed numerous cost studies and written a handful of reports and articles on cost estimation. I also had the pleasure and exceptional learning opportunity to work more closely with both Lori Taylor and Bill Duncombe in separate settings and on separate occasions. As a result, my own thinking was starting to shift, both on the best methods for getting at the additional costs associated with differences in contexts and student needs and on the relationship between cost estimates and student outcomes. Bill and Lori had converted me.

Among other things, I had noticed a tendency in studies of proposed inputs provided by professional judgement panels to do two things: (1) to overstate the minimum costs of achieving the desired outcomes in the settings of lowest needs and costs (i.e., to overstate the base) and, concurrently, (2) to understate the additional needs of achieving those outcomes in higher-need settings (i.e., to understate the weights). This would often lead to unreasonably large required increases to statewide spending and in many cases involved increasing spending for districts that already exceeded the standards in question. This just didn't pass a basic smell test. How could these districts need substantially more funds to achieve a constitutional standard that they already exceeded? There's always some fuzziness in cost estimates, but this was more systematic. Of greater concern to me was that these approaches understated additional costs associated with student needs. Thrown into the political kerfuffle that determines the level and distribution of school funding, this evidence would most likely lead to some increase to base funding for everyone, but too little additional attention given to those with the greatest needs.

The next wave of cost analyses would require a tighter connection to outcomes and more accurate determination of how the costs of achieving specific outcomes varied from one setting to another and one child to the next. It was at this very point in time that the constitutional requirements in Kansas came together with the emerging technical developments in cost modeling. Timing really was a big part of it all, as was the unique constitutional structure of Article 6 of the Kansas constitution.

As explained in chapter 4, it was in the May 11, 2005, oral arguments before the Kansas Supreme Court that the state offered, as part of its remedy bill, a newly proposed cost study that would look at historical spending of Kansas districts and also at the bare-bones costs of inputs required for providing the core curriculum standards adopted by the state board of education—and nothing more! It was the state board's attorney, Dan Biles, who argued to the court on that day that any analysis proposed by the legislature must take full account of the outcome standards approved by the board and not merely bare-bones inputs.

In its June 3 opinion, the high court opined (regarding the legislature's proposed study in HB 2247):

> Although the language of the statute is not completely clear, it can be read to require post audit, among other things, to study historical costs in a sample of districts and then extrapolate from the collected data a reasonable estimate of the future cost of providing services and programs "required by state statute." Estimating future reasonable and actual costs based on historical expenditures can be acceptable if post audit ensures that its examination of historical expenditures corrects for the recognized inadequacy of those expenditures and ensures that a reliable method of extrapolation is adopted. Post audit must incorporate those components into its study, and its report to the legislature must demonstrate how the incorporation was accomplished.[15]

By this point, the court understood fully the problems of developing new policies based on the average characteristics of previous policies that had been found unconstitutional. Also at this point, Marla Luckert, who had raised concerns a decade earlier, was sitting on the high court—with far more extensive evidence in hand that perhaps she had been correct all along, even though she had been overruled in 1994. Further, the language in the June 3 statement suggests that it could be possible to use expenditure data in a way that does permit projection of costs, with sufficient corrections, as might be accomplished by cost function modeling.

Also, and perhaps most importantly, the high court accepted Biles's reasoning that the board's outcome standards must play an integral role in the estimation of costs: "It also appears that the study contemplated by H.B. 2247 is deficient because it will examine only what it costs for education 'inputs'—the cost of delivering kindergarten through grade 12 curriculum, related services, and other programs 'mandated by state statute in accredited schools.' It does not appear to demand consideration of the costs of 'outputs'—achievement of measurable standards of student proficiency."[16] I listened to the questioning in the May 11 arguments and read the June 3 decision and, coupled with my newfound understanding of education cost modeling, it became more apparent how the method served the Kansas context particularly well. And there really wasn't any way around it. The court, with Biles's advisement, had argued that the study must include direct consideration of outcomes, and there was no way that the legislature would mandate another study using the methods employed by A&M, which more loosely tied proposed inputs to outcomes anyway.

When the legislature completed its summer session homework in 2005, it proposed to hand off responsibility for conducting the originally proposed study, and a study that met the court's (and Biles's) demands, to the Legislative Division of Post Audit. The Division of Post Audit knew Kansas school finance and Kansas school districts plenty well, having conducted a number of previous studies. Post auditor Barbara Hinton and lead researcher Scott Frank were comfortable doing the input cost analyses and doing additional related analyses of district expenditure data, but, quite reasonably, they weren't sure how to go about more clearly estimating costs associated with outcome goals using existing data. As I mentioned back in chapter 4, I explained the work and methods of Bill Duncombe and Lori Taylor to them, and for this task they decided to contract Bill and his colleague, John Yinger of Syracuse. I personally had a preference for certain aspects of Duncombe and Yinger's methods and had been using them in my own work.[17]

The Study

The LDPA study consisted of three independent pieces. Some components were conducted directly by staff from LDPA, while others were conducted by William Duncombe and John Yinger of the Maxwell School of Citizenship and Public Affairs at Syracuse University. The study and eventual report included three basic components:

1. Input-based analysis (LDPA staff)
2. Cost function model analysis (Duncombe and Yinger)

3. Cost compilation and remedy estimate simulation (LDPA staff)

Staff at LDPA created estimates of the costs of providing the basic programs and services required under the state board's core curricular standards.[18]

Separately, Duncombe and Yinger estimated a model of the costs associated with achieving the state board's outcome standards for state assessments and graduation rates. Although Duncombe and Yinger's model included only general fund expenditures, it was able to reveal some complex relationships—showing, for example, that costs associated with child poverty escalated as population density increased. LDPA took a number of steps to combine Duncombe and Yinger's model with its own findings, which accounted for spending not included in the Duncombe and Yinger model and subtracted federal dollars. Using these two sets of findings, LDPA created a table of projected per-pupil costs for each district to meet input and outcome standards. That table (in the report's appendix 16)—the combined findings, without federal aid—would become the proposed benchmark for the state legislature's constitutional obligation for making suitable provision for financing the educational interests of Kansas children. The study was unveiled in January 2006, at the outset of the legislative session.

TAYLOR/WESTED STUDY (2018)

The summer of 2017 found the Kansas legislature back in a position similar to where it had been in the summer of 2005. The high court had ruled in March that the current funding was constitutionally inadequate. As discussed in chapter 5, during oral arguments before the court in July 2017, the state provided a set of successful schools estimates of base costs to the court in an attempt to assert that the funding levels it proposed for schools for the 2017–2018 school year met the adequacy demands the court laid out in March of 2017. These were the arguments in which I noted that Dan Biles, in his line of questioning, was on fire.

Leaning on the fact that A&M had also included successful schools analysis in its original study, the legislature had tasked the Kansas

Legislative Research Department (KLRD) with doing similar analyses to propose a base funding figure. In their oral arguments, the state's lawyers offered calculations by the KLRD of the average spending of forty-one districts it had identified as successful.

KLRD's approach was actually somewhat more complex than a typical successful schools analysis. It involved identifying four sets of successful districts, by different criteria, and then relating, via regression analyses and scatterplots, the outcomes and shares of low-income children from these districts. Finally, it involved calculating the average spending of districts where outcomes exceeded expectations. The fatal flaw underlying these analyses was that they had established a standard of adequacy that was based on whether a district's students performed better than expected, given the share of low-income students served, not on whether those outcomes actually met the standards. Although the state had not provided the list of districts to the court, the plaintiffs' attorneys (Alan Rupe and John Robb) did, revealing that many in fact did not meet the necessary standards.

As explained in chapter 5, Dan Biles was especially tough on the state's counsel during arguments before the court, first critiquing the outcome standard applied and then raising questions about whether the estimates provided were at all useful for projecting costs of meeting standards in other districts that may have differed significantly from the selected sample. The October decision of the court reflected Biles's concerns. Among other issues, the court explained that the legislature's outcome metric—performing better than expected—was the wrong metric for determining constitutional adequacy.[19] The decision goes on to systematically debunk the legislature's calculations for determining the costs to achieve adequate outcomes across all districts, as would be needed to meet the court's demands, concluding: "Stated simply and starkly, the State's 'successful schools' model does not contain enough schools or districts meeting student performance standards—much less constitutional standards of adequacy—to warrant that label."[20] Given the specificity of the language in the ruling and the critique of the successful schools approach, the legislature rightly assumed it would need to provide the court with something as comparably rigorous as what it offered in the 2006 post audit study. The bar had been raised, in part because of the past record of studies and the judicial record of those studies and methods, but also because those on the court had significant personal knowledge of all that had brought them to this point.

The Kansas legislature scrambled in the fall of 2017 to establish the parameters for its new study, knowing also that the study would require external credibility to be acceptable to the court. The legislature relied on former Republican state senator Jeffrey King[21] to identify and line up experts who might (a) provide the cost modeling analysis itself and (b) provide an external review and comparison of the new study in relation to the prior two studies. The study would have a quick turnaround, starting around January 2018 and to be completed by March 15, 2018, with the external review to be completed within two weeks of the March 15 date.

The Study

This time around, the study prepared by Lori Taylor and WestED would only involve cost modeling. Taylor would estimate a model relating current spending, existing outcomes, and a variety of district and student population characteristics, which could be used to project the costs for each district associated with meeting specific outcome targets. This is basically what Bill Duncombe and John Yinger had provided to LPA in December of 2005, but their report was relegated to an appendix in a larger post audit report, which used their findings to construct a hybrid set of policy recommendations. This time around, it was just the cost model. No other methods, no further attempts to merge and combine the results with other data to construct policy recommendations. There really wasn't time for either.

Taylor and Willis's approach was largely similar to that of Duncombe and Yinger, except for (a) the outcome standards that were selected for cost prediction, (b) the fact that Taylor modeled district size–related costs differently (using a curved function rather than a step down function), and (c) a few other highly technical issues, which can be found in my and Jesse Levin's competing reviews![22] Duncombe and Yinger also had been tasked with identifying just the underlying general fund expenditures associated with achieving specific outcome goals, excluding supplemental funds, special education, and transportation costs. Because this was a multipronged study, those could be added back in through the post audit analyses.

COMPARING FINDINGS ACROSS STUDIES

Recall that in both *Montoy* and *Gannon*, the state's central legal theory of defense for why the court should not intervene in matters pertaining to the equity or adequacy of school funding was that the amount of money schools had really didn't matter that much. Schools had more than enough money to get the job done and just needed to use it more efficiently, the theory went. Moreover, it proposed, cutting funds from schools would be unlikely to cause harm and could serve as a useful experiment on inducing greater efficiency in schooling. Judge Bullock was the first to call out state's experts on this point, stating, "Money doesn't matter? That dog won't hunt in Dodge City." The three-judge panel of the trial court in *Gannon* similarly exclaimed: "Educating students costs money."

These statements were affirmed by the state's own studies—and especially the two latter studies, which evaluated the statistical relationship between existing spending and student outcomes. For their 2006 model, Duncombe and Yinger said: "We found a strong association between the amounts districts spend and the outcomes they achieve. In the cost function results, a 1.0% increase in district performance outcomes was associated with a 0.83% increase in spending—almost a one-to-one relationship. This means that, all other things being equal, districts that spent more had better student performance. The results were statistically significant beyond the 0.01 level, which means we can be more than 99% confident there is a relationship between spending and outcomes."[23] The Taylor/WestED model echoes this conclusion, with new and different outcome measures, thus revealing differences in the magnitude of the relationship. The authors note:

> Table 17 presents coefficient estimates and standard errors from the cost function analysis. As the table illustrates, the analysis finds a strong, positive relationship between educational outcomes and educational costs, once differences in scale, need and price are taken into account. Consider first the Condition NCE scores. The estimation indicates that a one percentage point increase in academic performance is associated with a 5 percent increase in cost. Similarly, a one percentage point

increase in the graduation rate is associated with an 1.2 percent increase in cost at lower grades and a 1.9 percent increase in cost at the high school level.[24]

And this is why a *Kansas City Star* headline exclaimed: "Kansas School Funding Report Blows a Hole in Conservative Doctrine."[25] But in fact, the hole in question had already been created by a growing body of academic research, and by the Kansas legislature's own report from twelve years earlier.

The first conclusion is that it costs more to achieve higher than lower outcomes. The second is that it costs more in some places, with some children, than in others to achieve any given level of outcomes—with the possible exception that the costs of achieving nothing at all don't vary. Cost variation, like costs themselves, increases as one raises the standards. The Duncombe and Yinger and Taylor/WestEd studies, twelve years apart, provided similar estimates of which districts within the state faced higher or lower costs of achieving target outcomes.

Table 7.1 shows the correlations across districts among all three studies. Basically, the correlations tell us the extent to which the differences in cost estimates across districts from one study to another are consistent. If they were perfectly matched, the correlation would be 1.0. Correlations near and above .80 show a quite strong relationship. The point here is that the evidence provided to the Kansas legislature over time, while varying in methods and evolving in terms of the quality of the data and methods used over time, remained quite consistent. The correlation between the A&M study and the Duncombe and Yinger study for all districts (treating each district as an equal unit) is .88, mainly picking up similarities in low enrollment–related costs. The correlation across large districts (with more than two thousand pupils) is also over .8, mainly picking up large districts that serve student populations needing higher costs to achieve specific outcome goals.

Correlations between the Duncombe and Yinger model and the alternative scenarios estimated by Taylor are also very high among large districts—but lower when small districts are included because of a quirk that both Jesse Levin and I discuss about the size adjustment in Taylor's model. But this chapter is already too long to explore this issue in detail!

TABLE 7.1   Correlations between cost study findings.

	All		All (Weighted)		Large (Weighted)	
	Duncombe & Yinger 2006	A&M 2002	Duncombe & Yinger 2006	A&M 2002	Duncombe & Yinger 2006	A&M 2002
Duncombe & Yinger 2006						
A&M 2002	0.88		0.73		0.82	
Taylor 2018 maintenance	0.77	0.76	0.87	0.56	0.90	0.67
Taylor 2018 scenario A	0.65	0.63	0.81	0.48	0.86	0.62
Taylor 2018 scenario B	0.65	0.63	0.83	0.51	0.88	0.65

Source: Author brief, *Gannon v. Kansas.*

SETTING OUTCOME GOALS

One final issue is how the use of an outcome-based modeling approach changes the legislative and judicial conversations around education costs and constitutional obligations. The Kansas constitution itself forces this conversation by placing setting of outcome standards in the hands of one government body and the financing of the system to meet those standards in the hands of another, while positioning the court to mediate any differences. As the cost studies found, higher outcomes cost more. While the state board has authority to set those outcome standards without worrying directly about the cost of meeting the standards, decisions about outcomes can't be made entirely in a vacuum. The point may come at which the state actually cannot afford to achieve the outcome standards set without consideration for costs. I don't believe that's the case in Kansas, and I believe the split roles with judicial mediation has thus far worked exceptionally well, especially when combined with cost model evidence.

That said, I would argue that the setting of standards, when using state assessments as tools to represent those standards, requires careful consideration of exactly what those standards mean and how they relate to the larger goals of the state's public education system. The Duncombe and Yinger study and the Taylor/WestEd study took different approaches to setting outcome goals. Further, in between those studies, the state significantly changed and renormed (raised the bar for) the assessments used for evaluating student proficiency. As the state had opined in its own defense at trial in *Montoy*, "Our education system is strong and is producing meaningful results for most children."[26] The Duncombe and Yinger cost model largely accepts the premise that the average Kansas school district is meeting the constitutional standard and thus sets out to estimate the costs per pupil for each district to be able to achieve what the average Kansas school district already achieves. Duncombe and Yinger describe the outcome target as follows: "We use the performance outcomes set by the Kansas State Board of Education for the three math exams, the three reading exams, and the graduation rate. To construct a performance standard comparable to the outcome index used in the cost model, we took a simple average of the standards for these seven performance measures."[27] This is certainly a reasonable approach to the extent that the court accepts that the average of current circumstances does in fact meet constitutional adequacy. It exists and is observable. And by applying this approach, the researchers will be able to specifically identify those school districts that do require more resources to provide their children with equal opportunity to achieve what the average child in the state already achieves.

The shortcoming of this purely relative, within-the-boundaries-of-Kansas approach is that it ignores the possibility that Kansas children may not be sufficiently competitive for the larger world around them, that the adequacy standard has no external anchor or validity. The relevance of this point is for the court to decide. But it is important to note that test developers at the University of Kansas had never really evaluated whether achieving so-called proficiency levels on their state assessments were actually predictive of achieving any larger goal, like being sufficiently prepared to succeed in college or the workforce. In studies conducted by the National Center for Education Statistics that mapped the relationship between state proficiency scores and the National Assessment of Educational Progress (NAEP), researchers found that Kansas's assessment standards were quite low at the time of the Duncombe and Yinger study.

Twelve years later, when Lori Taylor was setting outcome standards for her cost model, the state had adopted new assessments, with a much higher bar set for proficiency. Taylor's team relied (rightfully so) on guidance from the state board of education to use existing assessment and other data to set two different bars against which costs would be projected. These scenarios both set a graduation rate of 95 percent but identified different performance thresholds for student assessments (see table 7.2). Scenario A is described as "approaching on track for college readiness" and makes use of the percentage of students meeting Level 2 on the Kansas Assessment Program (KAP) ELA/ math tests. The more stringent Scenario B is described as "on track for college readiness" and uses the percentage of students scoring at Level 3 or above on the same assessments.[28]

Taylor and colleagues explain in their report that Scenario A approximates the expected performance levels under former assessments during the No Child Left Behind era.[29] These are the standards that were in place at the time of the Duncombe and Yinger (2005) and Kansas LDPA (2006) studies. Scenario B is based on Kansas's updated college- and career-readiness standards and uses a more stringent performance threshold.

To put the different standards used in the Kansas study into perspective, table 7.3 shows the following for fourth- and eighth-grade reading and math: (a) NAEP cut scores denoting proficiency, (b) Smarter Balanced Assessment Consortium (SBAC) proficiency cut scores equated

TABLE 7.2 Percentage of students meeting performance thresholds under two different scenarios.

	ELA (Level 2+)	Math (Level 2+)	ELA (Level 3+)	Math (Level 3+)	Graduation Rate
Scenario A	90	90			95
Scenario B			60	60	95

Source: Lori Taylor, Jason Willis, Alex Berg-Jacobson, Karina Jaquet, and Ruthie Carpas, *Estimating the Costs Associated with Reaching Student Achievement Expectations for Kansas Public Education Students* (Topeka, KS: WestEd, 2018), table 15.

TABLE 7.3 Relationship between NAEP, SBAC, and Kansas assessments, then and now.

Test	NAEP 2017	SBAC 2017	Kansas 2009	Kansas 2017
Reading Grade 4	238	224	186	228
Reading Grade 8	281	266	236	290
Math Grade 4	249	241	217	251
Math Grade 8	299	291	265	310

Notes: For mapping of Kansas 2009 standards to NAEP, see National Center for Education Statistics (2011).[30] For mapping of Kansas 2017 standards to NAEP, see Bandeira de Mello et al. (2019).[31]

to NAEP, (c) 2009 Kansas proficiency cut scores equated to NAEP, and (d) 2017 Kansas proficiency cut scores equated to NAEP. The SBAC assessments are tests in which cut scores are set with the more specific intent of representing college and career readiness. They are included here to show that cut scores for NAEP are somewhat higher than this goal.

The table shows that Kansas proficiency standards in 2009 were quite low, aligned with "basic" levels or below on NAEP and surpassed by most children in the state. Kansas's updated "college- and career-ready" assessment standards are more stringent, especially at the eight-grade level, and current proficiency rates are therefore much lower. Thus, raising the rates of children surpassing these higher standards (cut scores) is a more difficult task requiring a larger investment of resources. In turn, the projected cost of providing an adequate education under Scenario B was higher than for Scenario A despite setting a lower percentage of students meeting the more stringent 2017 standards (60 percent instead of 90 percent).

The high standards set in the Taylor study were the basis for the *shock effect* cost estimate that caught headlines when the study was released. But again, achieving lofty goals is more expensive than achieving more modest goals. The virtue of this method in this context is that it provides the direct connection between the two and forces parties—in this case, the state board and the legislature, with the court as a mediator—to determine just where the constitutional standard lies and how best to measure whether that standard has been met.

REFLECTING ON THE INFLUENCE OF COST EVIDENCE IN KANSAS

Not once has the Kansas legislature simply taken the recommendations of one the cost studies and adopted those recommendations in full as their new state school finance formula. Not once has the court simply said, "Adopt this!" or "Spend that!" But the various cost studies over time have provided benchmarks and the evidentiary basis for both the court and legislature to understand when and how much more funding might be needed, as well as where that funding should be targeted. The presence of such empirical evidence can, at the very least, help to bend existing policy toward equal opportunity and adequacy.

Many elements of the 2006 LDPA report appeared to influence what became SB549, a three-year school finance plan adopted in 2006. However, the funding formula that was ultimately adopted included a number of differences from the cost estimates. The translation of empirical evidence to policy is a complex and challenging process, particularly when deliberated among legislators. In the case of the post audit study, many of the changes occurred within the process overseen by LDPA, picking and choosing which elements to include or exclude and how to combine them into a policy recommendation. Although the A&M study had a less direct influence on policy, that study too involved some adaptation by consultants themselves to achieve more politically palatable recommendations—specifically, the choice to combine the lower successful schools base figure with the weights derived from professional judgment to reduce the overall sticker shock.

I personally have reservations about handing over to the legislature an already compromised set of estimates, which is why throughout the debate over SB549 in 2006 (the end of *Montoy*) and *Gannon*, I stubbornly made all of my comparisons against the cost predictions generated by Duncombe and Yinger themselves and not the policy recommendations provided by the Legislative Division of Post Audit. We can hope that unadulterated evidence will influence the state school finance system that comes out of the other side of the legislative process. By relying on that evidence, courts can help that happen. But surely that which comes out the other side as legislation will be imperfect. There's no need to introduce those imperfections on the front end.

Few other states have given as close consideration to cost analyses for guiding state school finance policy as Kansas, and no other state has done so with such an emphasis on outcomes and the costs of achieving those outcomes. Wyoming has continued a process of recalibrating its input-based model for changing needs and costs.[32] New York drives the base figure for its state aid formula on updates to successful schools estimates.[33] Of course, they've never fully funded the formula, and New York policymakers long ignored that it was researchers in their own back yard (at Syracuse) who pioneered the use of cost modeling like that applied in Kansas.

The institutional history and individual knowledge in the Kansas courts cannot be ignored. Sitting on the state's high court are Marla Luckert, who in an earlier era intuitively grasped the problems of building new school finance policies based on the averages of disparities that existed in the old policies, and Dan Biles, who brings to the table a unique combination of seeing the importance of linking the financing of schools to the desired goals of schooling and an understanding of the data and methods needed to accomplish this task. As I've listened to legislative deliberations in Kansas on these same topics, including questioning of Lori Taylor as she presented her findings, I've noticed a level of technical understanding that I simply don't see elsewhere, due largely to the fact that many of the same individuals have been grappling with these issues for years.

8

STABLE INSTITUTIONS, COMMITTED INDIVIDUALS

"We who believe in freedom cannot rest."

—Ella Baker, as quoted by Bernice Johnson Reagon
in "Ella's Song"

This chapter explores the persistent individuals and institutions that have over the decades accumulated deep knowledge and understanding of Kansas school finance policy—both technical and legal/constitutional, as well as, perhaps most importantly, the relationship between the two. Achieving and maintaining an equitable and adequate system of publicly financed schools is not a one- or two-step process. Rather, it's an ongoing multilateral tug of war—one that requires an informed referee. I recall being on an academic panel, discussing the role of courts in resolving school funding inequities, when the question was raised: "When does it ever end?" The implication is that it is somehow problematic if courts retain oversight for long or indefinite periods of time. The same logic was a mantra of the desegregation era—and when the courts stopped mediating, states and districts stopped trying, and progress came to a halt.

The reality is that constitutional rights persist whether in a moment of judicial oversight or not. If it takes persistent oversight to protect those rights, then so be it. As revealed within the pages herein, when the courts step back, it's only a matter of time before they are asked to chime in again. Those lapses in continuous oversight may lead to entire generations of students lost in the lag before bringing the next case full cycle. Persistence, either with continuous or discontinuous oversight, is critical to achieving and maintaining an equitable and adequate system of school finance.

This chapter is part soap opera and part lessons in good state governance, a bizarre mix to say the least. Kansas has some especially stable institutions, primarily because of how they're established in the state constitution. Kansas has a process of judicial selection and retention that reduces the extent to which the judiciary can be politicized. Yes, there are frequent attempts to displace politicized judges through the state's retention vote process, but those efforts have largely failed, and the high court in particular has been relatively stable over time, retaining a wealth of knowledge and understanding of school finance.

Similar stories may exist in other states, but one thing that still strikes me about Kansas is how a relatively small handful of key figures have rotated through critical roles in this long-running soap opera. Marla Luckert heard the *USD 229* case in the 1990s, later heard the *Montoy* and *Gannon* cases while on the high court, and now sits as the high court's chief justice, replacing Lawton Nuss. Dan Biles spent a few decades arguing before the court on behalf of the state board of education, framing the legal theory of the application of the state's constitution from a defendant's standpoint, only to later sit on the high court for the most recent round of school finance litigation. Others remain constant, including the ever-persistent team of Alan Rupe and John Robb; Schools for Fair Funding, continuously monitoring the status of the state school finance system; and Dale Dennis, who since the adoption of the education clause has overseen the implementation of that formula.

This chapter explores institutional structures and individual players, including legislators, lower court and high court judges, advocates, and the media. As noted, some individuals move across organizations over time. For example, state senator John Vratil, who was instrumental in several adjustments to the state school finance formula over time, also sat on the Vision 21st Century Task Force and served as legal counsel before the court on behalf of affluent suburban school districts in *USD 229 v. State*. Edward O'Malley served as a liaison for Governor Graves, traveling with the Vision 21st Century Task Force. He was later appointed to then reelected to a seat in the legislature. He resigned to head the Kansas Leadership Center and recently penned his own book, *What's Right with Kansas?*, while mounting an unsuccessful run in the Republican primaries for governor in 2018. Since the departure of Vratil from the legislature, recent school finance deliberations have involved legislators who were neophytes during the early *Montoy* years (Clay Aurand), as well as Melissa Rooker (who recently lost a reelection bid).[1] Finally, despite some recent significant departures (e.g., Topeka statehouse reporter Peter Hancock headed to Illinois), the media continues to play a role in informing the Kansas public about the history and complexities of the long-running school finance saga.[2]

LONGEVITY IN GOVERNMENT INSTITUTIONS

The Kansas State Board of Education in its current constitutional form has existed only since 1966. The state has had a significant school aid program for about the same time through a few iterations, from the School Foundation Act to the School District Equalization Act to the School District Finance Act and subsequent modifications. From the very beginning, one man, Dale Dennis, has overseen the implementation of those formulas. And for several decades, one man, Dan Biles, served as legal counsel to the state board of education. These two characters are among the most persistent forces in the Kansas school finance saga over time. And these are perhaps the two characters I appreciated least during my time in Kansas but now appreciate most in retrospect.

Dale

When I first encountered Dale, I was a cocky young academic who had just moved to Kansas from New York City. Well, Yonkers, actually, but my grad program was in New York City. At some point during my first year at the University of Kansas (1997–1998), I was informed that Dale would be speaking to the United School Administrators of Kansas conference in Wichita. I was new to the state, living in the Kansas City area and working at the University of Kansas in Lawrence, and hadn't really ventured out much yet. My colleagues suggested I make my way down to Wichita to meet some administrators and hear Dale talk about school finance. After all, he had already been running the show for thirty years. Knowing I had grown up in Vermont, my senior colleague George suggested that I might enjoy the drive through the Flint Hills on my way to Wichita. I had no idea what George was talking about, and still wasn't sure by the time I actually reached Wichita. (For those who haven't driven across Kansas, the Flint Hills don't really seem like hills per se, but more like an undulating ocean floor—which is actually how they were formed, as part of the vast inland sea, during the mid- to late Cretaceous period, as well as the very early Paleogene.)[3]

That day, I heard Dale speak about the current status of school funding and what administrators could expect in the coming year, including how to handle all of their reporting and filing requirements for their annual school district budgets. At least part of his talk was dedicated to warning administrators that another Bruce (Cooper, of Fordham University) from New York City was trying to pitch a new school accounting and reporting software tool that he (Dale) didn't think brought much value to the table. In retrospect, though I knew the other Bruce quite well, I now agree with Dale. To me, each time Dale mentioned New York City, all I could hear in my head was the Pace picante salsa commercial in which one of two cowboys turns to the other, reads the contents of the salsa he's eating, and says, "This stuff's made in New York City!"

I perceived Dale to be a typically parochial school administrator type, looking to maintain control over his own domain, disinterested in academic theories about equity and adequacy, and skeptical of carpetbaggers like me. That last part is certainly correct, but also appropriate. Up to this point in my new career, I had been studying states from the outside: I had written grad school papers on Connecticut and Wisconsin school finance, but I hadn't had much contact yet with the insiders actually running the numbers for their state. I did come to realize nearly two decades later, when preparing testimony for a Connecticut school finance case (2011), that the insider in the Bureau of Grants Management (Brian Mahoney, who retired in 2013) who had provided me with data for that grad school paper back in the 1990s was still there running the show. Unfortunately, Connecticut lacked many of the other key elements of the Kansas puzzle needed to achieve the same positive long-term school funding outcomes.

The primary skill I had honed early in my career was developing simulations of state school finance formulas in Microsoft Excel. And the Kansas School District Finance Act was relatively simple in that regard, as were Dale's spreadsheets of the formula, which were readily accessible on the state's website—if not in my first year in Kansas, soon thereafter (I believe they were accessible all along). At the time, I didn't realize either (a) how rare this was (that they were understandable and publicly accessible) or (b) the virtues of the relative simplicity of the formula.

I also didn't realize at the time that a lot of states—especially smaller states—have their own Dale. That one person who, in a spreadsheet only that person understands, lays out the calculations of the state school finance formula. Often, that means one person is gathering the data on which the formula is built, taking the letter of the legislation that describes the formula, and putting that into column calculations to distribute what in many cases amounts to hundreds of millions or even billions of dollars. In different states, these people play marginally different roles and may answer to different branches of state government. And in different states, the degree of transparency into and accessibility of their source data and formula runs varies.

What do I mean by *source data*? Well, calculating the amount of funding any school district should receive from the state depends on specific data from each local school district, including the numbers of enrolled children, numbers of children in each category to be provided with additional "weighted" funding, and so on. There should be publicly accessible and official, audited, and uniformly collected versions of these numbers, on which the calculations are based. There should also be accurate measures of each district's taxable property wealth to determine what share of funding will be raised by the required local tax rate and what share will be distributed as state aid. A lot of money gets shuffled around based on these measures and data, which get multiplied by large sums of taxpayer dollars.

In Kansas, Dale's role involved preparing those final "runs" of the formula each year at the close of the legislative session (or once a plan was passed into law), and it also involved running any interim proposals along the way. Dale's run of a proposal was considered the official run of the proposal. The Kansas Legislative Research Department (KLRD) would provide supplemental information. Even if a legislator simply wanted to know how an idea would play out—a formula change—they'd ask for an official Dale run of the numbers before sharing the result with their colleagues. I worked with representative Ed O'Malley on a few of these in the mid-2000s; we would play with our own simulations over lunch at St. Louis Bread Co. (now Panera Bread) in Overland Park, and once we had a clearer idea of what we were looking for, Ed would request that Dale provide an official run.

Dale also served as a single point of data and information access for any outsider, including plaintiffs and their expert witnesses. As an institution, the Kansas State Department of Education, under direction of the state board of education, maintained (and still does to this day) a website that includes a lengthy archive of Excel spreadsheets for the School District Finance Act.[4] At the same time, the Kansas Legislative Research Department maintained an extensive archive of documentation on the formula and changes to the formula over time.[5]

By contrast, in New Jersey, I have to file an open public records request each year just to get the underlying measures on which the formula is calculated and the results of those calculations (not provided with actual calculations). The state publishes only the final numbers, or end points of the calculations, for public access.[6] Other states with which I've worked recently have single separate worksheets for each district—not publicly accessible and not compiled as a statewide formula—and a single Excel workbook, involving layers of linked spreadsheets that have evolved over time into a bizarre Rube Goldberg device, lacking any documentation and being handed off from one internal source to another but never publicly posted.

During my time in Kansas, Missouri also maintained a pretty good website of archived school finance data. I also had begun consulting on the development of simulation tools for the State of Texas and realized that Texas had very comprehensive data. What I didn't realize is that many other states had far less than these three. Texas, perhaps due to its size and complexity, also had multiple entities checking each other on aid formula calculations: the Legislative Budget Board had the final official word (and simulation), and the Education Agency reconciled its numbers with its own model. (I'll talk about each one more later in this chapter.)

It seems that in the 1990s through the mid-2000s, as web-based access to data and documents became easier and internet access became more ubiquitous, more became available. But strangely, as technologies continued to advance in the decade since, many states actually removed much of their accessible information on their state school funding formulas in particular. They've created searchable query tools to see individual districts or schools, but limit access to underlying data and all but prohibit outright access to the actual calculations. Very few other than Kansas provide an archive of downloadable formula worksheets (for all districts) with active calculations embedded. That's actually a big deal (even if just a super geeky big deal).

Dale kept a clean and impressive archive. He had the trust of school district officials that his calculations were on the up-and-up and the trust of legislators, who could rely on Dale to give a test run of even their most wacky ideas. Of course, there are upsides and downsides to placing so much responsibility and ultimately power in the hands of a single person. Dale didn't work alone running the numbers. During my time in Kansas, Dale's staff included Veryl Peter (who was still there as recently as 2018). I upset a few people a few years back when Dale came under fire for how he had been implementing the calculations for district transportation aid. There were always a few legislators who would take aim at Dale or the state board of education, but they were clearly in the minority. In January 2018, an audit revealed that these calculations had distributed an overpayment of $45 million in transportation aid, as reported by Celia Llopis Jepsen.[7] For context, that's over a total aid package of $4 billion, or about 1 percent for the time period.

With no intent to criticize Dale personally, I pointed out the potential problem: "'We're talking about shuffling millions and millions of dollars,'" Rutgers University education professor Bruce Baker said. 'It's a lot of money to be subject to however one person has decided to organize the columns in their spreadsheet.'"[8] I also pointed the reporter to Texas for comparison purposes: "Texas legislative budget experts run annual school funding calculations. The state education department checks the results independently. 'Any discrepancies that arise are brought to light and reconciled,' Lauren Callahan, a spokeswoman for the Texas Education Agency, wrote in an email. That's good policy, Baker argues, because translating finance formulas from law to math is tricky, with risk for controversy. Agencies are often stuck with deciding arcane details that can make a difference—such as when to round numbers or in what order to factor in various data."[9] Interestingly, while Kansas had no formal interagency process for agencies to check each other's math, the issue came to light because another Kansas agency, headed by an experienced individual—Scott Frank—caught the problem: "'We had some inkling' it needed to be checked, auditor Heidi Zimmerman said. She said that head auditor Scott Frank saw an education department spreadsheet that sparked his concern. 'So,' she said, 'he gave us a heads-up that he thought something was not quite right.'"[10] A number of folks were not happy with me for raising the concerns I voiced in this article, seeing it as an attack on Dale. This is perhaps when I realized just how widely respected and appreciated Dale was.

In the spring of 2020, Dale retired after fifty-three years. Scott Frank has moved on to another state (Washington). I often wondered, What happens when Dale retires? This guy ran the state's school finance system for fifty years, and in effect is the only person ever to run it! Upon his retirement, the media tributes poured in.[11] In his own words: "I've tried to be as helpful as possible," Dennis said of his career. "If you can make a difference and help a school district—which will help students—it's all about that. It's about making a difference."[12] One can hope that the legacy Dale has left behind can be not only maintained but improved upon. That the state will continue to make transparent runs of the state school finance formula publicly available. That the state board, in collaboration with the legislative research division (KLRD) and Division of Post Audit (LPA), will continue to provide responsive and accessible reports and analyses of the state school finance system. All three of these governmental entities have played a critical role over time and have been exceptional in maintaining integrity and independence.

Dan Biles

Dan Biles also wasn't my favorite Kansan the first time I met him. My first encounter with Dan Biles was when I was retained as an expert witness by Alan Rupe and John Robb in the *Montoy* and *Robinson* cases; Dan Biles was the legal counsel for the state board of education—the "other side," shall we say. I was still the outsider. By the spring and summer of 2003, I had prepared two obscenely long and technical reports (185 pages for *Montoy*; 160 for *Robinson*) on all the things I thought were wrong with the Kansas school finance formula. I was not one for brevity or clarity back then, or use of plain language. As Senator Vratil had shown me in our time on the task force, I did not have much skill for precision in word selection. I was developing my understanding of Kansas school finance but did not have sufficient respect for the volume of institutional knowledge possessed by those who'd been through all this for more than a decade already.

Then there's the adversarial context of school finance litigation to consider—and it was this adversarial context that first shaped my opinions of Dan Biles. As a general matter, and at this point in Kansas history (2003), it was in the state board's interest (and its legal position) that the courts should leave determining what's right for school finance to the state board and the legislature. Having the court intervene restricts the board's flexibility. It was the state board's official position that SDF-QPA established a reasonable, workable, and, most importantly, constitutional framework, even if the board would have preferred the legislature to fund it more robustly. It was the plaintiff's position, that of Schools for Fair Funding, represented by Alan Rupe and John Robb—that there were significant problems with the formula that could only be fixed with court intervention. And in the federal case, primarily, some of those problems were rooted in racial discrimination. I got the feeling at many points in time that at least some state policymakers really took this claim personally and considered it an unwarranted and mean-spirited attack. After all, Kansans prided themselves on the fact that the state had been founded as a free state. Dan Biles did not seem amused by this line of argument. It also seemed that Biles, Rupe, and Robb, while cordial with each other, had

developed a bit of a rivalry before my arrival, and I was being thrown
right into the middle of it all: an east coaster elitist carpetbagger calling
Kansans racist.

Prior to going to trial, experts submit their reports. Then, still
prior to the trial, the opposing counsel gets some time to depose those
experts on their reports—to better understand the claims involved, the
data used, and how the analyses were conducted. This is the *discovery*
process in litigation, which allows for all sides to get as complete a picture as possible of the arguments and evidence being presented. It also
gives each side the opportunity, between deposition and trial, to find
ways to poke holes in the work of the experts on the other side. And
it gives lawyers the opportunity to get experts to say certain things, to
make certain admissions on the record, providing a chance for the lawyers to revisit that transcript at trial to reinforce those points or high-
light contradictions. For example, it would be important for lawyers in
my deposition to get me to agree that I did not believe that the racial
disparities were created intentionally (except that I had come to realize
they probably were!). It's especially important to understand where all
of this fits in the long game of complex litigation of this type. It's also
why, at times, I even question how useful this adversarial process is for
improving state school finance systems. I didn't understand much of
this the first time I encountered Dan Biles.

Thankfully, depositions in federal cases are limited to seven hours
(though I learned much later about running out the clock). Sadly, I
had to be deposed by Biles in both the federal (*Robinson*) and state
(*Montoy*) cases, and Dan Biles was far more concerned about detail and
thoroughness than time. These were my first depositions as an expert
in school finance—my first depositions of any kind, in fact. Luckily
for me, Dan Biles worked out of a law firm in Overland Park, down
the road from the KU branch campus and not far from where I lived. I
spent what felt like days on end across the table from Biles, with Alan
Rupe and John Robb by my side, an additional attorney representing the state from the attorney general's office, and a court reporter.
Actually, it *was* days on end. Really. What I learned was (a) that Dan
Biles was a stickler for detail, (b) that Dan Biles was persistent in his
pursuit of the answer he was looking for, and (c) that Dan Biles knew,
exceptionally well, the substance—technical and legal—and history of

the case(s). As a stickler for detail, for what seemed like days on end, perhaps in his desire to understand every word, every number, and every claim in my reports, Dan Biles walked me line by line, page by page through my two voluminous reports. He then walked me line by line through spreadsheets of numbers (on the three hundred or so Kansas school districts at the time) to ask about apparent discrepancies. It was like a weeks-long root canal.

What I've learned from this in retrospect was just how unique Dan Biles's approach was. Yes, it was conducted in the usual adversarial context. Yes, his goal was to win. But his goal was also to legitimately understand the nature and details of the critique and underlying data. I was perhaps fooled on this occasion into believing that cases I would become involved in thereafter, in other states, would also be focused on substance and detail and would be conducted with professional and personal respect. While that has been true in some cases, the *Montoy* and *Robinson* cases, as handled by Biles, were unique. In fact, by the time Biles had moved to the high court in *Gannon*, the state's own approach had shifted to personal attacks and theatrics over substance.

Especially problematic are cases in which, on one or both sides, the actual trials are carried out by hired gun attorneys from the outside. It doesn't matter how good they are or how much they may pretend to care about the issue. It becomes more about "winning" and the adversarial process than about informing and improving policy. I recall testifying in one case in which the counsel for the plaintiffs had been the lead counsel for big tobacco, and the counsel for the defense had spent much of his career defending segregation (or at least fighting against school desegregation orders). Both were and are exceptional trial attorneys and learned about or knew the substance of the issue better than many. But it was still more about the game and winning. Often these trials, with leading roles played by hired guns, are heard by judges who themselves are new to the substance of school finance and to cases involving the requirements of their state education articles. I've seen lower court judges new to these issues write favorable rulings for plaintiffs, but base those rulings on misunderstandings of history and precedents, leading the rulings to be overturned by the high court and leaving severely underfunded districts serving low-income and minority children with no subsequent recourse.[13] (A more thoughtful high court would have remanded the case, clarifying the application of the relevant precedents for the lower court.)

I can only imagine that Biles's measured and thoughtful approach in *Montoy* was similar to that he had taken in the earlier period of the *USD 229* and *Mock* cases. Based on a 1996 interview with Biles, reflecting on Bullock's prejudgment of the flaws in SDEA, Charles Berger explains: "Faced with the uncomfortable prospect of defending such a law, Dan Biles, attorney for the State Board of Education, was more relieved than anything else when Judge Bullock issued his opinion on points of law before trial, which cast serious doubt on the constitutionality of the SDEA. 'I just did you a big favor,' confided Judge Bullock to him afterwards."[14] From the outset, Biles, like Dale, was interested in good policy. From the moment of my first encounter with him, he believed, or at least was willing to argue, that SDF-QPA was a reasonable framework that didn't require judicial intervention. But it was also Biles, with the history of the two previous rounds of litigation behind him, who could see the fraught future of Kansas schools if the court failed to recognize the independent roles of the state board and legislature and permitted the legislature to set the spending bar wherever it desired.

It took Biles's experience and large-picture, long-view game view to lay this out for the court on which he would eventually sit. Biles had, in effect, helped add clarity to plaintiffs' arguments for why it was important that the legislature include the state boards' outcome standards in determining the costs of meeting its own constitutional obligation. It was Biles's experience advantage that mattered over the remaining counsel arguing on behalf of the state for complete deference to the legislature and the legislature alone.[15] Biles, Rupe and Robb, and multiple members of the sitting court held shared knowledge of Kansas's constitutional history and Kansas school finance. They also shared a law school alma mater (Biles, Rupe, Robb, Luckert, and McFarland were all Washburn grads), which perhaps infused some common understanding of Kansas constitutional history. Increasingly, I wonder just how much this may matter. Biles's institutional knowledge, constitutional understanding, and lived experience would go on to shape the court's reasoning in *Gannon*, and perhaps whatever comes next.

Legislative Division of Post Audit

In about half of states, including Kansas, the position of state auditor is appointed.[16] As described back in chapter 2, the Division of Post Audit is governed by a Legislative Post Audit Committee. The division conducts performance audits intended to address "the following types of questions:

- Is the program or agency complying with the law?
- Is the program or agency accomplishing what it is supposed to accomplish?
- Could the program or agency operate more efficiently?
- What might happen if the agency or program were changed?"[17]

Those audits may be requested (as described on the LPA's own website) by the Legislative Post Audit Act:

> The Legislative Post Audit Act (K.S.A. 46-1114) gives our office broad authority to conduct audits of state and local agencies, as well as certain private individuals and organizations. Those auditable entities include:
> - any state agency
> - any local government agency that receives funding from or through the state
> - anyone who receives a grant from the state
> - anyone who contracts with the state
> - anyone who is licensed or regulated by any state agency
>
> Although state law gives us authority to audit any state agency, in practice we do not directly audit the legislative branch of government because we would not be viewed as impartial and independent.[18]

One might imagine that such an entity could be highly politicized and as a result experience substantial turnover over time. Certainly, some of the reports and findings by LPA have created political firestorms, including the 2006 cost study. I was first alerted to the fact that Kansas might have something a bit unique going on in this division—in terms of technical capacity and independence—when I first engaged with its staff and leadership just prior to that process. Bill Duncombe reinforced this when he told me at a later point, after completing his work, that he was thoroughly impressed by LPA's technical capacity and research integrity.

Given that public education spending is the largest single chunk of state and local expenditure in Kansas, or most states, it stands to reason that LPA has conducted numerous audits on K–12 school finance over the years.[19] In the wake of the transportation aid controversy, I, among others, argued that perhaps LPA could play a more consistent role in reconciling state aid runs, though ongoing reporting of this type is beyond LPA's stated purpose.

Despite, or perhaps because of, LPAs delicate positioning in the political structure, it has been able to maintain relatively consistent staffing and leadership, at least in recent decades. Scott Frank, who departed in 2018, had been with LPA for eighteen years and had been head auditor since 2010, surviving significant shifts in legislative political balance. Although Frank was not around anywhere near as long as Dale, like other long-time government employees in Kansas, he carried with him an institutional knowledge and history that was of immeasurable value—allowing him, for example, to catch the transportation aid problem in 2018.

LONGEVITY ON THE HIGH COURT

I've not been able to uncover much research literature on the longevity of state high court judges or the composition of state high courts. There exists a body of literature on election, appointment, and retention procedures and constitutional requirements for high court positions. Fifteen states have nonpartisan, elected state supreme courts; four have partisan elections; and two have partisan elections followed by a retention election.[20] It should not go unnoticed that the two in this last category—Pennsylvania and Illinois—happen to be persistently two of the least equitable states in the nation on school funding, home to two of the least well-funded major urban districts in the nation (Philadelphia and Chicago), and two states where school funding challenges have largely been avoided by courts declaring those challenges to be nonjusticiable political questions. Pennsylvania does have a current case moving forward as of the time of the writing.

A study of state high court judges published in 1984 found the following: "Based on a study of 694 judges who sat on 16 selected American state supreme courts between 1900 and 1970, this article finds that the appellate judiciary was drawn from a variety of legal and political backgrounds rather than from any single career line. The judges came from both non-elite and elite law schools. About half had no substantial lower court judicial experience. Over one-third had been public prosecutors, another third had held other elective political office, and only a small minority had practiced in multi lawyer big-city law firms."[21] Table 8.1 provides a list of Kansas Supreme Court Judges, from Kay McFarland to the present court. A few features are notable. First, most recent Kansas high court judges have been appointed by Democratic governors. Further, even though the current chief justice was appointed by a Republican governor, Graves (a moderate), she has been a staunch advocate for equitable and adequate school funding and upholding the constitutional requirements. While I downplayed Sebelius's role as governor in providing any strong support for school finance remedies, Sebelius's most significant contribution may be her appointments of Beier, Biles, and Rosen to the high court.

Several state high court justices held long terms on the court, with Luckert presently at seventeen years (two rounds of school finance litigation on the high court and one in the lower court), and Nuss and Beier also having held seventeen-year terms before retiring. Although Kansas judges are put up for retention votes, none have actually been removed through the process. Robert Davis, who was briefly the chief justice upon McFarland's retirement, also served seventeen years. Moritz's term was shortened by her appointment to the tenth circuit federal court. Allegrucci and Crocket sat on the court for twenty years, and Kay McFarland tops them all in recent decades with twenty-two years on the court.[22] McFarland was also among the minority being appointed by a Republican governor, and though her approach to judicial intervention on school finance was indeed more conservative than many of her peers on the court, she was not entirely averse to holding the legislature to their constitutional obligation, though she may have pressured the court to step back prematurely at times.

Nearly all of the justices listed in table 8.1 attended law school within Kansas, and the majority attended Washburn. This was one of those Kansas things that I really didn't think too much about when I was there. It didn't seem like most lawyers I encountered—other than Rupe, Robb, and Biles—had attended Washburn. But clearly the influence of Washburn in Kansas politics was a force to be reckoned with. Of course, not every Washburn graduate was a stellar advocate for human rights. For example, Westboro Baptist Church founder Fred Phelps also received his JD from Washburn. Justice Harold Herd's biography notes that early in his tenure on the court, he was among those who voted to disbar Phelps.

Most importantly, from the perspective of this book, the Kansas Supreme Court has maintained a political balance and membership stability that has permitted consistency in ruling on matters of the state's education article, applied to school funding. Throughout the past few decades, the courts' memberships have also included justices with intimate knowledge of the complexities of school finance policy— most notably, Biles and Luckert. As I mentioned earlier, the provision of elementary and secondary public schooling is one of the major responsibilities of states and the largest share of total state and local expenditures in most states. It stands to reason that just as legislators need to become familiar with these issues, state high courts and relevant district courts need judges who understand the educational rights of citizens. But these issues are complex, are boring to many, and don't necessarily launch politicians or judges into the national spotlight like more contentious issues, including immigration, gay marriage, and abortion—or even the teaching of evolution. But within the boundaries of Kansas, in the Kansas media, and in Kansas's political races, positions on school funding matter.

LEGAL ADVOCATES

Alan Rupe and John Robb have been fighting the school finance fight in Kansas since the *Mock* case, with their primary nemesis at the time being Dan Biles. Both are deeply embedded Kansans, but they're very different individuals in many regards. Alan Rupe is a big city (Wichita)

TABLE 8.1 Kansas Supreme Court justices of the modern era (since McFarland)

Name	Term Dates	Chief Justice	Total Years	Prior	Law School	Appointed By
Marla J. Luckert	13 Jan 2003 to present	17 Dec 2019 to present	17	District court	Washburn	Graves (R)
Eric S. Rosen	18 Nov 2005 to present		15	District court	Washburn	Sebelius (D)
Dan Biles	6 Mar 2009 to present		11	Attorney	Washburn	Sebelius (D)
Caleb Stegall	5 Dec 2014 to present		16	Appeals court	KU	Brownback (R)
Evelyn Z. Wilson	24 Jan 2020 to present		1	District court	Washburn	Kelly (D)
Keynen "KJ" Wall Jr.	3 Aug 2020 to present		1	Attorney	KU	Kelly (D)
Nancy Moritz	7 Jan 2011 to 29 Jul 2014		3	Appeals court	Washburn	Parkinson (D)
Lee A. Johnson	8 Jan 2007 to 8 Sep 2019		12	Appeals court	Washburn	Sebelius (D)
Carol A. Beier	5 Sep 2003 to 18 Sep 2020		17	Appeals court	KU	Sebelius (D)
Robert L. Gernon	13 Jan 2003 to 30 Mar 2005		2	Appeals court	Washburn	Graves (R)
Lawton R. Nuss	17 Oct 2002 to 3 Aug 2010	3 Aug 2010 to 17 Dec 2019	17	Attorney (first in over twenty years)	KU	Graves (R)
Edward Larson	1 Sep 1995 to 4 Sep 2002		7			
Robert E. Davis	11 Jan 1993 to 12 Jan 2009	12 Jan 2009 to 3 Aug 2010	17	Appeals court	Georgetown	Finney (D)
Bob Abbott	1 Jan 1990 to 6 Jun 2003		13			
Frederick N. Six	1 Sep 1988 to 13 Jan 2003		15			
Donald L. Allegrucci	12 Jan 1987 to 8 Jan 2007		20	District court	Washburn	Carlin (D)
Tyler C. Lockett	11 Feb 1983 to 13 Jan 2003		20	District court	Washburn	Carlin (D)
Harold Herd	18 Mar 1979 to 11 Jan 1993		14		Washburn	Carlin (D)
Kay McFarland	19 Sep 1977 to 1 Sep 1995	1 Sep 1995 to 12 Jan 2009	22	District court	Washburn	Bennett (R)

Source: https://www.kscourts.org/About-the-Courts/Supreme-Court/Historical-Listing-of-Supreme-Court-Justices.

employment lawyer who has made the rounds with various major regional and national law firms over the years. As his current firm bio explains:

> He receives ongoing national attention and recognition for his successful prosecution of cases relating to the constitutionality of the funding of K-12 public education, and received the Demetrio Rodriguez Champion of Educational Justice Award from Education Law Center, Inc. for "years of outstanding lawyering and lobbying and perseverance in the face of many obstacles, including brash insults" for his work on a series of lawsuits on behalf of Kansas school children. The lawsuit culminated in a court ordering the State of Kansas to increase spending on public schools by nearly $1 billion each year from 2006-2009, and approximately $440 million in 2014 and 2015.[23]

John Robb, by contrast, is a small-town Kansas lawyer (from Newton) in a family law firm. Robb is a third-generation lawyer in the town, partnered with his brother to take over the family firm from his father. He's been practicing law in the family firm since 1978. The family firm's website maintains an impressive archive of district and high court rulings on school finance, plus a complete archive of trial exhibits from *Gannon v. Kansas*.[24]

A unique feature of the Kansas school finance saga is that each of the cases brought along the way, since *Mock*, have been brought primarily by Rupe and Robb and have been argued at trial and to the high court by Rupe and Robb. Since *Montoy*, those cases have been backed by Schools for Fair Funding.

Other states have had persistent legal advocates and advocacy organizations backing them, but few with the persistence of Rupe, Robb, and Schools for Fair Funding. Again, history and knowledge matters. So too do resources. New Jersey is perhaps most similar in this regard in that the Education Law Center of New Jersey and lead counsel David Sciarra (and previously Paul Trachtenberg) have been engaged in several sequential rounds of school finance litigation in the state. For a period, New York State's Campaign for Fiscal Equity cases were similarly pursued by Michael Rebell. One thing that all of these plaintiffs have in common is that they are invariably and substantially outgunned financially when bringing these cases. Alan Rupe and John Robb, like Sciarra and Rebell, have attempted to balance the playing field by helping to organize alliances and advocacy efforts around them. States are still much bigger entities with much bigger budgets to spend, defending their "right" to not spend on actual schools and children. There is a delicate balance to be achieved between access to financial resources and maintenance of sufficient local knowledge and history. Rupe and Robb kept it small—and for them, small was effective.

Although their alliance of backers has grown, the value of their own persistence and their knowledge of the issues and the history behind them cannot be understated. This is another one of those things I'm not sure I fully appreciated at first, or until recently. I assumed that bigger guns—big-time civil rights lawyers with big budgets—might fight a better case. I've certainly worked with small-shop, low-budget, highly competent and passionate firms taking on cases well beyond their financial capacity to carry the fight, and this is unfortunate.[25] But sometimes, as is the case with Rupe and Robb and Schools for Fair Funding, smaller and more local has been advantageous. In part, everyone knows everyone—counsel on both sides, judges on the lower and high courts—and that may lead to more civil discourse.

ADVOCACY ORGANIZATIONS

The importance of advocacy organizations—in particular, Schools for Fair Funding—cannot be overstated. Schools for Fair Funding was founded in 1997 in part to explore and frame what would become the *Montoy* and *Robinson* cases.[26] Founding member school districts included those that had been represented by Alan Rupe and John Robb in *USD 229 v. State* and *Mock*. This included Newton, home to John Robb's law firm.

Schools for Fair Funding also engaged from relatively early on (1998) in lobbying efforts to influence changes to the School District Finance Act. Achieving long-run, successful school finance reform requires multipronged efforts. Litigation may be one necessary piece of the puzzle, but ongoing legislative lobbying and education on key issues is equally important. The court merely rules on the question of constitutionality, but the legislature is ultimately tasked with coming up with a reasonable fix. Achieving a legislative solution without court intervention—to head off judicial intervention—is a lot quicker than addressing the issues through litigation and waiting for a legislative response to a high court order.

Recall that Bullock convened his preruling meeting in 1991, and by 1992 Finney had convened a task force. In its veto session, the legislature had passed the School District Finance Act. By contrast, Rupe and Robb filed *Montoy* in 1999 and got a lower court ruling from Judge Bullock in December 2003 and a high court ruling in January 2005. The summer special session of 2005 led to a partial adjustment to the formula. In the summer of 2006, the legislature adopted a more substantial three-year plan, which never quite made it to full implementation. This was seven years after the case was filed, with full implementation to be achieved by 2009, a decade after the case was filed. During this time, a generation of Kansas children attended constitutionally inadequately funded schools from first to tenth grade. The same thing would happen all over again for the generation of first graders entering Kansas schools in 2009. So, advocacy organizations and preemptive efforts can matter.

Further, these advocacy organizations can help inform legislators during the remedy phase—that is, help legislators understand the nature of the problem and plaintiffs' claims and how to design remedies to resolve those claims. A second organization, one focused more on political action than litigation, was founded during the early *Montoy* years: Kansas Families United for Public Education, now referred to as Kansas Families for Education. This group was based in the Kansas City area and has specifically focused on state and local political races and candidate endorsements. As described on its website: "Kansas Families for Education has been endorsing candidates from Governor to local school boards since 2002. Endorsements are published shortly before Advance Voting begins. Kansas Families for Education endorses in Federal, statewide and legislative races throughout Kansas. Due to our limited resources as a volunteer-driven organization, KFE only endorses candidates in local school board elections for districts serving at least 10,000 students."[27] I recall seeing the organization's signs pop up around neighborhoods in Johnson County in the early 2000s. I believe, though I lack empirical evidence to this effect, that this organization has been significantly responsible for making sure that school funding is a top political platform issue, at least for legislators running for office in the Kansas City area, and that its backing may have helped at least some get elected.

The general public doesn't always pay close attention to down-ballot races. But school finance depends largely on state legislative action. It's those state house and senate elections that determine the future of school funding—specifically, the amount and the distribution of that funding in most states. Governors carry variable weight in the process, depending on the state. Having organizations that put a spotlight on these state races and explain their implications for the quality of public schools matters, even if the focus is on localism and self-interest.

Both of these organizations have political action arms, with Schools for Fair Funding also backing litigation. Kansas Families for Education is now nearly twenty years old and Schools for Fair Funding twenty-three. Other states have organizations analogous to both Schools for Fair Funding and Kansas Families for Education. In Texas, the Equity Center has backed several rounds of litigation and has existed since 1982.[28] The Equity Center focuses on information dissemination and training pertaining to understanding Texas School Finance and the equity concerns of its constituents (six hundred of the state's over one thousand districts). The Equity Center has also long operated its own simulation of the Texas school finance formula in order to evaluate equity implications of policy proposals before they are adopted. Legal challenges in Connecticut were long backed by an organization more analogous to Schools for Fair Funding: the Connecticut Committee for Justice in Education Funding (CCJEF).[29] New York litigation was backed by the Campaign for Fiscal Equity, and the Alliance for Quality Education continues to advocate for funding equity and adequacy in New York.[30] New Jersey has its Education Law Center, which has engaged in litigation strategies, information dissemination, and political advocacy for decades.

LEGISLATIVE LEADERSHIP

Legislatures and legislative leadership tend to have higher turnover rates than state high courts or individual advocates. Political winds change. Seats get flipped. Legislators come and go, and with them deep knowledge of complex policy issues. I have found over time that it tends to be a relatively few or even a single legislator in a given state that develops a high degree of mastery of understanding for how the state school finance system works. They know the trade-offs within the system and how to tweak or bend the system to best serve the needs of their constituents. These are the legislators who have a strong intuitive understanding, if not a deep mathematical understanding, of how the many moving parts of a state school finance system work and interconnect. Developing that understanding takes time. But it also puts state legislators who have developed that understanding in a position of power among their peers. State legislators have many complex policies to deal with, from insurance regulation to Medicaid expansion to K–12 and higher education funding. K–12 funding is certainly one of the biggest ticket items in terms of the state budget. It's also one of the clearest opportunities to bring money back to one's district—either in terms of additional funding for schools or in terms of local tax relief.

From the 1990s through 2013, John Vratil had become that individual who knew the inner workings and nuances of the School District Finance Act. Prior to running for the legislature, he had fought the formula as lead counsel for *USD 229*. Vratil learned, in particular, how to make the formula work for Johnson County by finding ways to quietly increase the ability of those districts to raise additional local taxes. Overlapping and outlasting Vratil, but in the house rather than senate, individuals like Clay Aurand (house education committee chair) have taken the lead on school funding issues. Aurand, who had served on his local school board, is also a Republican and perhaps more fiscally conservative than Vratil. Aurand served one house district from 1995 to 2013 and another from 2016 to 2019.

I met Aurand on one occasion in the mid-2000s after I had been toying with simulation options for school funding solutions with freshman representative and moderate republican Ed O'Malley. O'Malley had spent some time sitting through my KU school finance class, and not even for credit. We felt that we had come up with a workable solution that would fold some of the existing local option tax rates back into the base funding to reduce the total cost to the state of bringing general funds into compliance with the court order in *Montoy*. Ed's first instinct was that we needed to run it by his somewhat more conservative colleague, Clay Aurand, so we did. Our plan didn't end up going anywhere, but it gave me a bit more insight into the process and into individuals in Kansas at the time.

Aurand made news in 2018 when he helped to push through a modified restoration of Kansas teachers' due process rights, which had been eliminated in 2014.[31] This particular action is illustrative because it was not under the pressure of a judicial oversight or order, although it was eventually linked with a plan to boost school funding.[32] In the effort, he appeased neither side of the issue. Aurand has taken a similar approach on school finance, backing a degree of responsiveness to the court's demands rather than resisting outright, but including some signals of resistance in the process as a political compromise. Aurand was among the Republicans in the legislature who voted to rescind Brownback's tax cuts in 2017: "'I'm a supply-sider,' Aurand said. 'But the most important thing about supply-side (economics) is getting the tax rate right. It's not about raising or lowering taxes, it's about getting it right. And in no case is zero the right amount for a certain segment when others are paying.'"[33] Having been in the legislature since 1995, Aurand has become one of the legislature's leading keepers of knowledge on the technicalities of the school finance system.

By contrast, over much the same period, Colorado progressive Democrat Mike Johnston, who worked in the Obama administration, pushed through a teacher evaluation bill rigidly tying tenure status and removal to student test scores and generally weakening teacher employment protections.[34] Johnston ran for governor in 2018 against a similarly "progressive" Democrat with education policy interests, Jared Polis. Polis won and eventually became governor of Colorado. But neither Polis nor Johnston took as strong—or effective—a stand on funding public education as Kansas Republicans from Aurand to Johnson County's Melissa Rooker.[35] And Colorado school children and teachers continue to suffer the consequences.

Colorado provides the starkest contrasts with Kansas on education policy and finance at many levels. Colorado's courts have refused to involve themselves in mediating the conflict between that state's educational responsibilities and the state's restrictions on increasing taxes and government spending, adopted by statewide referendum in the early 1990s.[36] Meanwhile, on the national stage, Colorado is certainly perceived as far more liberal than Kansas. It's also wealthier, with more capacity to fund a robust public school system. And leading politicians in the state, like Johnston and Polis, proudly wear the moniker of progressive Democrats and are recognized on the national stage. Perhaps partly due to the constitutional and judicial context of Colorado, neither has taken a strong stand on school funding equity or adequacy, preferring instead to chip around the edges for revenue-neutral options under the headings of *innovation* and *efficiency*.[37] If anything, both at various points in their careers have pushed the narratives that schools simply need to be more efficient with what they have, that school choice and expanded charter schooling can serve as a substitute for adequate funding, and that changing employment protections for teachers can solve the "bad teacher" problem. Although these were national platform issues for progressives during the Obama era, Kansas legislators across the political aisle plugged away at seemingly more mundane questions of providing equitable and adequate financing for their schools. I'll lay out the vastly different results of these efforts in chapter 9.

STATE AND LOCAL MEDIA

For a subject many might find less than riveting, state and local media in Kansas have dedicated countless headlines and pages to the school finance saga. It's my impression that the dedication of these outlets to thorough and accurate coverage has led them to being more than passive onlookers. State and local media have informed and engaged the public and likely contributed significantly to civic engagement on school funding in Kansas.

But across the nation, local newspapers are dying. Print media in particular is suffering. Many local television and print media outlets are being snatched up by national media conglomerates and running larger and larger amounts of nonlocal content. In a 2018 article, Hays and Lawless raised concerns: "To the extent that the local news environment continues to deteriorate—a likely scenario as the industry continues to struggle—observers' concerns about political engagement in localities across the United States appear very much justified."[38] One particular recent study found that "cities served by newspapers with relatively sharp declines in newsroom staffing had, on average, significantly reduced political competition in mayoral races."[39] There is at least some evidence to also suggest that political satire can influence participation, particularly on issues observers find personally important.[40] Regional, state, and local media have played a critical role in keeping school finance on the minds of the Kansas public and voters of all ages. A significant body of academic research in political science links political participation to engagement with local media—in particular, local print media.[41]

A handful of individuals have covered the story for decades for the state's major news outlets. They—Tim Carpenter, Scott Rothschild, Peter Hancock, and even cartoonist Richard Crowson—bring to their stories the institutional knowledge and history of other key players, like Rupe, Robb, Biles, and Luckert. Newcomers in the *Gannon* era included Celia Llopis Jepsen. During many of the heated exchanges addressed in this book, these individuals were there in the rooms to cover them. They were at the trials, at the state supreme court hearings, and in the legislative hearings, including the special summer session of 2005, meeting with and asking questions of legislators behind closed doors. Their access was far more extensive than my own and in many cases spanned far more years.

Kansas spans a lot of land area, and the drive from one corner to another can take up to eight hours. The interests of constituents in Garden City and Dodge City are often substantially different from those of residents in Johnson County or Wichita, so it seems especially important that many parts of the state had their own viable local media outlets sharing localized versions of the story. Topeka is not sufficiently "local" for Garden City. The drive from Topeka to Garden City is slightly longer than the drive from Philadelphia to Boston. You've likely noticed citations throughout this book pointing to articles in the *Garden City Telegram* and *Salina Journal*, in addition to the state's larger outlets like the *Wichita Eagle* and *Topeka Capitol Journal*.

Maybe the coverage is strong because there just isn't that much else to report in Kansas, creating an opening for in-depth reporting on school finance, however bland. I myself have a stack of copies of newspapers from the 2000s with massive front-page headlines all about school finance, court rulings, cost studies, special sessions, and more. I've not seen the same extent of coverage elsewhere, to my recollection. Certainly not in New Jersey, which splits itself between New York– and Philadelphia-centric news coverage. I have been increasingly impressed by more specialized and alternative media outlets, including Chalkbeat's coverage of national and state issues (where Chalkbeat has established state or local outlets), CT Mirror's (ctmirror.org) in-depth coverage on inequality in Connecticut (including school funding), and VT Digger's (vtdigger.org) in-depth coverage of politics and policy in Vermont. But these more specialized, nonprofit media outlets may play to insiders more than they inform and engage the broader public.

Another unique thing about Kansas is how interest in the school finance saga has spanned media. Perhaps the least amount of coverage was on local television news, which operates more in the moment; even when a major ruling was issued at 10 a.m., a tornado warning at 4 p.m. would bump school funding from the evening news. Print media, including satirical cartoons, was the primary source of coverage. If I had enough out-of-pocket cash while writing this book, I'd have bought the rights to as many as I could of Crowson's cartoons like the one in chapter 1—each of which conveys a different moment in time in the Kansas school finance saga. Go figure. Not one, not a few, but multitudes of political cartoons capturing the Kansas school finance saga. And then, on top of it all, there was the role of *The Pitch*, along with local alternative radio personalities who got their kicks out of taking down Kansas legislative shenanigans, including school funding! Perhaps I'm misguided, but it seems to me that consistent local and state media focused on the Kansas school finance saga, with experienced and knowledgeable reporters, may have made a difference in keeping the public engaged and keeping the pressure on.

2020: THE END OF AN ERA AND UNCERTAINTY FOR THE FUTURE

Kansas enters this next decade in a precarious position. Like at the end of *Montoy*, the legislature has adopted a significant scaling up of base funding to be phased in over the next several years. Like at the end of *Montoy*, as soon as that process began, the state's economic condition became uncertain—this time due to a global pandemic. Kansas school districts had been expecting another $120 million dollar payment in 2020–2021 toward the phase in.[42] Hopefully, Kansas and Kansans will ride out this storm as well, relying on the institutional structures outlined in this chapter to help the system once again self-correct.

Some things have changed; most notably, a collection of key individuals with extensive institutional knowledge and history have departed. Dale Dennis retired after fifty-three years of running the show (and the numbers) on school finance. Scott Frank departed post audit in 2018. The structures around them and their legacy of transparency, consistency, and independence remain. Among other things, those district-by-district aid runs and formula calculations are still posted on the state website. Carol Beier also retired, but her seat will be filled by an appointee chosen by a Democratic governor.[43] Nonetheless, those will be big shoes to fill. With Luckert as chief justice and Biles on the court, significant institutional knowledge of school finance has been retained.

Finally, there has also been some reshuffling of media. Local NPR outlets seem to be providing more coverage these days. The *Kansas City Star* has faced financial woes similar to other print outlets, but I've heard (and found) less on smaller Kansas-specific outlets. Long-time statehouse reporter Peter Hancock has moved on to cover Illinois. Much to my dismay, my last regular connection to Kansas (other than my 913 cellphone number), the radio station I had intended to stream while writing this book—the station that introduced me to Tony Ortega of the *Pitch* and kept me in touch with ongoings in Kansas—went to national syndicated format in the fall of 2020.

To the best of my knowledge, however, Schools for Fair Funding, Alan Rupe, and John Robb aren't going anywhere anytime soon. That may be just what Kansas schools need to ride out this next storm.

9

WHEAT STATE WISDOM

Lessons from Flyover Country

"Ad Astra per Aspera."
(To the stars through difficulties.)

—John James Ingalls, Kansas state motto, 1861

In this final chapter, I ask: What did all of this accomplish? Is Kansas really better for it all? Are there lessons to be learned from Kansas for other states, including politically "bluer" states where legislatures are presumably more amenable to equitably and adequately funding public schools and to the progressive taxation required to accomplish this goal? To some extent, the impetus for writing this book was drawn from my realization one day, a few years back, that Kansas really does stand out among its peer states in its region. I had been very critical of Kansas during my time there. While states in many parts of the country and in particular those neighboring Kansas significantly disinvested in their public schooling systems over the past ten years, Kansas, despite the Brownback era setbacks, has remained ahead of the pack. Given the severity of the Brownback tax cuts, this is quite an amazing accomplishment. Kansas certainly isn't a national leader on any major measure of its K–12 schools. But it is without question better off than it might have been had all the forces considered in this book not come together and persisted over the past several decades. School finance reform does not happen for only a moment in time, as a legislative response to a singular judicial action. It's a process. A long, arduous process involving persistent multilateral forces.

A map like the one in figure 9 .1 was the signal for me of the Kansas difference. It's subtle but it's there, much like Kansas itself. It just caught my eye one day. The map comes from a project that was eventually published with interactive maps through the Century Foundation.[1] I know from years of my work developing indicators to describe the equity and adequacy of state school funding systems that Colorado and Oklahoma are both train wrecks, though it's Arizona that comes in last on most measures. Colorado and Oklahoma are two of the least well-funded states for K–12 schools in the nation, with among the least competitive wages for teachers. Missouri was always less equitable, outside of desegregation funding that had, for a period in the 1990s, been targeted to Kansas City and St. Louis.[2] That boost in funding has long since faded, and the state has slid from above average to the lower half among states, both on equity (forty-seventh place) and adequacy (twenty-sixth place) measures.[3]

Figure 9.1 shows, in darker shades, school districts where spending is more adequate to achieve national average outcomes, based on nationally equated state assessment scores in reading and math. Dark-shaded districts are those spending above what they need to achieve national averages. Lighter-shaded districts are those spending below what they need to spend. You can clearly see the western (Colorado) and southern (Oklahoma) borders of Kansas and, somewhat less clearly, the eastern (Missouri) border. Kansas is doing a bit better than each of these neighbors!

Nebraska, its own story for another day, blends in more with Kansas in the map, having generally more adequate funding. Wyoming has its own interesting story worth telling, and one that includes significant attention to cost studies tied to court rulings, as discussed in chapter 8. Wyoming also has very few children to serve (about eighty thousand, similar to Vermont) and has had access to vast natural resources for generating revenue. Kansas, even more than Oklahoma and certainly

FIGURE 9.1 Map of gaps between current (2018) spending and spending needed to achieve national average outcomes

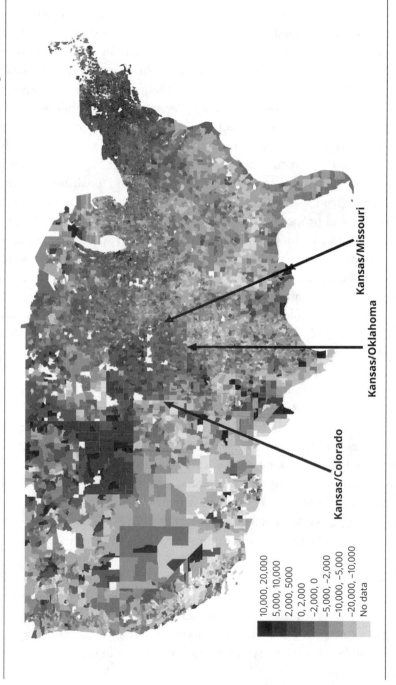

Kansas/Missouri

Kansas/Oklahoma

Kansas/Colorado

10,000, 20,000
5,000, 10,000
2,000, 5000
0, 2,000
−2,000, 0
−5,000, −2,000
−10,000, −5,000
−20,000, −10,000
No data

Source: Prepared by author; see https://tcf.org/content/report/closing-americas-education-funding/.

more than Colorado, is a state that gets painted as *the* caricature of American conservatism—from Brownback to Kobach to Fred Phelps. Playing to this national sentiment, *Wichita Eagle* cartoonist Richard Crowson penned a tune in 2015 titled "Kansan in Brownbackistan," with this opening lyric: "We don' like schoolin' here in Kansas, education is something we abhor."[4] An outsider might have assumed that the Brownback tax cuts, which certainly slammed K–12 public schools in Kansas, would have driven school budgets to nearly nothing—certainly much worse than Colorado, and maybe even worse than Oklahoma. But that's not the case, in part because Kansas entered the Brownback era in relatively good position. While Kansas's current position has yet to fully recover from Brownback, initial steps have been taken: rescinding the tax cuts and proposing substantial increases to base aid in the funding formula. Sadly, the COVID-19 crisis has interrupted that progress.

This final chapter provides contextual data illustrating that Kansas school funding is in fact *less bad than it might otherwise have been*, in comparison with national trends and with neighboring states. Also, in contrast with Colorado in particular, Kansas has largely avoided significant "anything but money" education reform distractions. These include dramatically expanding charter school enrollments—instead of funding—or adopting test-based teacher evaluations to "fire bad teachers"—also instead of funding. These policies were popular among self-anointed progressives during a period that ran parallel to the Brownback tax cuts and were often pitched as substitutes for, rather than possible complements of, equitable and adequate funding. To my frustration while working in Kansas, the state always seemed a bit averse to outside, disruptive influence. But that same Kansas skepticism and stubbornness may be one reason for how and why Kansas has stuck to basics on K–12 schools—focusing on equitable and adequate funding first and largely side-stepping popular (if not outright faddish) and national "reform" movements.

This chapter concludes with lessons for other states from Kansas. If the constitutional framing, government structures, individuals, and advocates in Kansas over the years have served to stabilize and strengthen the position of public schools in that state, Kansas may provide a template for other states—blue, red, and purple.

LONGITUDINAL LOOK AT KANSAS
SCHOOL FINANCE REFORM

Here, I'll provide a quick graphic rundown of longitudinal trends in school funding in Kansas from 1993 to 2018, using data from the School Finance Indicators Data System, a project originally funded by the William T. Grant Foundation and currently in collaboration with Matt Di Carlo of the Shanker Institute.[5] By 2018, even after the Brownback tax cuts, Kansas ranked sixteenth in *effort*, twentieth in *spending for high-poverty districts*, and twenty-second for *progressiveness of state and local revenue*. Kansas ranked worst on competitiveness of teacher pay (fortieth). That is, on most measures, Kansas was still above the median state.

Figure 9.2 shows the inflation-adjusted (adjusted for employment costs over time) per-pupil spending of Kansas school districts by poverty quintile. Especially during the period of persistent judicial pressure and legislative action, while Governor Sebelius was in office and during *Montoy*, school district spending climbed. It climbed fastest in districts serving higher-poverty student populations, peaking around

FIGURE 9.2   Per pupil spending by poverty quintile

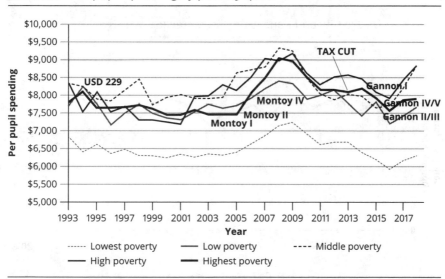

Data Source: School Finance Indicators Database, district-level data panel.

2009 as the final *Montoy* remedies were being phased in, but right before the economic collapse of the great recession. During the *Montoy* period, school funding became significantly more progressive in Kansas. But when the recession hit, much that had been gained was lost, with higher-poverty districts taking a larger hit than lower-poverty ones because of their greater dependence on state aid. That said, because additional local revenue raising is fixed to (capped at a percent above) the underlying general fund formula, low-poverty and higher-wealth districts also took a hit.

Figure 9.3 takes a closer look, focusing specifically on two of the state's high-need districts—one in each corner—and comparing their spending to the average of those around them during the period. The position of Dodge City changes the most—particularly in the early *Montoy* period, even before the lower court ruling. More than shifting the relative position of these districts, judicial pressure during the *Montoy* period elevated the system as a whole, largely maintaining the relative position of the districts (as shown in figure 9.2). That said, equity and progressiveness was maintained, if not marginally improved, while the system was lifted.

FIGURE 9.3   Dodge City and Kansas City vs. statewide averages

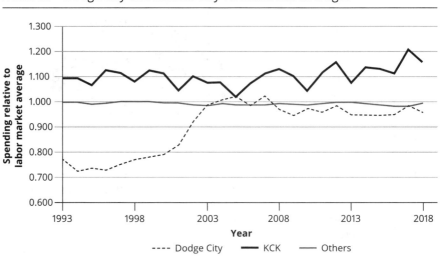

Data Source: School Finance Indicators Database, district-level data panel.

Figure 9.4 shows how Kansas's per-pupil spending levels stack up among its immediate neighbors during this period. From 1993 to about 2008, Kansas and Nebraska lead the pack, with Kansas school funding escalating especially during the *Montoy* period. First due to the recession and then due to the Brownback tax cuts, Kansas falls behind Nebraska but remains ahead of the others and well ahead of Colorado and Oklahoma. Nebraska uniquely weathered the recession and did so because Nebraska school funding continues to rely more heavily on property taxes. Property tax revenues tend to be more stable during economic fluctuations. Heavy dependence on property taxes can yield substantial inequity—as was the case in Kansas for years prior to *Mock*—and has done so in Nebraska. In this case, however, heavy reliance on property tax revenues buffered revenue losses for Nebraska school districts. Further, Nebraska has at times adopted creative strategies, including regional revenue sharing in the Omaha metro area, to mitigate those disparities.[6] (We'll save the long, contentious story of how this plan came about for another day.)

Table 9.1 shows the inflation-adjusted and regionally cost-adjusted per-pupil revenue by source for districts by poverty quintile in the five

FIGURE 9.4   Spending levels over time

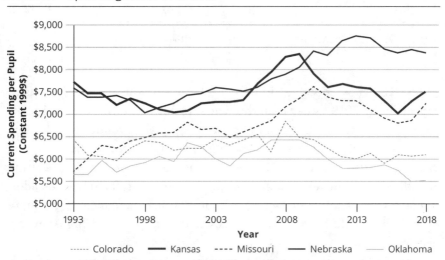

Data Source: School Finance Indicators Database, district-level data panel.

TABLE 9.1   Kansas and neighboring states' revenue by source for low- and high-poverty districts, 1993 and 2018.

Year	State	Poverty Quintile	Local	State	Federal
1993	CO	1, lowest	$4,480	$3,005	$175
1993		5, highest	$4,996	$2,638	$639
1993	KS	1, lowest	$4,007	$3,276	$283
1993		5, highest	$2,886	$4,578	$656
1993	MO	1, lowest	$3,568	$2,416	$180
1993		5, highest	$3,246	$4,887	$873
1993	NE	1, lowest	$4,475	$2,841	$501
1993		5, highest	$5,176	$3,549	$936
1993	OK	1, lowest	$2,287	$3,287	$210
1993		5, highest	$2,066	$3,737	$706
2018	CO	1, lowest	$3,773	$2,796	$276
2018		5, highest	$2,211	$4,747	$798
2018	KS	1, lowest	$2,903	$4,931	$351
2018		5, highest	$1,617	$6,434	$950
2018	MO	1, lowest	$4,615	$3,203	$359
2018		5, highest	$4,027	$3,690	$1,154
2018	NE	1, lowest	$5,336	$2,458	$323
2018		5, highest	$6,597	$4,391	$1,385
2018	OK	1, lowest	$2,988	$2,492	$396
2018		5, highest	$2,307	$3,312	$1,034

Data Source: School Finance Indicators Database, district-level data panel.

states. The most notable differences between Kansas and Nebraska, especially by 2018 (other than the wheat to corn ratio), is that Nebraska districts are substantially more reliant on local revenue. In addition, local revenue per pupil is actually higher in high-poverty districts than in low-poverty districts in Nebraska. Whether the underlying taxation of individuals, households, and property owners is fair requires additional investigation! On average, Nebraska also manages to be more progressive in its funding differences between low- and high-poverty districts.

Figure 9.5 compares the progressiveness of per-pupil spending across the five states. *Progressiveness* is measured as the ratio of predicted

FIGURE 9.5 Spending progressiveness over time

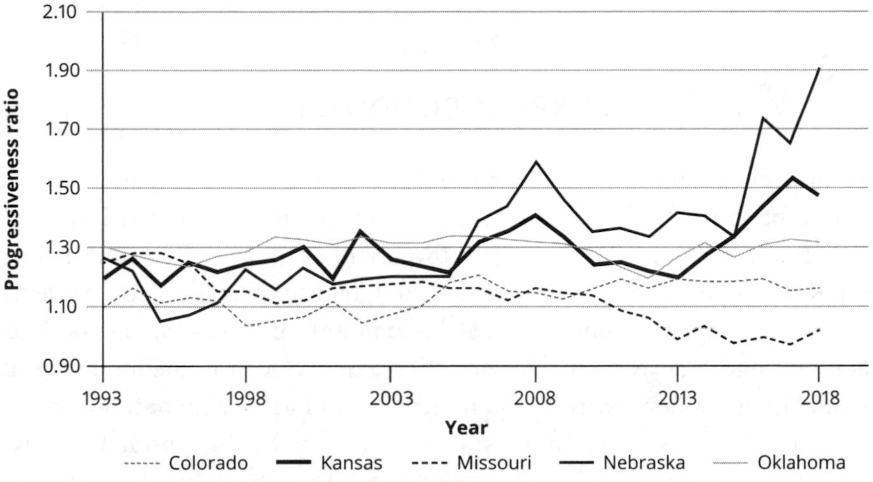

Data Source: School Finance Indicators Database, state-level data panel.

per-pupil spending for a high-poverty district compared to that of a low-poverty district, controlling for differences in regional labor costs and differences in district size. A progressiveness index of 1.2 would indicate that high-poverty districts—all else being equal—spend about 20 percent more than low-poverty districts. This information has to be considered along with the spending levels shown in figure 9.4. For example, figure 9.5 shows that Oklahoma has been relatively consistently progressive at around 1.3 over time—at times doing as well as Kansas. But the average spending in Oklahoma has been about 20 percent lower than the average in Kansas over the same period. In other words, in Oklahoma, low-poverty districts have very little funding—next to nothing at all—and higher-poverty districts have marginally more than next to nothing. Colorado's funding is not only low but also relatively flat with respect to child poverty concentrations.

Kansas and Nebraska led the pack in 2008 and again in the most recent years of data, despite the Brownback tax cuts and their disproportionate impact on high-poverty districts. Their funding is both higher *and* more progressive than that of their neighbors. Again, Kansas is no national model of excellence or progressiveness, and it comes in second to Nebraska in its own region. But Kansas also is no Colorado or Oklahoma!

CURRENT CONDITIONS

So how does Kansas stack up in the national picture on key indicators? Going back to the analyses underlying the map with which I started this chapter, figure 9.6 compares the share of personal income spent on K–12 schools for each state (x-axis) to the average gap between current per-pupil spending and the amount of spending needed to achieve national average outcomes (y-axis). Because the underlying model involves comparisons against the cost of achieving national average outcomes, about half of all states are above the line and half below. About half, on average, spend more than enough to be average, and about half fall short. I often cynically joked while in Kansas that the state's motto ought to be "Kansas? Eh . . . We're above average!" And it is, for the most part. It's true in figure 9.6, at least. On average,

FIGURE 9.6   Effort and funding gap

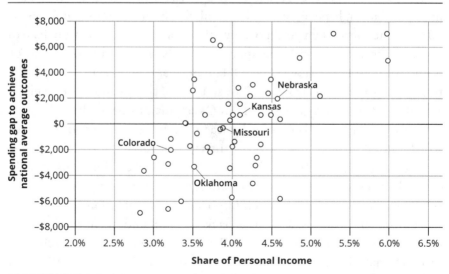

Data Source: School Finance Indicators Database, state-level data panel.

Kansas school districts spent slightly above what they'd need to spend to achieve national average outcomes in 2018.

Despite the Brownback tax cuts, Kansas is also still at about average effort in funding its schools. It spends a relatively average share of its economic capacity on K–12 schools. Kansas has not taken the path of Colorado or Oklahoma. Colorado and Oklahoma look worse than Kansas on nearly every measure of their states' education systems largely because they fail to make the effort to fund those systems. Instead, they've done anything and everything but.

Table 9.2 is drawn from data from the same study, using our National Education Cost Model (NECM) and comparing funding gaps to outcome gaps (differences from national average) using the Stanford Education Data Archive. Table 9.2 summarizes specifically the share of children in each state who attend districts where (a) spending is at or above targets and outcomes are at or above average and (b) spending is below targets *and* outcomes are below average. Some children in each state attend districts that do not fall clearly into these two categories, but most do. Colorado and Oklahoma top the list in terms of shares of children in underfunded and underperforming districts. Over half of children in Oklahoma and nearly a third in Colorado attend districts in these categories.

TABLE 9.2   Percent of children affected by spending gaps and outcome gaps in Kansas and neighboring states.

	Spending Above Target and Outcomes Above Average	Spending Below Target and Outcomes Below Average
Oklahoma	22.24	52.44
Colorado	47.72	29.03
Missouri	43.43	28.98
Kansas	58.12	13.24
Nebraska	65.89	0.58

Data Source: Author's estimates using data from B. D. Baker, A. Edwards, and H. Potter, "National Cost Model," in *Closing America's Education Funding Gaps* (Century Foundation, 2020), https://tcf.org/content/report/closing-americas-education-funding/; and S. F Reardon, A. D. Ho, B. R. Shear, E. M. Fahle, D. Kalogrides, H. Jang, and B. Chavez, "2016 District Standardized (NAEP Equivalent) Reading and Math Assessments, Grades 3–8," *Stanford Education Data Archive*, v. 4.0, Stanford Libraries, 2021, http://purl.stanford.edu/db586ns4974.

Costs to achieve average outcomes are higher where child poverty is higher. Among these states, Oklahoma has the highest child poverty rate, around 20 percent, and Missouri is second, around 16 percent. As such, their costs to achieve the target outcomes are somewhat higher than for the other three states, where child poverty sits around 12 percent. Colorado is the highest-income state among this group.[7] So, in Colorado, the cost of closing these gaps is smaller, more comparable to that of Kansas and Nebraska, and the state's capacity to close these gaps is greater—yet it chooses not to.

No doubt, defenders of my attack on Colorado will be quick to check the data and point out that Colorado does in fact have higher average scores on the National Assessment of Educational Progress than Kansas or Nebraska.[8] This is because Colorado has higher average income and many students attending school in more affluent school districts. It's just a richer state. And despite its low spending across the board, many Colorado children are doing okay on national assessments. Yet amazingly, despite the state's wealth and lower costs to achieve excellence, more than twice as large a share of children in Colorado compared with Kansas attend underfunded districts with outcomes below national averages.

Figure 9.7 shows a measure on which Kansas typically does quite poorly on the y-axis: the competitiveness of teacher salaries with respect to those of nonteachers holding the same degree levels and at the same age. Kansas's more robust funding has most often translated into more robust staffing ratios (quantities of staff) than into more competitive wages. As with figure 9.5, effort matters. States that put more effort into funding their schools also tend to have more competitive wages. Even here, Kansas does better than Colorado, Missouri, and Oklahoma, the latter of which comes in second (from the bottom) only to Arizona.

RESISTING SCHOOL REFORM FADS

During the Brownback administration, the Kansas legislature gutted teacher tenure protections. It did, however, partially restore those protections a few years later. Kansas does have a charter school law—but

FIGURE 9.7 Salary parity ratio at age 35

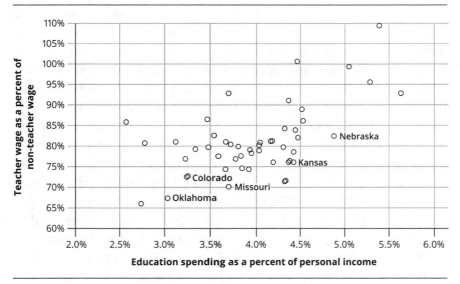

Data Source: School Finance Indicators Database, state-level data panel.

Kansas's charter school law is scorned by national charter school advocacy groups favoring unlimited charter school growth, expanded pathways to authorization, and limited government regulation and oversight of those pathways or operators. Using these preferences as guideposts, Kansas charter school law ranks forty-fourth among forty-five states with charter laws, ahead of only Maryland.[9] Colorado ranks as having the second-best charter school law in the country, implying that, somehow, the adequacy of funding for any schools (including charters) is inconsequential.

Perhaps because Kansas was governed by a conservative Republican when these policies were favored by a "progressive" Democrat's presidential administration, Kansas resisted the urge to rapidly adopt and expand policies that might otherwise be preferred by conservatives—like expanding school choice by use of private providers and weakening public employment protections. It certainly jumped on the latter, but only marginally chipped away at the former.[10] Kansas had already been resisting faddish reforms in earlier periods and continues to resist today. For example, Kansas also resisted adopting common standards and assessments from outside providers, relying instead on the testing center at the University of Kansas to develop and operate its state assessment system.[11] One might view this last preference as parochial and territorial, and perhaps to an extent it is. But it's my impression that KU's testing center has maintained a degree of independence and integrity comparable to that of the Legislative Division of Post Audit over time. Although early Kansas assessments set a relatively low bar for proficiency, as discussed in chapter 8 and reflected in the 2018 cost study, the new bar has been raised substantially and is well aligned with national consortium assessments.

Obama-era policy preferences were perhaps most clearly laid bare in the Race to the Top (RTTT) competition, which was framed in terms of getting states to adopt *innovative* strategies to improve their public school systems. Innovation, however, was narrowly defined as including three key components: (1) expanding the share of children in charter schools and loosening regulations on those schools, (2) adopting teacher evaluation legislation that would tie teacher evaluation to student test scores and requiring the removal of employment protections for low-performing teachers (on those measures), and (3) adopting Common Core and College-Readiness Standards and assessments designed to measure proficiency on those standards. These were the preferred progressive reforms du jour. Promoting equitable and adequate school funding was particularly unsexy in that moment—a moment peaking around 2011 and framed by Obama's education secretary, Arne Duncan, as "the new normal," a period when school districts were just going to have to learn to do more with less.

Because Kansas's RTTT application made no big promises on the first two components, reviewers systematically slammed that application.[12] A substantial percentage of the overall available points were allocated to these very specific subcategories. Again, the premise of RTTT was to promote innovation, but only as long as these were your proposed innovations. Kansas wasn't really buying it, so it really didn't have much chance at winning RTTT funds. But I'm not sure it cared. In this interstate education competition, Kansas scored below average (330 total points against an average of 359). By contrast, Colorado was a darling of the reviewers on the same measures (see table 9.3)![13]

TABLE 9.3 Race to the Top scores on teacher evaluation and charter schools.

	CO	KS
(D)(2) Improving teacher and principal effectiveness based on performance	48	32
(F)(2) Ensuring successful conditions for high-performing charter schools and other innovative schools	40	19
Total (All Areas)	**410**	**330**

Source: See https://www2.ed.gov/programs/racetothetop/phase1-applications/phase1-scores-detail.xls.

Figure 9.8 shows the rate of charter school enrollment growth for Kansas and its neighbors. While Colorado has continued to drive education spending and the share of economic capacity spent on K–12 schools into the ground, the state has increased the share of children enrolled in charter schools to over 12 percent—much higher than surrounding states. Missouri charter enrollments stand around 2 percent, with modest growth over time. Since 2010, charter enrollment has begun a rapid climb in Oklahoma, which sits near the bottom in terms of effort and spending, like Colorado. Oklahoma has followed the lead of Colorado rather than that of Kansas.

The irony of this approach—increasing the number of schools and fragmenting the provision of schooling while decreasing spending—is that a more fragmented system in fact costs more to operate than a less fragmented one, even if increased competitive pressures across the sectors may lead to small improvements in efficiency, offsetting some of those costs. More importantly, though, and more simply, providing high-quality schools—be they district-operated, privately managed, assigned, or chosen—requires adequate funding. Providing choices and charter schools doesn't negate the need for additional funding. It may in fact exacerbate that need. And even if one might make the argument that some schools and districts should learn to do more with less—that school districts can spend less and the kids will be just fine—that's a hard argument to make in Colorado and Oklahoma, which rank seventh and twelfth from the bottom among states on effort and eleventh and twelfth from the bottom on adequacy (Kansas, meanwhile, is fifteenth from the top).[14]

FIGURE 9.8   Share of students in charter schools over time

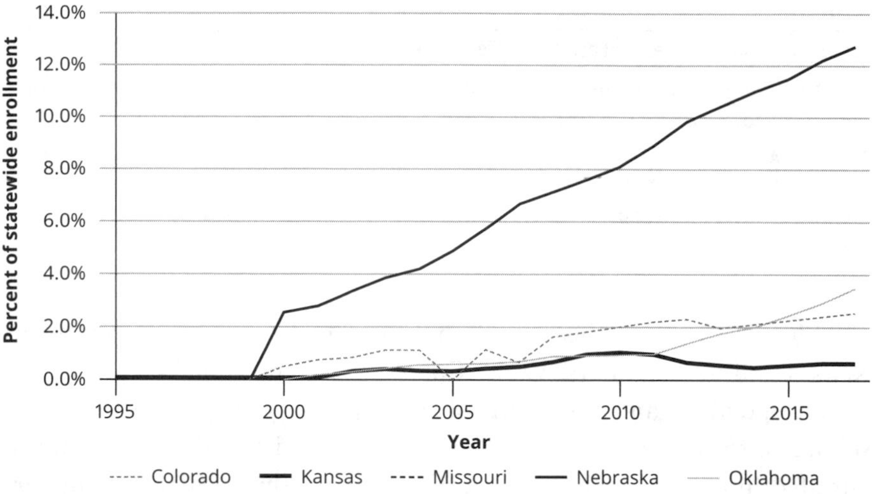

Data source: School Finance Indicators Database, state-level data panel.

A notable feature of Arizona's education system, one of the few states that fares consistently worse than even Colorado or Oklahoma on nearly every indicator in our database, is that Arizona has an even larger—in fact, the largest—share of children attending charter schools. This is not to suggest that charter schools or charter schooling in and of themselves are the problem, the drain on the financial resources of the district schools. But rather, that the political preference to view reforms like expanded charter schooling as a substitute for equitable or adequate funding can lead to an overall degradation of school quality. Kansas policymakers, perhaps because they've been forced by their courts, advocates, and the media, have kept their eye on the ball—at least, on the ball that's in play: the school finance ball!

WHEAT STATE WISDOM

What can other states learn from all of this? What great wisdom can be passed along from the Wheat State? Perhaps first and foremost, constitutions need not be viewed as static documents. State constitutions can be amended. The Kansas constitution was reshaped significantly regarding the structure of the judicial branch and the education article in the second half of the twentieth century. Constitutional amendments that have perhaps inflicted the greatest damage on the quality of public schools have also been adopted in recent decades, from California's Proposition 13 in the 1970s to Colorado's Taxpayer Bill of Rights (TABOR) in 1992.[15] In those cases, voters statewide approved strict limits (albeit in very different forms) on taxes and spending, which ultimately led to stagnating public school spending.[16] A California ballot initiative in November 2020, which would have chipped away at the restrictiveness of Proposition 13 by revaluing and separating commercial and industrial properties, failed.[17] Kansas legislators similarly have tried on a handful of occasions to weaken the constitutional requirements of Article 6 and they are trying once again in 2021.

Now may be a time to think boldly. If the goal is to affect permanent change in states, to reposition and reprioritize public education, then significant changes—including constitutional amendments—are worth considering. But I would argue that it's not necessarily enough to chip away at the edges, for two reasons. First, amendments that chip away at the edges, making more subtle changes, may be harder to explain to the public and thus harder to pass by statewide referenda. It just may not be sexy enough or simple enough to try to sell the general public on split roll reassessment of property values—certainly not as easy as selling the public on "we'll limit your property taxes in perpetuity" (saying nothing of what that does to your schools). While the operative phrasing and structure of Kansas's Article 6 isn't that simple or obvious, it still may provide a framework, and one that is sufficiently simple and sellable:

1. Obligate (*shall*, not *may*) the legislature and governor to provide suitable funding for schools.
2. Establish an independently elected entity to develop and set goals and standards for the school system.
3. Perhaps extend the same logic all the way through higher education governance.

Call it a children's bill of educational rights, if you will. At least in Kansas, the separate self-executing constitutional authority of the independently elected state board of education and legislature and the court's willingness to enforce those roles and mediate their disputes have been critical to keeping the state's public schools from falling off the funding cliff.

Constitutional amendments to restructure high court appointments and retention may be a harder sell, but they're worth consideration. Most importantly, models that achieve greater stability, leading to accumulated institutional knowledge on complex issues the court may have to revisit time and time again—like school funding—seem important. So too, for that matter, does professionalism. Kansas's approach of (a) having minimum professional requirements and (b) involving the professional legal community in generating a short list of potential nominees has served the state well, even where judges are subjected to a more political process for periodic retention.[18] States with the most purely political processes for appointment and retention of high court judges, like Illinois and Pennsylvania, have to date been abject failures in upholding the rights of children to equitable and adequate school funding. Constitutional rights are intended to be more permanent than political whims, preferences, and campaign platforms.

Most states have some form of state auditor or comptroller, but few in my experience have a division analogous to the Legislative Division of Post Audit in Kansas, which spends so much time on issues pertaining to education funding and school district financial management. Because the activities of the post auditor in Kansas are at the behest of legislators, it is *legislative interest* that drives that distribution. The charge of such an agency might be modified to include a series of ongoing annual or biennial evaluations. Other states, like Texas, have dedicated divisions within their education agencies and serving their legislatures that play similar roles. What I would suggest broadly is that (a) there must be at least one independent, state-operated research and analysis division that holds these responsibilities, and (b) that division should have staff with expertise in and dedicated to research on the state's public education system and its financing. It stands to reason that if a state were to adopt a constitutional structure governing education like Kansas's Article 6, the legislature would want to have its own independent research arm (or two) and the state board would have its own, providing a system of checks and balances between the two branches responsible for K–12 schooling in the state. Kansas did not formally have a system of checks and balances in place for the implementation of the school funding formula, and thus it was by chance that experienced state auditor Scott Frank caught the transportation funding problem in the education department's spreadsheets. A more formal mechanism like the one in Texas, where the Legislative Budget Board and Texas Education Agency each run the numbers and then reconcile any differences in underlying data and calculations, is preferred.

Further, public accessibility to all of this information, the data needed to perform the calculations underlying the state school finance system, the calculations as implemented, should be transparent and publicly available, enabling the public and advocacy organizations to see, understand, and critically evaluate how things are being done. Kansas has maintained an extensive archive of downloadable funding formula runs available to any and all who wish to geek out on this kind of thing.

I would argue that one additional assignment, perhaps also with responsibility split between legislative research (a post audit–like entity) and education department research, is the periodic evaluation of the costs of achieving the outcome standards adopted by the state board of education. Simply declaring that the state board sets the standards and the legislature must fund them creates an imbalance of power favoring the state board. Clearly, the state board can't just set whatever standard it wants in a vacuum, regardless of cost. That said, constitutional protections are not limited by cost. We saw in the 2018 cost study what happens when we estimate the cost of a high standard, where that standard is set without sufficient contextual analysis of just how high that standard is. The standard was really high and the costs to meet it astronomical. This occurred in part because the state board had reset its own standards to a higher bar and adopted new tests to align with that higher bar but had not yet really evaluated exactly how high that bar was. An ongoing deliberative process, involving periodic reviews (every three to five years) of standards and estimation of costs to meet those standards, with replication done by both responsible branches, would be desirable and would aid the courts in mediating any differences. Ideally, such an approach would aid the legislature and state board in recalibrating the state school finance system regularly so as to avoid the need for judicial intervention.

Finally, people and persistence matter—and this is a harder one to figure out how to replicate across states. Part of the Kansas story is about people who persisted in multiple roles, including on the high court. Persistence and institutional knowledge on the high court can only be achieved under appropriate constitutional structures, as mentioned earlier in this chapter. Even then, it may take some time before other state high courts find their Marla Luckert, Carol Beier, or Dan Biles. These are truly unique individuals with unparalleled knowledge of public school finance. Not lost in all of this is the prominent role of women in key leadership and mediation roles throughout the process. There are at least four other categories of individuals that have played key roles in maintaining the stability and adequacy of Kansas's schools:

1. Competent, stable, nonpartisan researchers and officials (like Dale and Scott)
2. Legislators who know the inner workings of the school finance system and are willing to use that knowledge for the broader public interest
3. Legal counsel who know the history and context of school funding in their states
4. Advocacy organizations that take at least a two-pronged approach, with political action and litigation support

All of these elements are necessary for making things happen and for making sure certain things *don't* happen. Kansas was lucky to have Dale for over fifty years. Other states have similar dedicated public servants. No academic institution I know of is specializing in producing similar individuals. So it's a bit of a crapshoot on the hiring end—and no doubt the labor pool for such jobs was different in 1967, when Dale was first hired. But these are critical roles, and because so much of the learning is on the job and in the trenches, experience and stability matters. State school finance formulas can get exceedingly complex, and learning them can take a long time. But someone has to, and these individuals in particular have to know their stuff down to the finest detail.

Finding, electing, and keeping state legislators who know their stuff well enough to advocate for the broader public interest is also critical.

These individuals can affect more change when they are around long enough to be heard and to assume leadership roles, even if in minority parties. They may not need to know the details quite like the technical support in their research divisions, but they also have to understand and respect the legislature's broader constitutional obligations, thinking beyond the boundaries of their own constituents and the core principles of school finance equity and adequacy. A few years ago, when my book on school finance was released, I was pleased, if not shocked, to come across a group of Johnson County, Kansas, legislators actually talking about the book on Twitter! Faced with complicated stuff like education cost studies and cost models, state legislators need these broader conceptual underpinnings, and I would argue that our field has come to a greater consensus in recent years on certain key points:

- First, money matters. That dog has retired and need not hunt anymore.
- Second, it costs more to achieve higher rather than lower outcome goals.
- Third, it costs more with some children and in some settings to achieve any given level of outcomes.

Full stop! There will always be those who hitch their wagons to dogmatic or extremist views like the Laffer curve. But it only takes one of their peers—like Clay Aurand, for example—to point out the simple illogic of zero ever being an optimal tax rate.

I've come to think, mostly in the process of writing this book, that persistent, local, knowledgeable legal counsel are critical to keeping the system in balance. While it perhaps should not be the case, it strikes me that the ongoing relationships between plaintiffs; counsel, defense counsel, and lower and high court judges led to a more civil process of mediating the state's school funding disputes. Alan, John, Dan, Terry, Marla, Lawton, and Carol all got to know each other pretty well over the decades, and while those relationships were contentious at times, they all seemed to work collectively toward the greater good for Kansas children, even if and when they might have taken slightly different paths toward that greater good. These ongoing personal relationships may be as important, if not more important, than being a renowned trial attorney. Further, these personal relationships are coupled with deep knowledge of the context and history of the litigation at hand.

Alan Rupe and John Robb know Kansas. They know their clients. They know the case, the constitution, and the stories along the way. Several members of the high court do, and have done so, as well. It was only the state—the attorney general's office—that on occasion relied on outside, non-Kansas counsel at various points in the litigation, and let's just say that it didn't go too well for them. The case has been similar in New Jersey, where David Sciarra and the Education Law Center have played the legal watchdog role for decades, with similar success. That said, even persistent and knowledgeable legal counsel can have limited influence.

Persistent institutions and individuals involved in both legal and political advocacy matter. Litigation is expensive and takes a long time to succeed. Those wishing to bring legal challenges against their states regarding their education rights will invariably be outgunned and outspent. Those most likely to have their constitutional rights deprived by their states are invariably those with the fewest available resources to fight the state for their rights. Organized and well-funded advocacy matters, and one way in which it matters is by supporting legal challenges to protect children's rights to equitable and adequate education.

I would, however, offer a specific focus in this regard based on my experiences in Kansas. Advocacy organizations should not be narrowly focused on gaining resources for organization members specifically. Legal advocacy should involve constant evaluation of the state education system to identify where the problems lie, who is most disadvantaged as a result, and whether those disadvantages rise to a level where litigation may be required and likely to succeed. Alan Rupe and John Robb knew in the aftermath of the *USD 229* case that certain districts, and the children they served, continued to be disadvantaged under Kansas school finance law. Schools for Fair Funding asked Alan Rupe and John Robb to evaluate potential federal and state causes of action to pursue. Then Rupe and Robb convened a group of experts to evaluate data with respect to those causes of action and to identify relevant plaintiff districts in advance of the cases. I'm unconvinced that allocating time, effort, and money to plaintiff-sponsored cost studies is the best use of time, though some form of cost analysis may ultimately inform plaintiffs' cases. Having constitutional requirements in place that require the legislature to make these determinations seems more useful.

Finally, political and policy advocacy organizations may play a key role in grooming and elevating legislators through local elections to state offices. Having an excellent statewide system of public schools under the model I propose herein requires both having an informed board of education to set good standards and having a legislature that knows how to craft a state aid formula to achieve those standards. That is no simple feat, and not an activity for a freshman legislator who wields too little influence. But you do have to start somewhere, and advocacy organizations like Kansas Families for Education can play a role in that. It's my belief that Kansas Families for Education in particular has helped shape the political landscape across party lines, in Johnson County in particular, over the past few decades and has kept school funding at the top of the agenda for any and all choosing to run for state office—Republican or Democrat—in the county. Electing and keeping informed legislators in place is key to the maintenance of equitable and adequate school funding.

After all, state school finance formulas are legislation—math written into law—adopted by politicians. What could possibly go wrong? They are a bunch of calculations that distribute hundreds of millions to billions of dollars—more than any other part of the state budget—to local public schools that serve the vast majority of the state's children. That's a messy process and one that within the legislature involves extensive multilateral bargaining. It also requires having at least a few legislators in positions of influence who have a sufficiently good handle on school finance that they can explain it to their peers. Advocacy organizations can help that to happen, either by helping existing legislators better understand the issues or by helping elect those who do.

APPENDIX

YEAR	Federal Courts	State Courts	State Legislation	Other Events
1940		Upholding Segregation and Denying Consolidation		
1954	*Brown v. Board*			
1963			Unification Act*	
1965			Unification Act (Revised) and School Foundation Act	Eleven-Member Task Force
1966			Constitution Ratified	
1967				Dale Starts at KSDE (1967)
1972		Caldwell (District Court)		
1973			SDEA	
1976		Knowles (District Court)		
1981		Knowles (District Court)		
1991		Bullock Preruling Letter		
10/14/91		Summit KSSC Chamber		Dale Provides Overview
November 1991		Finney Task Force		11/21 Task Force Report
March 11, 1992			House Bill Passes (Endorsed by Sen. Majority Leader Frahm)	

YEAR	Federal Courts	State Courts	State Legislation	Other Events
April 11, 1992			Session Ends Plan (Stalled)	
April 29, 1992		Trial Date Set For June 1; Shutdown Threat	Veto Session Senate Passes Bill	
May 20, 1992			SDF-QPA Adopted	
1994		*USD 229* (JoCo Court)		
Dec. 2, 1994		*USD 229* (KSSC)		
1996				Midsize Districts Organize
1997				Schools for Fair Funding Formed
1998				Rupe and Robb Hired; Feasibility Study
1999	*Robinson* Filed	*Montoy* Filed		
2000				
2002	Tenth Circuit			Task Force Report / Augenblick and Meyers Study
2003 Fall		Trial		
2003 December		Preliminary Order		
May 11, 2004		Shutdown Order		
Jan 3, 2005		KSSC Ruling		
April, 2005			HB2247/ SB 43	
May 11, 2005		Oral Argument (Biles)		
June 3, 2005		KSSC Ruling		
June 22, 2005			Special Session	
July 2, 2005		Fix it by 7/8 Or Close Schools		
Sept 9, 2005		Beyer's "Fundamental Right" Opinion		
January 9, 2006				LDPA Studies

YEAR	Federal Courts	State Courts	State Legislation	Other Events
May 22, 2006			SB 549	
June 21, 2006	Petrella (Intervene in Robinson)			
July 28, 2006		Montoy Dismissed By KSSC		
2009		_Gannon_ Filed		Chief Justice McFarland Retires Recession
2012		Gannon Trial		
2013		Trial Court Ruling		
2016		KSSC (Equity Compliance)		
2017		Trial Court (Overturns on Adequacy)		

NOTES

INTRODUCTION

1. Bruce Baker, Matt Di Carlo, Aja Srikanth, and Mark Weber, School Finance Indicators Database, accessed November 23, 2020, http://www.schoolfinance-data.org.

2. Marty P. Jordan and Matt Grossmann, *The Correlates of State Policy Project: Variable Codebook*, version 2.2 (East Lansing, MI: Institute for Public Policy and Social Research, 2020), http://ippsr.msu.edu/sites/default/files/Correlates Codebook.pdf.

3. 270toWin, "Kansas," 270toWin, accessed November 23, 2020, https://www.270towin.com/states/kansas.

4. Bonnie Fusarelli and Bruce Cooper, *The Rising State: How State Power Is Transforming Our Nation's Schools* (Albany, NY: SUNY Press, 2009).

5. Adam Bonica and Maya Sen, "Judicial Reform as a Tug of War: How Ideological Differences Between Politicians and the Bar Explain Attempts at Judicial Reform," *Vanderbilt Law Review* 70, no. 6 (2017): 1781–1811; Bonica and Sen, "The Politics of Selecting the Bench from the Bar: The Legal Profession and Partisan Incentives to Introduce Ideology into Judicial Selection," *Journal of Law and Economics* 60 (2017): 559–595.

6. Bruce Baker, Lori Taylor, and Arnold Vedlitz, *Adequacy Estimates and the Implications of Common Standards for the Cost of Instruction* (Washington, DC: National Research Council, 2008); Jay Chambers, Jesse Levin, and Thomas Parrish, "Examining the Relationship Between Educational Outcomes and Gaps in Funding: An Extension of the New York Adequacy Study," *Peabody Journal of Education* 81, no. 2 (2006): 1–32; Bruce Baker, "Evaluating the Reliability, Validity, and Usefulness of Education Cost Studies," *Journal of Education Finance* 32 (2006): 170–201; William Duncombe, "Responding to the Charge of Alchemy: Strategies for Evaluating the Reliability and Validity of Costing-out Research," *Journal of Education Finance* 32 (2006): 137–169.

7. Richard Norton Smith, "Four Kansas Governors to Assess State's Fiscal Crisis at Economic Policy Conference," University of Kansas Public Relations, September 25, 2002, http://archive.news.ku.edu/2002/02N/SeptNews/Sept25/roundtable.html.

8. Montoy v. State, 279 Kan. 817, 112 P.3d 923 (2005).

9. Gannon v. State, 319 P.3d 1196, 298 Kan. 1107 (2014).

10. Scott Rothschild, "Legislators on the Defense over School Finance Plan,"

Lawrence Journal-World, May 12, 2005, https://www2.ljworld.com/news/2005/may/12/legislators_on_the/.

11. C. J. Janovy, "Kansas School Board: Still Arguing About Evolution!," *Kansas City Pitch*, October 27, 2008, https://www.thepitchkc.com/kansas-school-board-still-arguing-about-evolution/.

12. Steven Rattner, "The Dangerous Folly of Lafferism," *New York Times*, June 25, 2019, https://www.nytimes.com/2019/06/25/opinion/the-dangerous-folly-of-lafferism.html.

CHAPTER 1

1. Craig E. Richards, Rima Shore, and Max Sawicky, *Risky Business: Private Management of Public Schools* (Washington, DC: Economic Policy Institute, 1996)

2. Bruce Baker and Craig Richards, "Exploratory Application of Systems Dynamics Modeling to School Finance Policy Analysis," *Journal of Education Finance* 27, no. 3 (2002): 857–883.

3. Bruce Baker and Craig Richards, "Equity Through Vouchers: The Special Case of Gifted Children," *Educational Policy* 12 (1998): 363–379.

4. Bruce Baker and Jill Dickerson, "Charter Schools, Teacher Labor Market Deregulation, and Teacher Quality: Evidence from the Schools and Staffing Survey," *Educational Policy* 20 (2006): 752–778.

5. Lisa Wolf-Wendel, Bruce Baker, Susan Twombly, Nona Tollefson, and Marc Mahlios, "Who's Teaching the Teachers? Evidence from the National Survey of Postsecondary Faculty and the Survey of Earned Doctorates," *American Journal of Education* 112 (2006): 273–300.

6. Bruce Baker, "Balancing Equity for Students and Taxpayers: Evaluating School Finance Reform in Vermont," *Journal of Education Finance* 26 (2001): 437–462.

7. Serrano v. Priest, 487 P.2d 1241, 5 Cal. 3d 584, 96 Cal. Rptr. 601 (1971).

8. Robinson et al. v. Cahill et al., 303 A.2d 273, 62 N.J. 473, 119 N.J. Super. 40 (1973).

9. Rose v. Council for Better Educ., Inc., 790 S.W.2d 186, 60 Ky. 1289 (1989).

10. Edgewood Indep. School Dist. v. Kirby, 777 S.W.2d 391 (Tex. 1989).

11. Brigham v. State, 692 A. 2d 384 (Vt. Supreme Court 1997).

12. Baker, "Balancing Equity for Students and Taxpayers."

13. Claremont School Dist. v. Governor, 142 NH 462 (NH Supreme Court 1997).

14. Eric Brunner and Jon Sostelie, "Homeowners, Property Values, and the Political Economy of the School Voucher," *Journal of Urban Economics* 54 (2003): 239–257; William Fischel, *An Economic Case Against Vouchers: Why Local Public Schools Are a Local Public Good*, Occasional Paper #54 (New York: National Center for the Study of Privatization in Education, 2002).

15. Tammy Kolbe, Bruce Baker, Drew Atchison, and Jesse Levin, *Pupil Weighting Factors Report* (Montpelier, VT: State of Vermont, House and Senate Committees on Education, 2019), https://legislature.vermont.gov/assets/Legislative-Reports/edu-legislative-report-pupil-weighting-factors-2019.pdf.

16. Bruce Baker and Michael Imber, "'Rational Educational Explanation' or Politics as Usual? Evaluating the Outcome of Educational Finance Litigation in Kansas," *Journal of Education Finance* 25 (1999): 121–139.

17. Bruce Baker and Preston C. Green III, "Tricks of the Trade: State Legislative Actions in School Finance Policy That Perpetuate Racial Disparities in the Post-Brown Era," *American Journal of Education* 111 (2005): 372–413.

18. Bruce Baker and Preston C. Green III, "Does Increased State Involvement in Public Schooling Necessarily Increase Equality of Educational Opportunity?," in *The Rising State: How State Power Is Transforming Our Nation's Schools*, ed. Bonnie Fusarelli and Bruce Cooper (Albany, NY: SUNY Press, 2009), 133.

19. Tony Ortega, "Funny Math," *The Pitch*, April 14, 2005, https://www.thepitchkc.com/funny-math/.

20. Joe Miller, "You Got Schooled," *The Pitch*, February 19, 2004, https://www.thepitchkc.com/you-got-schooled/.

21. Dugan Arnett, "Megan Phelps-Roper of Westboro Baptist Church: An Heir to Hate," *Wichita Eagle*, November 21, 2011, https://www.kansas.com/news/article1078345.html.

22. Baker and Green, "Tricks of the Trade."

23. Ortega, "Funny Math"; emphasis in original.

24. Tony Ortega, "The Wussies of Oz," *The Pitch*, June 16, 2005, https://www.thepitchkc.com/the-wussies-of-oz/.

25. Justin Kendall, "Kansas School Funding Fight Set to Resume in 2010," *The Pitch*, January 7, 2010, https://www.thepitchkc.com/kansas-school-funding-fight-set-to-resume-in-2010/.

26. Scott Rothschild, "Legislators on the Defense over School Finance Plan," *Lawrence Journal World*, May 12, 2005, https://www2.ljworld.com/news/2005/may/12/legislators_on_the/.

27. Crowson Cartoons, *Wichita Eagle*, June 29, 2005.

28. Kansas.com, December 30, 2005.

29. Scott Rothschild, "Kansas Supreme Court Ends Teachers' Legal Battle for Tenure," KCUR, June 15, 2018, https://www.kcur.org/post/kansas-supreme-court-ends-teachers-legal-battle-tenure#stream/0.

30. Tony Ortega, "Your Official Program to the Scopes II Kansas Monkey Trial," *The Pitch*, May 5, 2005, https://www.thepitchkc.com/your-official-program-to-the-scopes-ii-kansas-monkey-trial/.

31. Greg Allen, "Evolution and Intelligent Design in Kansas," *Weekend Edition Saturday*, NPR, May 7, 2005, https://www.npr.org/2005/05/07/4634563/evolution-and-intelligent-design-in-kansas.

32. Celisa Calacal, "Kansas Takes a Different Direction on Abortion Rights," *American Prospect*, May 29, 2019, https://prospect.org/health/kansas-takes-different-direction-abortion-rights/.

33. Bruce Baker and Douglas Elmer, "The Politics of Off-the-Shelf School Finance Reform," *Educational Policy* 23 (2009): 66–105.

34. Lawrence Picus, *Income Sensitive Property Taxes and School Finance Reform in Vermont* (Montpelier, VT: Vermont State Legislature, 1998).

35. Kolbe et al., *Pupil Weighting Factors Report*, https://legislature.vermont.gov/assets/Legislative-Reports/edu-legislative-report-pupil-weighting-factors-2019.pdf.

36. Bruce Baker, Drew Atchison, Jesse Levin, and Caitlyn Kearns, *New Hampshire Commission to Study School Funding: Final Report* (Durham, NH: University

of New Hampshire, Carsey School of Public Policy, 2020), https://carsey.unh
.edu/sites/default/files/media/2020/09/20-12685_nh_final_report_v10.pdf.

CHAPTER 2

1. Richard Norton Smith, "Four Kansas Governors to Assess State's Fiscal Crisis
   at Economic Policy Conference," University of Kansas Public Relations, press
   release, September 25, 2002, http://archive.news.ku.edu/2002/02N/SeptNews/
   Sept25/roundtable.html.
2. Charles Berger, "Equity Without Adjudication: Kansas School Finance Reform
   and the 1992 School District Finance and Quality Performance Act," *Journal of
   Law and Education* 27 (1998): 1–46, 8.
3. Gannon v. State, 319 P.3d 1196, 298 Kan. 1107 (2014).
4. Bruce Baker and Preston C. Green III, "Does Increased State Involvement in
   Public Schooling Necessarily Increase Equality of Educational Opportunity?,"
   in *The Rising State: How State Power Is Transforming Our Nation's Schools*, ed.
   Bonnie Fusarelli and Bruce Cooper (Albany, NY: SUNY Press, 2009), 133.
5. Michael Fuhlhage, "To Limit the Spread of Slavery: A *Boston Journal* Corre-
   spondent's Multiple Roles in the Kansas Free State Movement," *Journalism
   History* 43 (2017): 143–153.
6. Sharon Jessee, "The Contrapuntal Historiography of Toni Morrison's Paradise:
   Unpacking the Legacies of the Kansas and Oklahoma All-Black Towns," *American Studies* 47 (2006): 81–112.
7. Thomas Cox, *Blacks in Topeka Kansas, 1865–1915: A Social History* (New Orle-
   ans: LSU Press, 1999).
8. Baker and Green, "Does Increased State Involvement in Public Schooling Necessarily Increase Equality of Educational Opportunity?"; Brown v. Board of
   Education, 347 U.S. 483, 74 S. Ct. 686, 98 L. Ed. 873 (1954); Plessy v. Ferguson,
   163 U.S. 537, 16 S. Ct. 1138, 41 L. Ed. 256 (1896).
9. Kevin Fox Gotham, *Race, Real Estate, and Uneven Development: The Kansas
   City Experience, 1900-2000* (Albany, NY: SUNY Press, 2002).
10. Baker and Green, "Does Increased State Involvement in Public Schooling Nec-
    essarily Increase Equality of Educational Opportunity?"
11. Eric Adler, "Was J. C. Nichols Racist? 'He Had to Do What He Had to Do,'
    Kansas City Grandson Says," *Kansas City Star*, June 12, 2020, https://www
    .kansascity.com/news/politics-government/article243459771.html.
12. Michelle Tyrene Johnson, "Past Housing Discrimination Contributed to Wealth
    Gap Between Blacks and Whites in Kansas City," KCUR, August 10, 2018,
    https://www.kcur.org/community/2018-08-10/past-housing-discrimination-
    contributed-to-wealth-gap-between-blacks-and-whites-in-kansas-city.
13. Elle Moxley, "Who Was J. C. Nichols? The Mixed Legacy of the Man Whose Name
    Could Be Taken off Kansas City's Most Famous Fountain," KCUR, June 12, 2020,
    https://www.kcur.org/arts-life/2020-06-12/who-was-j-c-nichols-the-mixed-
    legacy-of-the-man-whose-name-could-be-taken-off-kansas-citys-most-famous-
    fountain.
14. *Kansas City Star*, "Curse of the Covenant Persists," *Kansas City Star*, February
    13, 2005.

15. "QuickFacts: Jackson County, Missouri; Wyandotte County, Kansas; Johnson County, Kansas; Kansas," US Census Bureau, accessed October 1, 2020, https://www.census.gov/quickfacts/fact/table/jacksoncountymissouri,wyandottecountykansas,johnsoncountykansas,KS/PST045219.
16. Tony Ortega, "Funny Math," *Pitch Weekly*, April 14, 2005.
17. Juliana Garcia, "Prairie Village Diversity Task Force Discusses Steps to Remove the City's Racist Deed Restrictions," *Shawnee Mission Post*, October 23, 2020, https://shawneemissionpost.com/2020/10/23/prairie-village-diversity-task-force-discusses-steps-to-remove-the-citys-racist-deed-restrictions-104700/.
18. James W. Drury and Marvin G. Stottlemire, *The Government of Kansas* (Lawrence: University of Kansas, Division of Continuing Education, 2001).
19. Stephen J. Ware, "Selection to the Kansas Supreme Court," *Kansas Journal of Law & Public Policy* 17 (2008): 368.
20. Ware, "Selection to the Kansas Supreme Court," 392.
21. Ware, "Selection to the Kansas Supreme Court," 395.
22. Drury and Stottlemire, *The Government of Kansas*.
23. Ware, "Selection to the Kansas Supreme Court," 395.
24. Drury and Stottlemire, *The Government of Kansas*.
25. Original Article 6, Section 2: "The Legislature shall encourage the promotion of intellectual, moral, scientific and agricultural improvement, by establishing a uniform system of common schools, and schools of higher grade, embracing normal, preparatory, collegiate, and university departments." See https://www.kansasmemory.org/item/90272/text.
26. Baker and Green, "Does Increased State Involvement in Public Schooling Necessarily Increase Equality of Educational Opportunity?"
27. Baker and Green, "Does Increased State Involvement in Public Schooling Necessarily Increase Equality of Educational Opportunity?"
28. Bruce Baker and Preston C. Green III, "Tricks of the Trade: State Legislative Actions in School Finance Policy That Perpetuate Racial Disparities in the Post-Brown Era," *American Journal of Education* 111 (2005): 372–413.
29. Baker and Green, "Does Increased State Involvement in Public Schooling Necessarily Increase Equality of Educational Opportunity?"
30. Baker and Green, "Does Increased State Involvement in Public Schooling Necessarily Increase Equality of Educational Opportunity?"
31. Bob Beatty, "Governor William Avery Interview," Kansas Memory, Kansas Historical Society, December 5, 2003, https://www.kansasmemory.org/item/212031.
32. Joey May, "Deputy Commissioner Dale Dennis Retiring from KSDE After 53 Years," *Atchison Globe*, September 9. 2020, https://www.atchisonglobenow.com/news/deputy-commissioner-dale-dennis-retiring-from-ksde-after-53-years/article_598e5a9c-f2ab-11ea-a945-2f0fecf7882d.html; Editorial Advisory Board, "Editorial: Dale Dennis Deserves Our Gratitude," *Hutchinson News*, September 17, 2020, https://www.hutchnews.com/opinion/20200917/editorial-dale-dennis-deserves-our-gratitude.
33. State, Ex Rel., v. Board of Education, 511 P.2d 705, 212 Kan. 482 (1973).
34. Baker and Green, "Tricks of the Trade."

35. Berger, "Equity Without Adjudication," 1.
36. Quoted in Unified School District No. 229 v. State (1994), 1177.
37. Knowles v. State Board of Education, 547 P.2d 699, 219 Kan. 271 (1976) at 273.
38. *Knowles*, at 273.
39. *Knowles*, at 273.
40. *Knowles*, at 279.

CHAPTER 3

1. Charles Berger, "Equity Without Adjudication: Kansas School Finance Reform and the 1992 School District Finance and Quality Performance Act," *Journal of Law and Education* 27, no. 1 (1998): 1–46, 17.
2. Lisa M. B. Harrington and Max Lu, "Beef Feedlots in Southwestern Kansas: Local Change, Perceptions, and the Global Change Context," *Global Environmental Change* 12 (2002): 273–282.
3. Mock v. State of Kansas, No. 91-CV-1009, 31 Washburn L.J. 489, October 14, 1991.
4. John Robb, personal communication, August 2019.
5. Berger, "Equity Without Adjudication," 18.
6. Berger, "Equity Without Adjudication," 18.
7. Berger, "Equity Without Adjudication," 18.
8. Berger, "Equity Without Adjudication," 23.
9. Berger, "Equity Without Adjudication," 24.
10. Peter J. McCormick, "The 1992 Secession Movement in Southwest Kansas," *Great Plains Quarterly* 15, no. 4 (1995): 247–258.
11. John Robb, personal communication, August 7, 2019.
12. John Robb, personal communication, August 2019.
13. John Deke, "A Study of the Impact of Public School Spending on Postsecondary Educational Attainment Using Statewide School District Refinancing in Kansas," *Economics of Education Review* 22 (2003): 275–284.
14. McCormick, "The 1992 Secession Movement in Southwest Kansas," 247.
15. McCormick, "The 1992 Secession Movement in Southwest Kansas," 248.
16. Bruce Baker and Michael Imber, "'Rational Educational Explanation' or Politics as Usual? Evaluating the Outcome of Educational Finance Litigation in Kansas," *Journal of Education Finance* 25, no. 1 (1999): 121–139.
17. Kansas Governor's Task Force, *Vision 21st Century Initiative: K–12 Education: Financing for Results* (Topeka, KS: State of Kansas, December 1, 2001), 1.
18. Helen Ladd, Rosemary Chalk, and Janet Hansen, *Making Money Matter: Financing America's Schools* (Washington, DC: National Academies Press, 1999); Helen Ladd, Rosemary Chalk, and Janet Hansen, *Equity and Adequacy in Education Finance: Issues and Perspectives* (Washington, DC: National Academies Press, 1999).
19. Kansas Governor's Task Force, *Vision 21st Century Initiative: K–12 Education: Financing for Results* (Topeka, KS: State of Kansas, December 1, 2001), 3.
20. Berger, "Equity Without Adjudication."

CHAPTER 4

1. See https://schoolsforfairfunding.org/.
2. Powell v. Ridge, 247 F.3d 520 (3d Cir. 2001).
3. African American Legal Defense v. New York State, 8 F. Supp. 2d 330 (S.D.N.Y. 1998).
4. Alexander v. Sandoval, 532 U.S. 275, 121 S. Ct. 1511, 149 L. Ed. 2d 517 (2001).
5. San Antonio Independent School Dist. v. Rodriguez, 411 U.S. 1, 93 S. Ct. 1278, 36 L. Ed. 2d 16 (1973).
6. Robinson v. Kansas, 295 F.3d 1183 (10th Cir. 2002). See also Preston C. Green III and Bruce Baker, "Circumventing Rodriguez: Can Plaintiffs Use the Equal Protection Clause to Challenge School Finance Disparities Caused by Inequitable State Distribution Policies?," *Texas Forum on Civil Rights and Civil Liberties* 7 (2002): 141–166.
7. Montoy v. State, 62 P.3d 228, 275 Kan. 145 (2003).
8. Robert Berne and Leanna Stiefel, *The Measurement of Equity in School Finance: Conceptual, Methodological, and Empirical Dimensions* (Baltimore, MD: Johns Hopkins University Press, 1984).
9. Jocelyn Johnston and William Duncombe, "Balancing Conflicting Policy Objectives: The Case of School Finance Reform," *Public Administration Review* 58 (1998): 145–158.
10. Bruce Baker and Preston C. Green III, "Tricks of the Trade: State Legislative Actions in School Finance Policy That Perpetuate Racial Disparities in the Post-Brown Era," *American Journal of Education* 111 (2005): 372–413.
11. Tony Ortega, "Funny Math," *The Pitch*, April 14, 2005.
12. Joe Miller, "You Got Schooled," *The Pitch*, February 19, 2004, https://www.thepitchkc.com/you-got-schooled/.
13. Case No. 99-C-1738, December 2, 2003, at 59.
14. Case No. 99-C-1738, December 19, 2003, at 13.
15. Case No. 99-C-1738, December 2, 2003, at 52 (emphasis added).
16. Case No. 99-C-1738, December 2, 2003, at 59.
17. Case No. 99-C-1738, December 2, 2003, at 47.
18. *Northeast Johnson County Sun*, "$1 Billion School Fix Ordered," December 4, 2003.
19. Miller, "You Got Schooled."
20. Miller, "You Got Schooled."
21. Case No. 99-C-1738, May 11, 2004.
22. 278 Kan. 769; 120 P.3d 306; 2005 Kan. Lexis 460, January 3, 2005, opinion filed.
23. *Montoy*, 279 Kan. 817, 112 P.3d 923 (2005).
24. *Montoy*, no. 92,032 (Kan. July 28, 2006).
25. *Montoy*, no. 92,032 (Kan. July 28, 2006).
26. *Montoy*, no. 92,032 (Kan. July 28, 2006).

CHAPTER 5

1. Max Ehrenfreund, "Kansas Republicans Raise Taxes, Rebuking Their GOP Governor's 'Real Live Experiment' in Conservative Policy," *Washington Post*, June 7, 2017, https://www.washingtonpost.com/news/wonk/

wp/2017/06/07/kansas-republicans-raise-taxes-rebuking-their-gop-governors-real-live-experiment-in-conservative-policy/?noredirect=on; Harold Meyerson, "Going Up in Economic Ratings? Then Lose Trickle-Down, *American Prospect* (blog), July 23, 2019, https://prospect.org/blog/on-tap/going-economic-ratings-then-lose-trickle-down.

2. "Kris Kobach," BallotPedia, accessed October 1, 2020, https://ballotpedia.org/Kris_Kobach.

3. Yael T. Abouhalkah, "Milestones of Gov. Sam Brownback's Tax Cut Debacle in Kansas: A Timeline," *Kansas City Star*, accessed October 1, 2020, https://www.kansascity.com/opinion/editorials/article6514956.html; Sam Brownback, "State of the State Message," Office of the Governor, State of Kansas, January 12, 2011, http://media.khi.org/news/documents/2011/01/12/2011stateofthestate.pdf.

4. Abouhalkah, Milestones of Gov. Sam Brownback's Tax Cut Debacle in Kansas"; Brad Cooper, "Reagonomics Guru Arthur Laffer Touts Brownback Tax Plan at Capitol," *Kansas City Star*, January 19, 2012, http://www.kansascity.com/news/local/article300536/Reagonomics-guru-Arthur-Laffer-touts-Brownback-tax-plan-at-Capitol.html.

5. Bruce Baker and Douglas Elmer, "The Politics of Off-the-Shelf School Finance Reform," *Educational Policy* 23 (2009): 66–105.

6. Brent D. Wistrom, "Economist Arthur Laffer Says Tax Cuts Will Help Kansas Grow," *Wichita Eagle*, August 14, 2012, https://www.kansas.com/news/article1097282.html.

7. Wistrom, "Economist Arthur Laffer Says Tax Cuts Will Help Kansas Grow."

8. Abouhalkah, "Milestones of Gov. Sam Brownback's Tax Cut Debacle in Kansas."

9. Alexandra Thornton and Galen Hendricks, "Kansas 'Real Live Experiment' in Trickle-Down Tax Cuts: A Flashing Warning Sign for Congress," Center for American Progress, November 2, 2017, https://www.americanprogress.org/issues/economy/reports/2017/11/02/441822/kansas-real-live-experiment-trickle-tax-cuts/.

10. Brad Cooper, "Kansas Revenues Will Fall $1 Billion Short of 2015 and 2016 Expenses, Fiscal Experts Say," *Kansas City Star*, November 10, 2014, https://www.kansascity.com/news/politics-government/article3729756.html.

11. Catherine Garcia, "Watch Seth Meyers Explain What Happened in Kansas when Taxes Were Cut Dramatically," *The Week*, March 22, 2016, https://theweek.com/speedreads/614134/watch-seth-meyers-explain-what-happened-kansas-when-taxes-cut-dramatically; Seth Meyers, "Kansas Tax Cuts: A Closer Look," *Late Night with Seth Meyers*, March 22, 2016, https://www.facebook.com/LateNightSeth/videos/629856370498379.

12. Michael Linden, "Kansas' Experiment with Tax Cutting Failed Spectacularly—on Its Own Terms," *Business Insider*, June 14, 2017, https://www.businessinsider.com/kansas-experiment-with-tax-cutting-failed-on-its-own-terms-2017-6.

13. Thornton and Hendricks, "Kansas 'Real Live Experiment' in Trickle-Down Tax Cuts."

14. Thornton and Hendricks, "Kansas 'Real Live Experiment' in Trickle-Down Tax Cuts."

15. Wade Goodwyn, "Kansas' 2012 Tax Cut Experiment Could Serve as a Cautionary Tale," *Morning Edition*, National Public Radio, December 13, 2017, https://www.npr.org/2017/12/13/570387479/kansas-2012-tax-cut-experiment-could-serve-as-a-cautionary-tale; Eric Levitz, "Kansas Just Proved That a Better GOP Is Possible," *New York Magazine*, January 9, 2020, https://nymag.com/intelligencer/2020/01/kansas-medicaid-expansion-plan-republican-party.html.

16. Chris Edwards, "Governor Brownback's Tax Cuts," *Cato Institute* (blog), October 10, 2014, https://www.cato.org/blog/governor-brownbacks-tax-cuts?queryID=ef27065526de39dd9d9abe071cfeadfc.

17. Leonard Gilroy and Harris Kenny, "Better Service. Better Price: How Privatization Can Streamline Government, Improve Services, and Reduce Costs for Kansas Taxpayers," Reason Foundation, January 28, 2013, https://reason.org/policy-study/kansas-privatization-study/.

18. Michael Leachman, "Timeline: 5 Years of Kansas' Tax-Cut Disaster," *Center on Budget and Policy Analysis* (blog), May 24, 2017, https://www.cbpp.org/blog/timeline-5-years-of-kansas-tax-cut-disaster.

19. Justin Kendall, "Kansas School Funding Fight Set to Resume in 2010," *Kansas City Pitch*, January 7, 2010, https://www.thepitchkc.com/kansas-school-funding-fight-set-to-resume-in-2010/; Justin Kendall, "Kansas Lawmaker Takes Shot at Supreme Court, Funding Schools," *Kansas City Pitch*, February 3, 2010, https://www.thepitchkc.com/kansas-lawmaker-takes-shot-at-supreme-court-funding-schools/.

20. District court ruling, Case No. 10C569, January 11, 2013, http://www.robblaw.com/PDFs/2013-01-11%20Gannon%20Trial%20Decision.pdf, emphasis added.

21. District court ruling, Case No. 10C569, January 11, 2013, http://www.robblaw.com/PDFs/2013-01-11%20Gannon%20Trial%20Decision.pdf, emphasis added.

22. District court ruling, Case No. 10C569, January 11, 2013, http://www.robblaw.com/PDFs/2013-01-11%20Gannon%20Trial%20Decision.pdf.

23. Gannon v. State, 319 P.3d 1196, 298 Kan. 1107 (2014).

24. "We further affirm the panel's rulings that the State failed to meet its duty to provide equity in public education as required under Article 6 of the Kansas Constitution. More specifically, we affirm the panel's holding that the State established unreasonable, wealth-based disparities by (1) withholding all capital outlay state aid payments to which certain school districts were otherwise entitled under K.S.A. 2012 Supp. 72-8814(c) and 108." *Gannon v. State*, 319 P.3d, at 1204.

25. "More specifically, the panel must assess whether the public education financing system provided by the legislature for grades K–12—through structure and implementation—is reasonably calculated to have all Kansas public education students meet or exceed the standards set out in Rose v. Council for Better Educ., Inc., 790 S.W.2d 186 (Ky. 1989), and as presently codified in K.S.A. 2013 Supp. 72-1127. (p. 110)." *Gannon v. State*, 319 P.3d, at 1237.

26. *Gannon v. State*, 390 P.3d, at 8, emphasis added.

27. Tim Carpenter, "Senate, House Narrowly Override Gov. Sam Brownback's Veto of $1.2 Billion Tax Bill," *Topeka Capital Journal*, June 6, 2017, https://www.cjonline.com/news/state-government/2017-06-06/senate-house-narrowly-override-gov-sam-brownback-s-veto-12-billion.

28. Gannon v. State, 402 P.3d 513, 306 Kan. 1170 (2017).

29. *Gannon v. State*, 402 P.3d.

30. For more about Bill's life, see "William D. Duncombe," obituary, *Syracuse Post Standard*, May 18–19, 2013, https://obits.syracuse.com/obituaries/syracuse/obituary.aspx?n=william-d-duncombe&pid=164845715.

31. Tim Carpenter, "Kansas Democrats Raise Questions About Texas Professor's History as School-Finance Expert," *Topeka Capital Journal*, February 23, 2018, https://www.cjonline.com/news/20180222/kansas-democrats-raise-questions-about-texas-professors-history-as-school-finance-expert.

32. See Bruce Baker, Lori Taylor, Jesse Levin, Jay Chambers, and Charles Blankenship, "Adjusted Poverty Measures and the Distribution of Title I Aid: Does Title I Really Make the Rich States Richer?," *Education Finance and Policy* 8, no. 3 (2013): 394–417.

33. Celia Llopis-Jepsen, "Report Suggesting $2 Billion For Kansas Schools Overshot Education Goals by $500 Million," KCUR, April 1, 2018, https://www.kcur.org/education/2018-04-01/report-suggesting-2-billion-for-kansas-schools-overshot-education-goals-by-500-million.

34. Wyatt Cenac, "Problem Areas in America's Schools," *Problem Areas*, HBO, June 15, 2018, https://www.youtube.com/watch?v=DFnIdq9fFhs.

35. Robert Gebeloff, "The Numbers That Explain Why Teachers Are in Revolt," *New York Times*, June 4, 2018, quoted in Cenac, "Problem Areas in America's Schools."

CHAPTER 6

1. Jodi Wilgoren, "In Kansas, Darwinism Goes on Trial Once More," *New York Times*, May 6, 2005, https://www.nytimes.com/2005/05/06/us/education/in-kansas-darwinism-goes-on-trial-once-more.html.

2. John Hanna, "Kansas Anti-abortion Measure Fails; Medicaid Plan Targeted," ABC News, February 7, 2020, https://abcnews.go.com/Health/wireStory/kansas-anti-abortion-measure-short-passage-delaying-vote-68825946.

3. Wikipedia contributors, "List of Female Governors in the United States," Wikipedia, accessed October 1, 2020, https://en.wikipedia.org/wiki/List_of_female_governors_in_the_United_States.

4. Laila Robbins, "State Supreme Courts Are Overwhelmingly White and Male," Brennan Center for Justice, November 2, 2018, https://www.brennancenter.org/blog/state-supreme-courts-are-overwhelmingly-white-and-male.

5. Laurenz Ensser-Jedenastik, "How Women's Political Representation Affects Spending on Family Benefits," *Journal of Social Policy* 46 (2017): 563–581.

6. Scott Rothschild, "Legislators on the Defense over School Finance Plan," *Lawrence Journal World*, May 12, 2005, https://www2.ljworld.com/news/2005/may/12/legislators_on_the/.

7. Alan Greenblat, "The Long Road to Recovery After Years of Severe Budget Cuts," *Governing Magazine*, August 2019, https://www.governing.com/topics/politics/gov-kansas-governor.html.

8. "History of Women Governors," Center for American Women and Politics, Rutgers University, Eagleton Institute of Politics, accessed October 1, 2020, https://cawp.rutgers.edu/history-women-governors.

9. "History of Women Governors."

10. Zach Oberfield and Bruce Baker, "Political Influences on School Funding Fairness" (presented at the Annual Meeting of the Association for Education Finance and Policy, Fort Worth, TX, 2020).

11. Bruce D. Baker, Ajay Srikanth, Preston C. Green III, and Rob Cotto, "School Funding Disparities and the Plight of Latinx Children," *Education Policy Analysis Archives* 28 (2020): 135, https://doi.org/10.14507/epaa.28.5282.

12. Erin B. Logan, "Teacher Walkouts: A State by State Guide," National Public Radio, April 25, 2018, https://www.npr.org/sections/ed/2018/04/25/602859780/teacher-walkouts-a-state-by-state-guide.

13. Maya Riser-Kositsky, Madeline Will, and Daarel Burnette II, "Over 170 Teachers Ran for State Office in 2018. Here's What We Know About Them," *Education Week*, November 21, 2018, https://www.edweek.org/ew/section/multimedia/teachers-running-for-state-office.html.

14. David Williams, "16 Oklahoma Educators Elected to Office on Tuesday," CNN, November 7, 2018, https://www.cnn.com/2018/11/07/politics/oklahoma-teachers-election-trnd/index.html.

15. Bruce Baker, Matt Di Carlo, Aja Srikanth, and Mark Weber, School Finance Indicators Database, accessed November 23, 2020, http://www.schoolfinancedata.org.

16. KOLD News 13 staff, "Arizona Decides 2020: Arizona Residents Approve Proposition to Fund Education," KOLD, November 3, 2020, https://www.kold.com/2020/11/04/arizona-decides-arizona-expected-approve-prop-increased-income-tax/.

17. Wikipedia contributors, "List of Female State Supreme Court Chief Justices: Female Chief Justices," Wikipedia, accessed October 1, 2020, https://en.wikipedia.org/wiki/List_of_female_state_supreme_court_justices#Female_chief_justices.

18. Debbie Mauldin Cottrell, "All-Woman Supreme Court," in *Handbook of Texas Online* (Austin: Texas State Historical Association, accessed September 26, 2014), http://www.tshaonline.org/handbook/online/articles/jpa01.

19. Richard E. Levy, "Gunfight at the K-12 Corral: Legislative vs. Judicial Power in the Kansas School Finance Litigation," *University of Kansas Law Review* 54 (2005): 1021–1115.

20. Mark Fonstad, William Pugatch, and Brandon Vogt, "Kansas Is Flatter than a Pancake," *Annals of Improbable Research* 9, no. 3 (2003), http://www.usu.edu/geo/geomorph/kansas.html.

21. Bruce D. Baker and Michael Imber, "'Rational Educational Explanation' or Politics as Usual? Evaluating the Outcome of Educational Finance Litigation in Kansas," *Journal of Education Finance* 25, no. 1 (1999): 121–139.

22. Bryan Lowry, "High Stakes in Kansas Supreme Court Retention Vote," *Wichita Eagle*, September 5, 2016, https://www.kansas.com/news/politics-government/article100083347.html.

23. Charlene Smith, "Women at Washburn," *Washburn Lawyer* 41, no. 1 (2002–2003): 4–9, https://washburnlaw.edu/publications/washburnlawyer/issues/41-1/04-09.pdf.

24. J. Phillip Thompson and Sarah Tobias, "The Texas Ten Percent Plan," *American Behavioral Scientist* 43 (2000): 1121–1138.

25. Around 2010, antiabortion activists called on voters to oust the justice via their "Fire Beier" campaign.
26. Jonathan Shoreman, "Kansas Gov. Kelly Will Pick Third Supreme Court Justice After Beier Leaves the Bench," *Wichita Eagle*, June 12, 2020, https://www.kansas.com/news/politics-government/article243497651.html#storylink=cpy.
27. Joe Miller, "You Got Schooled," *The Pitch*, February 19, 2004, https://www.thepitchkc.com/you-got-schooled/.
28. See http://www.sebeliusresources.com/about-2.
29. Rothschild, "Legislators on the Defense over School Finance Plan."
30. Montoy v. State, 120 P.3d 306, 278 Kan. 769 (2005).
31. *Montoy v. State*, 120 P.3d.
32. *Montoy v. State*, 120 P.3d.
33. *Montoy v. State*, 120 P.3d.
34. Gannon v. State, 390 P.3d 461, 305 Kan. 850 (2017).
35. Hodes and Nauser, MDs, PA v. Schmidt, 440 P.3d 461, 309 Kan. 610 (2019).
36. Hanna, "Kansas Anti-abortion Measure Fails."
37. Jonathan Shorman, "Kansas Lawmakers Differ on Meaning of School Funding Ruling," *Topeka Capital-Journal*, March 2, 2017, https://www.gctelegram.com/393fa6e0-0373-5ea5-8b9e-8ca0305ea12b.html.
38. Shorman, "Kansas Lawmakers Differ on Meaning of School Funding Ruling."
39. Jay Senter, "Final Results Have Challenger Rui Xu Defeating Incumbent Rep. Melissa Rooker by 121 Votes," *Shawnee Mission Post*, November 16, 2018, https://shawneemissionpost.com/2018/11/16/final-results-have-challenger-rui-xu-defeating-incumbent-rep-melissa-rooker-by-121-votes-75219/.
40. "Governor Laura Kelly," Office of the Governor, State of Kansas, accessed October 1, 2020, https://governor.kansas.gov/governor/.
41. Justin Kendall, "Unnatural Selection," *The Pitch*, August 18, 2005, https://www.thepitchkc.com/unnatural-selection/.
42. Steve Fry, "Luckert's Installation as Chief Justice Helps Women Make History on KS Courts," WIBW, December 17, 2019, https://www.wibw.com/content/news/Women-are-making-history-on-Kansas-courts-566295631.html.
43. Denise Neil and Jaime Green, "Kansas Makes History, Elects Retired Wichita Teacher as Its First Transgender Legislator," *Wichita Eagle*, November 3, 2020, https://www.kansas.com/news/politics-government/election/article246927272.html.

CHAPTER 7

1. Tony Ortega, "Your Official Program to the Scopes II Kansas Monkey Trial," *The Pitch*, May 5, 2005.
2. Bruce Baker, Lori Taylor, and Arnold Vedlitz, *Measuring Educational Adequacy in Public Schools* (Austin, TX: Joint Select Committee on Public Finance, 2004).
3. Campbell County School Dist. v. State, 907 P.2d 1238, 1995 W.Y. 184 (Wyo. 1995).
4. Baker, Taylor, and Vedlitz, *Measuring Educational Adequacy in Public Schools*.
5. William Duncombe and Jocelyn Johnston, "The Impacts of School Finance Reform in Kansas: Equity Is in the Eye of the Beholder," in *Helping Children*

Left Behind: State Aid and the Pursuit of Educational Equity, ed. John Yinger (Cambridge, MA: MIT Press, 2004), 147–193.

6. Timothy Gronberg, Dennis Jansen, Lori Taylor, and Kevin Booker, *School Outcomes and School Costs: The Cost Function Approach* (College Station: Texas A&M University, 2004).

7. Bruce Baker, Lori Taylor, and Arnold Vedlitz, *Adequacy Estimates and the Implications of Common Standards for the Cost of Instruction* (Washington, DC: National Research Council, 2008).

8. Bruce Baker, "Living on the Edges of State School-Funding Policies: The Plight of At-Risk, Limited-English-Proficient, and Gifted Children," *Educational Policy* 15 (2001): 699–723.

9. William Duncombe and Jocelyn Johnston, "The Impacts of School Finance Reform in Kansas: Equity Is in the Eye of the Beholder," in *Helping Children Left Behind: State Aid and the Pursuit of Educational Equity* (Cambridge, MA: MIT Press, 2004): 147–193.

10. Bruce Baker, "The Emerging Shape of Educational Adequacy: From Theoretical Assumptions to Empirical Evidence," *Journal of Education Finance* 30 (2005): 259–287.

11. Jay Chambers, *Measuring Resources in Education: From Accounting to the Resource Cost Model Approach* (Washington, DC: National Center for Education Statistics, 1999); Henry M. Levin, *Cost Effectiveness: A Primer* (Thousand Oaks, CA: Sage Publications, 1983). As a brief tangent on this point, resource cost model is the method used in the original Illinois and Alaska studies in the early 1980s, developed by Jay Chambers, a senior colleague of Jesse Levin at the American Institutes for Research. The ingredients method is the name used for the same method, outlined in Henry (Hank) Levin's 1983 book on education cost analysis. Hank is Jesse's dad. Jesse reappears later in this chapter as the external reviewer of the three Kansas cost studies.

12. John Augenblick, John Myers, Justin Silverstein, and Ann Barkis, *Calculation of the Cost of a Suitable Education in Kansas in 2000–2001 Using Two Different Analytical Approaches* (Topeka: Kansas Legislative Research Department, 2002), http://www.kslegresearch.org/KLRD-web/Publications/Education/Education_Cost_Study/SchoolFinanceFinalReport.pdf.

13. Joe Miller, "You Got Schooled," *The Pitch*, February 19, 2004, https://www.thepitchkc.com/you-got-schooled/.

14. Montoy v. State, 279 Kan. 817, 112 P.3d 923 (2005).

15. *Montoy v. State.*

16. *Montoy v. State.*

17. Bruce Baker, "Exploring the Sensitivity of Education Costs to Racial Composition of Schools and Race-Neutral Alternative Measures: A Cost Function Application to Missouri," *Peabody Journal of Education* 86, no. 1 (2011): 58–83.

18. LDPA, *Cost Study Analysis: Elementary and Secondary Education in Kansas: Estimating the Costs of K–12 Education Using Two Approaches* (Topeka, KS: Legislative Division of Post Audit, 2006), http://www.kslegresearch.org/KLRD-web/Publications/Education/Education_Cost_Study/Cost_Study_Report.pdf.

19. Gannon v. State, 402 P.3d 513, 306 Kan. 1170 (2017), at 25.

20. *Gannon v. State.*

21. Wikipedia contributors, "Jeff King (Politician)," Wikipedia, accessed October 1, 2020, https://en.wikipedia.org/wiki/Jeff_King_(politician).

22. Jesse Levin, *Review of Kansas Education Cost Studies* (Topeka: Kansas Legislative Research Department, 2018); Bruce Baker, *Review of Kansas Cost Studies* (Newton, KS: Somers, Robb & Robb, 2018), http://www.robblaw.com/PDFs/991454%20BBaker.KS.CostReview.3-26-18_FINAL_rl.pdf.

23. William Duncombe and John Yinger, *Estimating the Costs of Meeting Student Performance Outcomes Adopted by the Kansas State Board of Education* (Topeka, KS: Legislative Division of Post Audit, 2005), https://www.maxwell.syr.edu/uploadedFiles/cpr/research/cpr_research_education_finance_policy/Kansas_Report.pdf.

24. Lori Taylor, Jason Willis, Alex Berg-Jacobson, Karina Jaquet, and Ruthie Carpas, *Estimating the Costs Associated with Reaching Student Achievement Expectations for Kansas Public Education Students* (Topeka, KS: WestEd, 2018), 61, https://kasb.org/wp-content/uploads/2018/03/Kansas_Adequacy-Study_Cost-Function_20180315FINAL_02.pdf.

25. Editorial board, "Kansas School Funding Report Blows a Hole in Conservative Doctrine," *Kansas City Star*, March 16, 2018, https://www.kansascity.com/latest-news/article205595439.html#storylink=cpy.

26. Case No. 99-C-1738, December 19, 2003, at 13.

27. Duncombe and Yinger, *Estimating the Costs of Meeting Student Performance Outcomes*, C-33.

28. The KAP performance levels range from 1 to 4 as follows: at Level 1, a student is below grade level; at Level 2, a student is at grade level but not on track for college or career readiness; at Level 3, a student is at grade level and on track for college or career readiness; at Level 4, a student exceeds grade-level expectations and is on track for college or the workplace.

29. Taylor et al., *Estimating the Costs Associated with Reaching Student Achievement Expectations.*

30. V. Bandeira de Mello, *Mapping State Proficiency Standards onto the NAEP Scales: Variation and Change in State Standards for Reading and Mathematics, 2005–2009 (NCES 2011-458)* (Washington, DC: Government Printing Office, National Center for Education Statistics, Institute of Education Sciences, US Department of Education, 2011).

31. V. Bandeira de Mello, T. Rahman, M. A. Fox, and C. S. Ji, *Mapping State Proficiency Standards onto the NAEP Scales: Results From the 2017 NAEP Reading and Mathematics Assessments (NCES 2019-040)* (Washington, DC: U.S. Department of Education, Institute of Education Sciences, National Center for Education Statistics, 2019).

32. Seth Klamann, "Legislators Approve Bill to Create Committee to Recalibrate Wyoming's Education System," *Casper Star Tribune*, November 14, 2019, https://trib.com/news/state-and-regional/govt-and-politics/education/legislators-approve-bill-to-create-committee-to-recalibrate-wyomings-education-system/article_6a4e489f-4dc6-5569-a313-73f650021641.html.

33. Bruce Baker, *School Funding Fairness in New York State: An Update for 2013–14* (New York: Alliance for Quality Education, 2014), http://www.aqeny.org/

wp-content/uploads/2012/03/School-Funding-Fairness-in-New-York-State-An-Update-for-2013-14.pdf.

CHAPTER 8

1. Jonathan Shorman and Suzanne Perez Tobias, "How Kansas Lawmakers Made an $80 Million Error in School Funding Bill," *Wichita Eagle*, April 11, 2018, https://www.kansas.com/news/politics-government/article208464269.html.

2. Celia Llopis-Jepsen, "5 Themes at the Heart of Kansas' School Finance Lawsuit," KCUR, July 10, 2017, https://www.kcur.org/post/5-themes-heart-kansas-school-finance-lawsuit#stream/0.

3. Carol Yoho, "Turnpike: Flint Hills: Nothing?," Washburn University, April 2013, https://washburn.edu/cas/art/cyoho/archive/KStravel/turnpikeApr2013/index.html.

4. Kansas State Department of Education, "Legal Max General Fund, School Finance Studies," Kansas State Department of Education, accessed October 1, 2020, https://www.ksde.org/Agency/Fiscal-and-Administrative-Services/School-Finance/Legal-Max-General-Fund-School-Finance-Studies.

5. See the Kansas Legislative Research Department archive at http://www.kslegresearch.org/KLRD-web/Publications/Education/. See also Kansas Legislative Research Department, *Kansas School Finance System* (Topeka: Kansas Legislative Research Department, November 19, 2019), http://www.kslegresearch.org/KLRD-web/Publications/Education/2019Nov-School-Finance-System-Overview.pdf.

6. State of New Jersey Department of Education, "2020–21 State Aid Summaries—Revised," State of New Jersey Department of Education, accessed October 1, 2020, https://www.nj.gov/education/stateaid/2021/.

7. Celia Llopis-Jepsen, "Push Is on for Double-Checking Kansas School Money Spending," *Wyandotte Daily*, January 31, 2018, http://wyandottedaily.com/push-is-on-for-double-checking-kansas-school-money-spending/.

8. Llopis-Jepsen, "Push Is on for Double-Checking Kansas School Money Spending."

9. Llopis-Jepsen, "Push Is on for Double-Checking Kansas School Money Spending."

10. Llopis-Jepsen, "Push Is on for Double-Checking Kansas School Money Spending."

11. Editorial Advisory Board, "Editorial: Dale Dennis Deserves Our Gratitude," *Hutchinson News*, September 17, 2020, https://www.hutchnews.com/opinion/20200917/editorial-dale-dennis-deserves-our-gratitude.

12. Joey May, "Deputy Commissioner Dale Dennis Retiring from KSDE After 53 Years," *Hiawatha World Online*, September 9, 2020, https://www.hiawathaworldonline.com/news/deputy-commissioner-dale-dennis-retiring-from-ksde-after-53-years/article_14f448ec-f2ab-11ea-815f-13099c6e9b30.html.

13. Kathleen Megan, "Supreme Court Tries to Interpret Judge's Meaning in School Funding Case," *Hartford Courant*, September 28, 2017, https://www.courant.com/education/hc-news-ccjef-supreme-court-20170927-story.html.

14. Charles Berger, "Equity Without Adjudication: Kansas School Finance Reform and the 1992 School District Finance and Quality Performance Act," *Journal of Law and Education* 27 (1998): 1–46, 18.

15. The state's case was argued by Kenneth L. Weltz, of Lathrop & Gage based

in Overland Park. He was joined by Curtis L. Tideman, Alok Ahuja, and Jeffrey R. King of the same firm. Interestingly, after Weltz publicly crashed and burned in these particular oral arguments, he was replaced by Alok Ahuja in later arguments, who seemed to handle contentious interactions with the court much more professionally and respectfully than Weltz. It's my personal impression that Tideman had deeper knowledge of the issues at hand as well. Over a decade later, it would be Jeffrey King that would first serve on the legislature and then aid the legislature in its search for external consultants to conduct the 2018 cost study. All were members of the same law firm as Senator Vratil. To this day, it perplexes me that the state didn't pull Weltz from the game long before he started throwing one wild pitch after another.

16. See "Auditor (State Executive Office)," Ballotpedia, accessed October 1, 2020, https://ballotpedia.org/Auditor_(state_executive_office).

17. Kansas Legislative Division of Post Audit, "Audit Education," Kansas Legislative Division of Post Audit, accessed October 1, 2020, https://www.kslpa.org/audit-education/.

18. Kansas Legislative Division of Post Audit, "Audit Education," Kansas Legislative Division of Post Audit, accessed October 1, 2020, https://www.kslpa.org/audit-education/.

19. See Kansas Legislative Division of Post Audit, "Audit Report Library," Kansas Legislative Division of Post Audit, accessed October 1, 2020, https://www.kslpa.org/audit-report-library/?fwp_audit_subject=education-k12.

20. Wikipedia contributors, "State Supreme Court," Wikipedia, accessed October 1, 2020, https://en.wikipedia.org/wiki/State_supreme_court.

21. Robert Kagan, Bobby Infelise, and Robert Detlefsen, "American State Supreme Court Justices 1900–1970," *Law & Social Inquiry* 9 (1984): 371–408.

22. "Donald L. Allegrucci," obituary, Midwest Cremation Society, November 10, 2014, http://www.midwestcremationsociety.com/2014/11/donald-l-allegrucci/.

23. "Alan L. Rupe," Lewis Brisbois, accessed October 1, 2020, https://lewisbrisbois.com/attorneys/rupe-alan-l.

24. "School Finance Litigation," Somers, Robb and Robb, accessed October 1, 2020, http://www.robblaw.com/html/school_finance.html.

25. CG v. Pennsylvania Dept. of Educ., 734 F.3d 229 (3d Cir. 2013).

26. See https://schoolsforfairfunding.org/.

27. See https://www.fundourpublicschools.com/ and https://www.fundourpublicschools.com/political-action-committee.

28. See https://www.equitycenter.org/.

29. See https://ccjef.org/.

30. See https://www.aqeny.org/equity/.

31. Tim Carpenter, "Kansas House Moves to Restore Public School Teacher Due-Process Rights Stricken in 2014," March 8, 2018, https://www.cjonline.com/news/20180307/kansas-house-moves-to-restore-public-school-teacher-due-process-rights-stricken-in-2014.

32. Max Power, "Some Guaranteed Tenure Could Become Part of a Boost in Public School Spending," KNSS 98.7 Wichita, June 3, 2017.

33. Andy Marso, "In Tax Bill Battle, 16 Senators Save Brownback's Plan," KCUR,

February 22, 2017, https://www.kcur.org/government/2017-02-22/in-tax-bill-battle-16-senators-save-brownbacks-plan.

34. Todd Engdahl, "Final Senate Vote Endorses SB 10-191," Chalkbeat Colorado, May 11, 2010, https://co.chalkbeat.org/2010/5/11/21102506/final-senate-vote-endorses-sb-10-191; Jeremy Meyer, "Colorado Teacher Bill Ignites Firestorm of Support, Opposition," *Denver Post*, April 4, 2010, https://www.denverpost.com/2010/04/24/colorado-teacher-bill-ignites-firestorm-of-support-opposition/.

35. Eric Meltzer, "In State of the State, Colorado Governor Points to 'Systemic Problem' in School Funding, Pitches Preschool Expansion," Chalkbeat Colorado, January 9, 2020, https://co.chalkbeat.org/2020/1/9/21109383/in-state-of-the-state-colorado-governor-points-to-systemic-problem-in-school-funding-pitches-prescho. Even when Polis has taken a stand, as in his 2020 State of the State address, he has repeatedly ducked the issue of attempting a significant increase in the state's effort to fund schools or setting forth the steps needed to amend or remove the state's TABOR amendment. Instead, Polis continues to push a reshuffling of deck chairs in Colorado: "Because of our fiscal rules, the state spends far too much money backfilling some of the wealthiest districts not only in the state but in the country," he said. "That is truly at the root of our school funding issues. Together we can fix this systemic problem and finally raise pay for our hardworking educators." Meltzer, "In State of the State."

36. Legislative Council Staff, Colorado Legislature, *Taxpayer Bill of Rights*, https://leg.colorado.gov/agencies/legislative-council-staff/tabor; Lobato v. State, 218 P.3d 358 (Colo. 2009).

37. Jason Gonzales, "Gov. Jared Polis Launches $32.7 Million Fund to Incubate Ideas to Improve Student Learning During the Pandemic," Chalkbeat Colorado, September 9, 2020, https://co.chalkbeat.org/2020/9/9/21429483/polis-launches-fund-to-incubate-ideas-coronavirus-improve-student-learning.

38. Danny Hayes and Jennifer Lawless, "The Decline of Local News and Its Effects: New Evidence from Longitudinal Data," *Journal of Politics* 80 (2018): 332–336.

39. Meghan Rubado and Jay Jennings, "Political Consequences of the Endangered Local Watchdog: Newspaper Decline and Mayoral Elections in the United States," *Urban Affairs Review* 56 (2019): 1327–1356.

40. Hsuan-Ting Chen, Gan Chen, and Ping Sun, "How Does Political Satire Influence Political Participation? Examining the Role of Counter- and Proattitudinal Exposure, Anger, and Personal Issue Importance," *International Journal of Communication* 11 (2017): 3011–3029.

41. Patricia Moy, Michael McCluskey, Kelley McCoy, and Margaret Spratt, "Political Correlates of Local News Media Use," *Journal of Communication* 54 (2004): 532–546; Julie Firmstone and Stephen Coleman, "The Changing Role of the Local News Media in Enabling Citizens to Engage in Local Democracies," *Journalism Practice* 8 (2014): 596–606; Martin Baekgaard, Carsten Jensen, Peter Mortensen, and Soren Serritzlew, "Local News Media and Voter Turnout," *Local Government Studies* 40 (2017): 518–532.

42. Ellen Moxley, "Kansas School Funding Looks Good on Paper, but Deep Cuts Are Expected Due to the Pandemic," KCUR, June 3, 2020, https://www.kcur

.org/education/2020-06-03/kansas-school-districts-funding-looks-good-on-paper-but-deep-cuts-are-expected-this-fall-due-to-the-pandemic.

43. Deja Bickham, "Carol Beier Announces Her Retirement," KSN, June 14, 2020, https://www.fourstateshomepage.com/news/carol-beier-announces-her-retirement/.

CHAPTER 9

1. Bruce Baker, Alex Edwards, and Halley Potter, *Closing America's Education Funding Gaps* (New York: Century Foundation, 2020), https://tcf.org/content/report/closing-americas-education-funding/.

2. Preston C. Green III and Bruce Baker, "Urban Legends, Desegregation and School Finance: Did Kansas City Really Prove That Money Doesn't Matter," *Michigan Journal of Race & Law* 12, no. 57 (2006): 106.

3. "State School Finance Profile 2016–2017 School Year—Missouri," *School Finance Indicators Database*, http://schoolfinancedata.org/wp-content/uploads/2020/10/Profiles17_MO.pdf.

4. KMUW, "Richard Crowson's 'A Kansan in Brownbackistan,'" YouTube, February 10, 2015, https://www.youtube.com/watch?v=UysJ3gx0ksY.

5. See http://schoolfinancedata.org/.

6. John Brittain, Larkin Willis, and Peter Cookson Jr., *Sharing the Wealth: How Regional Finance and Desegregation Plans Can Enhance Educational Equity* (Palo Alto, CA: Learning Policy Institute, 2019), https://learningpolicyinstitute.org/product/sharing-wealth-regional-finance-desegregation-plans-report.

7. US Bureau of the Census, *Current Population Survey: 2019 Annual Social and Economic (ASEC) Supplement* (Washington, DC: US Census Bureau, 2019), www2.census.gov/programs-surveys/cps/techdocs/cpsmar19.pdf. Information is available on confidentiality protection, sampling error, nonsampling error, and definitions within the report.

8. "Nation's Report Card," National Assessment of Educational Progress, accessed October 1, 2020, https://www.nationsreportcard.gov/.

9. National Alliance for Public Charter Schools, "New State Rankings Report Compares Charter School Laws State by State," January 27, 2020, https://www.publiccharters.org/latest-news/2020/01/27/new-state-rankings-report-compares-charter-school-laws-state-state; Todd Ziebarth, *Measuring Up to the Model: A Ranking of State Public Charter School Laws* (Washington, DC: National Alliance for Public Charter Schools, January 2020), https://www.publiccharters.org/sites/default/files/documents/2020-01/2020_model_law_ranking_report-single-draft2%20%281%29.pdf.

10. Kansas State Department of Education, "Tax Credit for Low Income Students Scholarship Program," Kansas State Department of Education, accessed October 1, 2020, https://www.ksde.org/tax-credit-for-low-income-students-scholarship-program.

11. See https://ksassessments.org/.

12. See https://www2.ed.gov/programs/racetothetop/phase1-applications/comments/kansas.pdf.

13. See https://www2.ed.gov/programs/racetothetop/phase1-applications/phase1-scores-detail.xls.

14. See http://schoolfinancedata.org/wp-content/uploads/2020/02/SFID_Annual Report_2020.pdf.

15. Theresa McGuire and Kim Reuben, "The Colorado Revenue Limit: The Economic Effects of TABOR," *State Tax Notes* 40 (2006): 459–473.

16. Thomas Downes and David Figlio, "Tax and Expenditure Limits, School Finance and School Quality," in *Handbook of Research in Education Finance and Policy*, ed. Helen Ladd and Leanna Stiefel (Cambridge, MA: MIT Press, 2008), 373–388.

17. "California Proposition 15, Tax on Commercial and Industrial Properties for Education," Ballotpedia, accessed October 1, 2020, https://ballotpedia.org/California_Proposition_15,_Tax_on_Commercial_and_Industrial_Properties_for_Education_and_Local_Government_Funding_Initiative_(2020).

18. Bryan Lowry, "High Stakes in Kansas Supreme Court Retention Vote," *Wichita Eagle*, September 5, 2016, https://www.kansas.com/news/politics-government/article100083347.html.

ACKNOWLEDGMENTS

Support for the research behind this book was provided by the William T. Grant Foundation (Grant #189354, What's Not the Matter with Kansas? Lessons from Kansas for the Future of State School Finance Reform). The William T. Grant Foundation also provided support for the development of the School Finance Indicators Database used throughout this book (Grant # 183939, Indicators of Educational Inequality in US States 1993–2011).

This book is dedicated to all of the tireless advocates for Kansas school children who helped bring this story to life and others like them across the country.

ABOUT THE AUTHOR

BRUCE D. BAKER is a professor in the Department of Educational Theory, Policy and Administration at Rutgers Graduate School of Education in New Brunswick, NJ.

He previously served on the faculty at the University of Kansas from 1997 through 2008. In addition to publishing numerous articles, chapters, and a textbook on school finance, he has testified on school funding inequities and inadequacies in state and federal courts in Kansas, Arizona, Missouri, Texas, Pennsylvania, New Jersey, Connecticut, and New York. He has also worked with state legislatures and boards of education in Kansas, Texas, Missouri, and Maryland, and most recently in Vermont and New Hampshire to inform and reform various aspects of state school finance systems. He blogs at Schoolfinance101 .wordpress.com and can be found on twitter @schlfinance101.

INDEX